# TO LOSE A WAR

# TO LOSE
# A WAR

## THE FALL AND RISE
## OF THE TALIBAN

### Jon Lee Anderson

PENGUIN PRESS

NEW YORK

2025

PENGUIN PRESS
An imprint of Penguin Random House LLC
1745 Broadway, New York, NY 10019
penguinrandomhouse.com

"A Lion's Death," "The Warlord," "In the Court of the Pretender," "The Surrender,"
"City of Dreams," "Holy and Other Warriors," "Mullah Omar's Favorite Songs," "The Assassins,"
"The Man in the Palace," "The Americans' Opium War," "Day of the Superwadi," "Force and Futility,"
"Annals of Assassination," "An American Way of Killing," "The Ballad of Mullah Omar,"
"Kunduz Falls Again," "The Return of the Taliban," "The End of the American Empire?,"
and "After the Fall" appeared, in slightly different form, in *The New Yorker*.

Book design by Daniel Lagin

LIBRARY OF CONGRESS CATALOGING-IN-PUBLICATION DATA
Names: Anderson, Jon Lee, author.
Title: To lose a war : the fall and rise of the Taliban / Jon Lee Anderson.
Description: New York : Penguin Press, 2025. | Includes bibliographical references and index. |
Summary: "From one of the greatest foreign correspondents of our time, whose on-the-ground reporting
from Afghanistan has shaped our understanding of the country and its fate, comes the complete accounting
of the era from before 9/11 to the return of the Taliban to power in 2021" —Provided by publisher.
Identifiers: LCCN 2025000837 (print) | LCCN 2025000838 (ebook) |
ISBN 9780593493090 (hardcover) | ISBN 9780593493106 (ebook)
Subjects: LCSH: Taliban. | Afghan War, 2001–2021. | Afghanistan—History—2001–2021.
Classification: LCC DS371.412 .A554 2025 (print) | LCC DS371.412 (ebook) |
DDC 958.104/7—dc23/eng/20250510
LC record available at https://lccn.loc.gov/2025000837
LC ebook record available at https://lccn.loc.gov/2025000838

First published in the United States of America as *The Lion's Grave*,
by Grove Press, an imprint of Grove Atlantic, Inc., in 2002.

This revised and updated edition published by Penguin Press in 2025.

Printed in the United States of America
1st Printing

The authorized representative in the EU for product safety and compliance is
Penguin Random House Ireland, Morrison Chambers, 32 Nassau Street,
Dublin D02 YH68, Ireland, https://eu-contact.penguin.ie.

# CONTENTS

The site of Kabul's former stadium and onetime Taliban execution ground has become a place of swirling dust where, every afternoon, Afghan youths gather to play cricket. December 2021.   MOISES SAMAN/MAGNUM PHOTOS

# PREFACE

Afghanistan has always been more of a battleground of history than it has been a nation. Landlocked, bounded by deserts and rugged mountains, it is a geographically strategic crossroads between Central Asia, South Asia, and the Middle East, and has drawn foreign powers with visions of conquest since ancient times. Pivotal invasions were made by Alexander the Great in 330 BC, and by the Mongols in 1222. These were followed by two British colonial forays in the nineteenth century and another in 1919. All of them were ultimately defeated in warfare with the hardy Afghans, who earned a reputation for cunning, bravery, and mercilessness on the battlefield. Six decades after the British departed, the Soviets invaded, but after a bloody military occupation that lasted ten years, they too were forced to withdraw, having not only failed to subjugate the Afghans, but sparking off an armed resistance that has become endemic and hydra-headed over time.

For most Americans, awareness of Afghanistan probably began with the 9/11 terror attacks orchestrated by Osama bin Laden, the Saudi jihadist who had found sanctuary there. Bin Laden's hosts were the Taliban, an army of pious Islamists who had seized power violently a few years earlier, during the chaotic backwash of the Soviet retreat.

Following 9/11, the Americans launched an invasion of Afghanistan with the goal of unseating the Taliban and punishing bin Laden's Al Qaeda terror network. They quickly achieved both these aims, but then stayed on for another twenty years, variously engaged in counterinsurgency and nation-building efforts. It all ended in 2021, when, after failing to thwart a steadily growing Taliban resurgence, the war-weary US pulled out its last troops, and the Taliban marched back into Kabul.

I spent time on Afghanistan's battlegrounds in the late 1980s, during the prolonged Soviet retreat, as rival mujahideen factions united in an unsuccessful campaign to wrest control from Moscow's client regime. (My observations on those experiences can be found in *Guerrillas*, a book I wrote about a number of modern insurgencies.*)

In the wake of 9/11, I returned to Afghanistan and spent most of the next year reporting there for *The New Yorker*. In 2002, I published *The Lion's Grave*, a book-length collection of my Afghan articles that was intended to serve as a chronicle of the first year of the American presence in Afghanistan. At that point, the mission of the US and its coalition allies appeared to have been a qualified success, thanks to its partnership with an array of Afghan warlords. The Taliban had vanished into the hills, as had Al Qaeda, and a pliant new pro-Western regime had been installed.

A parallel narrative of *The Lion's Grave* was the story of the death of Ahmad Shah Massoud, a charismatic mujahideen leader who was assassinated by Al Qaeda operatives in Afghanistan two days before the

---

*Guerrillas* was originally published as *Guerrillas: The Men and Women Fighting Today's Wars* (Times Books, 1992), and reissued as *Guerrillas: Journeys in the Insurgent World* (Penguin, 2004).

9/11 attacks took place in the United States. Massoud's killing appeared to have been an essential part of the larger Al Qaeda conspiracy, yet had remained largely unexamined. Intrigued, I investigated the circumstances of Massoud's murder, and on the first anniversary of his death, attended a ceremony held at a new mausoleum erected in his honor in his home village in the Panjshir Valley. I chose to end my book with the scene of that ceremony, which also gave the book its title. During the anti-Soviet resistance war waged by the mujahideen, Massoud had earned acclaim as the "Lion of the Panjshir" for his leadership role in thwarting successive Soviet military offensives launched into the narrow mountain valley. The road that ran through the Panjshir was still littered with destroyed tanks and vehicles from those days, but, in the end, the Panjshir had also become Massoud's tomb.

I had always found Afghanistan a deeply compelling place, and was happy to be reporting there again, but unexpectedly soon I found myself drawn to a new theater of war in Iraq—the next battleground in the so-called war on terror that had been declared by President George W. Bush.

I left Afghanistan, but before long, I was back. The Taliban were having a resurgence, and the American project in Afghanistan had begun to acquire the look and feel of a quagmire. I traveled there in 2005, in 2007, in 2010, and again in 2011. Eventually, distracted once more by new conflicts erupting in Libya, Syria, and elsewhere, it would be an entire decade before I returned, in late 2021, a few months after the catastrophic American retreat and the Taliban's momentous return to power.

Given everything that has happened, it feels appropriate to look back over the entire twenty-year arc of the American presence in Afghanistan. To do so, I have reconceived *The Lion's Grave*, expanding its focus to include the stories I wrote on my return trips in the hope they provide a narrative chronology to my growing apprehension about the

US project there. *The Lion's Grave* has therefore become *To Lose a War*, an altogether different book, one that examines the American enterprise in Afghanistan from its dramatic beginning all the way to its hapless end.

Some of my apprehensions came early on. As I sought out a ground-level understanding of Afghanistan in the run-up to the US invasion, as it took place, and then in its aftermath, I had glimpses of a society that didn't fit easily into the "good Afghans versus bad Taliban" box. In the earliest chapters, "The Warlord" (chapter 2), "In the Court of the Pretender" (chapter 3), "The Surrender" (chapter 4), and "City of Dreams" (chapter 5), I share encounters I had with some Afghans who felt threatened by the sudden arrival of Westerners in their country, and who, perhaps, retained an allegiance to the archconservative Taliban. In the newly liberated capital, Kabul, a shopkeeper upbraided me angrily for speaking with a burkha-clad woman who had approached to ask me for help. During my excursions on the city's outskirts, curious groups of boys invariably assembled, and then began throwing stones, whenever a Western woman appeared.

In chapter 6, "Holy and Other Warriors," I describe a December 2001 trip to the mountainous redoubt known as Tora Bora, where the US military believed they had cornered bin Laden, but where, after several weeks of fighting, they had lost track of him. I recount my meetings with wildly unreliable mujahideen commanders, men who had presented themselves as American allies, but who were also suspected of having helped bin Laden escape. Another unreliable figure was Jack Idema, a bombastic former US Special Forces officer who had cut his own deals with Afghan warlords. Idema went on to run a rogue anti-terror operation, for which, after being found torturing suspects in a private jail, he was arrested, convicted, and sentenced to prison for his crimes. Idema's murky official affiliations and his ability to operate unhindered in the lee of the US war in Afghanistan for several years seemed to say something about the creeping, and chaotic, nature of the American mission.

Following the Taliban retreat from their stronghold in the southern city of Kandahar, things still felt tenuous in January 2002. It was there that the Taliban had made their final stand several weeks before, only to mysteriously vanish from the battlefield. A young man assisting the new government authorities, who had previously worked for the Taliban, disclosed that his former employers had all decamped across the border to the southern Pakistani city of Quetta, where they enjoyed the backing of the Pakistani intelligence services, who were playing both sides in the US war against the Taliban and Al Qaeda. As time would show, he was telling the truth: The Taliban had made a tactical withdrawal, but were still intact, having resolved to remain in the shadows until they felt ready to resume the fight.

In Kandahar, I paid a visit to Mullah Naquib, who had been my mujahideen host years earlier, during the anti-Soviet war. In a story I tell in chapter 7, "Mullah Omar's Favorite Songs," Naquib was under a cloud of suspicion from the American newcomers for his friendly ties to the former Taliban leaders, including its fugitive spiritual leader Mullah Omar, who had bequeathed him his fleet of luxury Toyota Land Cruisers before making his escape. Where did Naquib's loyalties lie in the new Afghanistan? It was difficult to know. He was, first and foremost, a survivor.

In the spring of 2002, I returned to Kabul and, together with the photographer Thomas Dworzak, my friend and companion since the first days of the war, rented a traditional Afghan house to live in. It was located on a street with many florist shops, appropriately named Flower Street, in the old city center. For the several months we lived there, I investigated the conspiracy behind Ahmad Shah Massoud's assassination. The story I eventually told, "The Assassins," in chapter 8, is about how Al Qaeda, with the complicity of the Taliban and other accomplices, managed to infiltrate two of its jihadists posing as journalists into rebel-held northern Afghanistan, and kill Massoud during an interview in his home. The more I dug into the story, the more I smelt the whiff of betrayal, especially when it came to the suspicious role played in the chain of events by Abdul Rasul Sayyaf. He was an archconservative warlord with close past links to Osama bin Laden who had nonetheless remained on the scene with a degree of power and influence. To my eye, the new Afghanistan was not a place of easy definition, but a witch's cauldron of newfound loyalties and old deceits.

Three years went by before I returned to Afghanistan. By 2005, the initial American-led coalition had morphed into a fully-fledged NATO mission, with multiple countries involved, and many thousands of American and other foreign troops on the ground. Aid money and investment had poured into Kabul, which had transmogrified from a ruinous near ghost town into a bustling city full of people, shops, and newly bought vehicles. Western expats hung out at a handful of stylish new restaurants; many lived in a nouveau-riche neighborhood where warlords and drug barons had built ostentatious homes. I had come to write a profile of President Hamid Karzai, an exile politician hand-picked by the Western powers to lead Afghanistan after the Taliban's removal. Lauded as the man who had "rescued" his country from the grip of Islamist extremists, Karzai was feted and lionized whenever he went abroad—the Volodymyr Zelensky of his day.

Karzai was polite and charming, but I found him in a private state of mounting distress over his lack of real authority. The more I investigated, the more I could see why he felt that way. Sitting in on meetings Karzai held with Afghan delegations from remote areas, I watched as he promised them his government's assistance. Following up afterward, I found him unable to meet his promises because, to fulfill them, he was dependent on American goodwill and resources, which the US was not always inclined to provide. I came away concerned that the Americans had not invested Karzai with enough sovereign power to do very much without them, much less earn the respect of his countrymen. Chapter 9, "The Man in the Palace," is the portrait of a man who was only ever the nominal president of his own country; real power lay elsewhere, with the Americans.

TWO YEARS LATER, IN 2007, I RETURNED TO AFGHANISTAN TO join a team of American military contractors and Afghan soldiers on a mission to tackle the booming opium industry in Uruzgan, a rural province that also happened to be the homeland of the Taliban. This is the story I tell in chapter 10, "The Americans' Opium War." After the team was repeatedly ambushed by gunmen following a meeting with the Uruzgan governor—a man suspected of being a Taliban proxy—the mission fell apart before it had even begun. To me, the episode exposed the extreme superficiality of the relationships forged between the Americans and their putative allies and pointed to the tenuousness of their project in Afghanistan.

By 2010, it was no longer possible to travel safely outside of Kabul. The armed Taliban resistance had gathered in strength and spread across the country, while in the capital itself, security had become tight as Westerners and Afghan government officials were targeted in so-called complex attacks launched by suicide bombers and gunmen against hotels and restaurants they frequented. Several journalist friends had been kidnapped and taken hostage; others had been killed. Suicide blast walls had popped up around the buildings in Kabul's government district; the massive new US embassy was a veritable fortress.

I opted for an "embedded" experience with a US Army battalion in Maiwand, in the south, a province adjacent to Kandahar. Flown in on American military aircraft and housed alongside soldiers in fortified camps, I ended up in a military outpost from which American soldiers launched raids to track down and clear Taliban from a series of nearby villages. Chapter 11, "Day of the Superwadi," is the story of that experience, in which the Afghans around me were kept at a remove and perceived by the Americans to be mostly hostile, likely loyal to the Taliban's "shadow government." Traveling with American soldiers outside the fortress walls meant moving around inside a bombproof armored vehicle, which seemed to say everything about their lack of a connection with the Afghan people. I left Maiwand in October 2010 feeling so detached from the Afghanistan I had once known that although I wrote up the story of my experience, I asked my editor not to publish it; it appears here in print for the first time.

Frustrated by my previous experience, I returned to Afghanistan several months later, in early 2011. I sought to overcome the sense of alienation I'd felt in Maiwand by making another attempt to understand what was happening in Afghanistan. Again, I was embedded, this time with a small unit of Afghan and American troops on Afghanistan's rugged border with Pakistan's tribal territories, a jihadi stronghold. Although I remained cut off from Afghan civilians, I had access to the Afghan soldiers fighting alongside the Americans, and found such a degree of ill will and suspicion between them that I concluded that the US-led campaign in Afghanistan had failed. The article I wrote, which appears as chapter 12, "Force and Futility," was subtitled "Is It Time to Leave Afghanistan?"

The subsequent decade was the chronicle of a disaster foretold, something I only reported on irregularly and from a distance. I have included some of these reports here, as a series of short, dated chapters: "Annals of Assassination" (chapter 13), "An American Way of Killing" (chapter 14), "The Ballad of Mullah Omar" (chapter 15), "Kunduz Falls Again" (chapter 16), "The Return of the Taliban" (chapter 17), and "The End of the American Empire?" (chapter 18). They include the obituaries of several prominent Afghans, whom I knew personally, following the news of their violent deaths, while the last pieces deal with the inexorable Taliban comeback. It was still a profound shock when the end came in August 2021. In the wake of the historic American debacle, I felt compelled to return to Afghanistan, and did so several weeks later, in November and December 2021, during the onset of the Central Asian winter.

DURING THE TWO DECADES OF THE AMERICAN PRESENCE, THE Afghan capital underwent a dramatic transformation. In 2001, after the Taliban were chased off into the hills following several weeks of B-52 bombardments and ground offensives by CIA-backed mujahideen, Kabul was a forlorn, empty place, much of it in ruins. By the spring of 2002, with thousands of US and coalition troops in place, the city had begun to fill up again. Millions of refugees returned after spending years in exile in Pakistan, Iran, and other countries.

Since then, Kabul's estimated 2001 population of two million people has more than doubled, to nearly five million, while the country's overall population of some twenty-one million people has ballooned to forty million. The average Afghan age is a mere eighteen and a half years.

In the months after the Taliban's return, Old Kabul was still discernible, but only barely, as it had been swallowed up by chaotic growth. From a city that was almost exclusively one of single-family dwellings, with almost no buildings, other than mosques, over ten stories high, it had transmogrified into one with dozens of apartment buildings soaring fifteen and even twenty stories into the sky. It was a bustling commercial city, full of cars and traffic, but its endemic social and sectarian inequities remained in place. The Mongol-looking men of the Shiite Hazara community, who rank the lowest in Afghanistan's social pecking order, still pulled carts through the streets with straps attached to their heads; people were everywhere, and numerous beggars. The hard-scrabble slums on the rocky hills had expanded, but there were now gaudy wedding palaces, men's hairdressers, and wedding-dress shops, as well as snooker clubs and weight-lifting gyms. Billboards around the city advertised a bewildering variety of Turkish energy drinks, while thousands of heroin addicts gathered in huddled throngs along median strips and under bridges, smoking or injecting the drug.

WITH THE TALIBAN AS THEIR RULERS ONCE AGAIN, KABUL'S IN-habitants carried on in a semblance of normality, moving around the city on foot and in vehicles, hauling cargoes, buying and selling food and other goods from roadside stalls, but there was a palpable sense that things were different.

To start with, there were no foreigners visible anywhere, while the ascendant Taliban were ubiquitous, manning roadblocks and access points, riding pickup trucks or US military Humvees with their guns cocked and held at the ready. Some wore their hair long, jihadi style, and were dressed in the traditional Afghan tunic and pantaloon outfits known as *shalwar kameez*—sometimes in incongruously bright hues of blue, orange, or yellow, and with their eyes dramatically adorned with black kohl. Others affected a US Special Forces look, right down to the camouflaged uniforms, boots, and wraparound sunglasses and weapons they had inherited as booty from the bases of the departed US fighters.

To most Kabulis, the Taliban were still as foreign-seeming as the Americans had once been, and I saw few interactions between the Afghan civilians and the Taliban on the streets, other than perfunctory exchanges. They seemed to ignore each other, as if they came from different worlds but had been forced to coexist. Occasionally, I detected what looked like flashes of fear in the eyes of civilians as they walked past Taliban gunmen. They were involuntary, cautionary glances that were quickly concealed behind neutral expressions. If an army of pro-life, gun-toting anti-vaxxers from Texas took over New York City, I thought, it might be something like this.

Whatever their political beliefs, most Kabulis adhere to a standard operating procedure of life-goes-on pragmatism. It was hardly surprising: In a forty-five-year period, they had lived through a decade-long Russian military occupation followed by a police state dictatorship followed by a bloody civil war followed by a six-year Taliban tyranny followed by twenty years of a Western-leaning quasi-democracy, only to revert to Taliban control.

At a prominent traffic circle, a man sold black-and-white satin flags, the Taliban's official flag, which bears the invocation "There is only one God, Allah, and Muhammad is his messenger" on it in Arabic script. One day, I stopped to speak to him. I asked him how he had earned a living before the Taliban came to power. Until the Taliban marched into town, he told me, he had been a government soldier. Since becoming unemployed, he had turned to selling the flags. He smiled and cupped his hands in the air, as if to say: "It's a job."

For the most part, the Taliban had left the people of Kabul to their own devices, and except for a few disturbing incidents, including the beating of women who came out to protest the curtailment of their rights to education and employment, there had been little overt repression. The Taliban had gone so far as to reassure Afghans, and the outside world, that they were not bent on revenge against their former enemies; they had even declared an amnesty. This was a far cry from their behavior when they had seized Kabul the first time in 1996. The Taliban of the 1990s and early 2000s were obsessive-compulsive and frequently violent in their zeal to bring about a society based on strict conformity with their interpretation of Islam. One of their pet peeves was the graven image. In the wake of the Taliban's removal from power in 2001, I had found shops in which the illustrations of mothers and

babies on packages of baby soap had been fastidiously crossed out by
Taliban morality commissars who had wielded brown magic markers.
Even road-crossing signs for livestock and pedestrians had been painted
over. No longer. Nowadays, most of the fighters carried around smart-
phones that, obviously, showed human images, the contemplation of
which, evidently, was no longer an issue.

A moralistic pall hung over the city, but it felt lackadaisical and ill-
defined. Many storefront advertisements that had previously featured
the images of women had been chastely painted over, but most had been
done preemptively by the shopkeepers themselves, to forestall trouble.
Signboards above wedding-dress shops continued to boast flamboyant
Bollywood-style images of women, however, the kind of transgression
that would have meant a beating for the proprietors, at the very least, by
the former Taliban. The imagery of the Taliban's political enemies had
not been uniformly destroyed either. The portrait of Ahmad Shah Massoud had been removed from the iconic red stone obelisk erected in his
honor some years earlier, but elsewhere his portrait—and indeed, those
of other Taliban adversaries—had remained intact.

Similarly, although women and girls had been provisionally banished from workplaces and high schools, they remained visible on the
streets. All wore hijabs—headscarves—but few had yet donned the all-
concealing burkhas. Most dressed in three-quarter-length tunics and
leggings, and some even wore makeup.

AT THE TIME OF MY VISIT, WHICH I DESCRIBE IN THE BOOK'S
final chapter, "After the Fall" (chapter 19), the degree to which the Taliban would continue to exhibit some tolerance was still unquantifiable.
They were a deeply committed, ideologically fervent insurgent force
that had prevailed after years of war against an army funded and armed
by the United States. By every conventional measure, they had achieved

a stunning victory, and their leadership's avowed commitment to bringing about a *truly* Islamic state suggested that Afghanistan was in the throes of a revolution that was as fully-fledged as Ayatollah Khomeini's in neighboring Iran four decades earlier, Fidel Castro's once-upon-a-time socialist revolution in Cuba, or, for that matter, Mao's earlier Communist triumph in China.

To gain a sense of where the Taliban 2.0 intended to take Afghanistan, I sought out and questioned Taliban officials for their latest "truth." In a combative exchange with Suhail Shaheen, the Taliban ambassador-designate to the United Nations, in the elegant garden of the Serena Hotel, I pointed out the incongruity of our meeting in a hotel that his comrades had twice attacked in previous years, singling out foreign guests as targets of assassination. Shaheen scowled and shrugged. When I asked him about Taliban intentions toward women, he fired back that Western sanctions were condemning Afghanistan's women and girls to lives of poverty.

The crafty ambiguity of Shaheen's responses, as well as those of other Taliban officials I met, suggested a tactical insincerity as to their ultimate intentions. I came away from Afghanistan feeling unsettled, and worried about the future of its people, who appeared doomed to be ruled by men who claimed the right, with force of arms, to be the custodians of their destinies, over and over again.

And what does the defeat in Afghanistan mean for the United States? More than anything else, occurring when it did, in the immediate aftermath of the calamitous Trump presidency and his instigation of the January 6, 2021, assault on the Capitol, it signaled the decline of the US, both as a global policeman and as a model of democracy. It was a mere six months later when Vladimir Putin, clearly buoyed by the spectacle of the ignominious American evacuation of Kabul, seized the moment to launch his full-scale invasion of Ukraine. Putin could perhaps be excused for his hubris: Afghanistan is not known as the graveyard of empires for nothing. Just as the Soviet retreat from Afghanistan in 1989 seemed to presage the collapsing power of the USSR, the images of Afghan men desperately clinging to the undercarriage of a departing American military aircraft, then falling to their deaths, suggested a precipitous American decline.

But then, this strategic game had occurred before. The American retreat from Vietnam had led to a decade of Soviet advances across the geostrategic chessboard, from Angola and Ethiopia to Nicaragua and Afghanistan. But in the end, the Soviet Union proved unsustainable, and it had collapsed. How will this round end? We don't yet know.

Dorset, England
March 2025

# A NOTE ON
# TITLE CHANGES

I have changed the titles of a few of the chapters that originally ran as *New Yorker* magazine articles. "The Americans' Opium War" was originally "The Taliban's Opium War," for instance, while "Mullah Omar's Favorite Songs" was originally titled "After the Revolution." Most of the articles also appeared with subtitles, which do not appear here. The short pieces dated from 2011, 2015, and 2021 were articles that were published in digital form, most of which I have renamed and edited very slightly to better reflect their content and my purpose in writing them.

# TO LOSE A WAR

# 1

## A LION'S DEATH

I met Wali Massoud a little over ten years ago, at a friend's house in Wimbledon. He was in his mid-twenties, a slight, amiable man with black hair and a mustache. Wali was the youngest son of an ethnic Tajik officer in the Afghan Army and had come to Britain to study international relations. He had a famous older brother, Ahmad Shah Massoud, the Lion of Panjshir, who led a band of mujahideen that fought off seven major offensives by Soviet forces in the great mountain valley of Panjshir, in northern Afghanistan, during the 1980s. In 1992, three years after the Soviets withdrew from the country, Massoud's forces—the Jamiat-i-Islami (Society of Islam), a moderately conservative group composed mostly of ethnic Tajiks and led by the Islamic scholar Burhanuddin Rabbani—defeated the brutish regime the Soviets had left in power. Ahmad Shah Massoud became the defense minister and, later, vice president of the new Islamic State of Afghanistan.

---

This chapter was originally published as "A Lion's Death," *The New Yorker*, October 1, 2001.

In 1996, when the Taliban militia gained control of Kabul, the capital city, and most of the rest of the country, Massoud and Rabbani returned to the mountains in the north. With limited backing from Iran, Russia, and India, they fought off the Taliban and managed to hold on to somewhere between 5 and 20 percent of the country. Massoud led a motley coalition of tribal-based guerrilla forces that are usually referred to as the Northern Alliance but are officially called the United Islamic Front for the Salvation of Afghanistan.

Wali Massoud stayed in London. He got married, had two daughters, and earned an MA in diplomacy. He is now the chargé d'affaires at the Afghan embassy to the Court of St. James's. The Northern Alliance controls Afghanistan's UN seat and all of its forty-odd embassies, except for the one in Pakistan, which is run by the Taliban. The Taliban is officially recognized only by Pakistan, the United Arab Emirates, and Osama bin Laden's homeland, Saudi Arabia.

The London embassy is a cream-colored early Victorian building across the street from Hyde Park in Knightsbridge. I met Wali Massoud there at eleven a.m. on Friday, September 14, 2001, while Londoners were standing for three minutes of silence in memory of the victims of the attack on the World Trade Center. Wali, who is just as thin and amiable as he was a decade ago, wore a gray pin-striped double-breasted suit and held a cell phone, which rang again and again, and which Wali answered each time, with an apology to me. The previous Sunday, his brother had been attacked at his headquarters while giving an interview to two Arabs carrying Belgian passports. They were posing as television journalists and carrying a bomb. When it went off, it killed one of the "journalists" and one of Massoud's men and wounded Massoud and several other people. The second attacker tried to flee but was killed.

The suicide bombers had come into Northern Alliance territory from Taliban-controlled Afghanistan, across the front lines, which was an unusual breach of security and has thus far not been explained. "They arranged this with someone at headquarters," a Northern Alliance official in London told me. "We are investigating." He said that the men are believed to have been either Moroccan or Algerian, and that they traveled from London to Pakistan before reaching Afghanistan. They are suspected of having links to an extremist group, the Islamic Observation Centre, in London.

Initial press reports said that Massoud had died in the attack, but all week Wali had been telling me that his brother was recovering. He was about to leave for Afghanistan, he said, to be with him. Wali was concerned about the stability of the coalition. Massoud was an extraordinarily gifted military tactician and was revered by his people. "The opposition can continue to function," Wali said, "but not the same as before." Then the phone rang again, and this time, as he listened, Wali hunched forward in his chair, holding his knees tightly together. He repeated the Farsi word *bale*—"yes"—and his voice became barely audible. He seemed about to weep.

Later that evening, the BBC confirmed Massoud's death. After the attack, he had been taken to a hospital in Tajikistan by helicopter. On Saturday, September 15, his body was brought back to his hometown, the mountain village of Bazarak, where he was buried. His thirteen-year-old son, Ahmad, spoke. "I want to be my father's successor," he said. While Massoud's bereaved relatives and thousands of followers were observing a period of mourning, the Taliban launched a large-scale military offensive against the Northern Alliance.

The timing and circumstances of the attack on Massoud, which came just two days before the strike on the United States, do not appear to be coincidental. Anyone who knew that the United States was going to be attacked and that Osama bin Laden and the Taliban would be blamed would also have known that Massoud would suddenly become an important ally for the West. "Without very good intelligence in Afghanistan, you can't do anything," an Afghan living in London said to me. "Bin Laden has a thousand caves to hide in." Ahmad Shah Massoud had been waging war in Afghanistan for more than twenty years, and he knew most of its hiding places.

A poster of the late Ahmad Shah Massoud (1953–2001) at a fruit and vegetable stand, December 2001.   THOMAS DWORZAK/MAGNUM PHOTOS

# 2

## THE WARLORD

A few days before the American and British air strikes in Afghanistan began, I visited a man being held prisoner in a hole in the desert. The hole was near Dasht-i-Qala, a northern Afghan town a few
miles from the Tajikistan border, not far from a hogback ridge of dusty
hills that the Taliban had, for some time, been trying to wrest from
their main opponents, the Northern Alliance. The Taliban and the
Northern Alliance fighters had come to within three hundred yards of
one another in places, and on the exposed ridges, where the powdery
earth was a grim geometry of sandbagged dugouts and trenches, they
traded shots with sniper rifles and heavy machine guns, while their rearguard positions lobbed tank shells back and forth.

The prisoner, a Taliban fighter who said his name was Bashir, had
been in the hole for about a month, since the night he was caught by
the Northern Alliance mujahideen wandering around on his own in

This chapter was originally published as "The Warlord," *The New Yorker*, October 22, 2001.

no-man's-land. His hole-prison was ten feet deep and three feet wide, and it was covered most of the time by a piece of heavy metal tread from a Russian tank. At the bottom, the hole turned into a cavity that, according to his captors, was a comfortable six feet by six feet. When Bashir was brought up to ground level, he had to climb a wooden ladder. This was not an easy thing to do, because he also wore leg irons.

On the day I met Bashir, or, rather, observed him—for he was in a trancelike state of detachment—his leg irons had been removed. He was forced to walk over to where I stood, but he appeared to be weak, and he soon squatted down against a mud wall. He was about thirty, very thin, with a black goatee and short-cropped black hair. He wore a filthy green smock and his skin was smeared with dirt. His arms were tattooed with green dots, and there was a string around his neck from which hung a little purple book containing verses from the Koran. He was barefoot. His captors said that he had needle tracks on his arms, although I didn't see them. I did see a scar from a bullet hole on his right collarbone.

A group of mujahideen guards and curious children gathered to watch. Despite promptings from Mullah Omar, the warlord who was holding Bashir and wanted to exchange him for five of his own soldiers who were being held prisoner by the Taliban, he didn't say very much—just his name, and that he was from Kandahar, more than four hundred miles to the southwest, where the Taliban had their headquarters. (And where the better-known Mullah Omar, the head of the Taliban, lived. Many Afghans use only one name, which can be confusing to Westerners.) "All the Kandaharis are like this," Mullah Omar said to me. "They never talk." They were not to be trusted, he said, which was why Bashir had to be kept in a hole. Mullah Omar was a slight, thirty-five-year-old man of Tajik ancestry. He said that the Taliban had offered him only three of his soldiers in exchange for Bashir, and that he and they were haggling about this over their field radios. I asked him why Bashir kept spitting, and he said it was because he was suffering from drug withdrawal. Some of what he had been spitting appeared to be brown, though. Was it blood? Had Bashir been beaten? "No, no," Mullah Omar reassured me. "We give him bread, milk—everything he wants. But we don't give him *charas*"—hashish, or opium. "He asks for it every day."

After a few minutes, Bashir was taken back to the hole, and Mullah Omar led me inside his compound to meet his sons. He assembled two groups of boys, all barefoot. One of the groups consisted of his ten sons, aged one month to twelve years, including a set of identical twins. The other group was made up of the five sons of his own twin brother, who was killed a few months ago by the Taliban. A few months before that, their eldest brother, Qari Kamir Alem, a relatively famous mujahideen commander, had been murdered. Mullah Omar captured six men who he said had betrayed Qari Kamir Alem and were responsible for his death, and he had them hanged. He had inherited his brother's command on the front line, and he claimed to have two thousand fighters, but this was almost certainly an exaggeration. He told me that he had begun fighting in 1979, when he was twelve years old and the Soviets invaded Afghanistan. As for his title of "mullah," he said that he had earned it by studying the Koran and other holy books in his home village—which is in the Khoja-i-Gar district, and is now occupied by the Taliban—and then at a madrasah in Pakistan. I left Mullah Omar as dusk approached and he and his men prepared for the sunset prayers.

The day after the air strikes began, I drove past Mullah Omar's compound, again at sunset, and looked out at the desert, toward Bashir's hole. His guards had brought their captive up for air, and he was standing in a shallow ditch they had dug for him. He was visible only from the torso up. He appeared to be rooted in place, half swallowed by the earth.

DASHT-I-QALA IS IN TAKHAR PROVINCE, AND UNTIL THE YEAR 2000 the provincial capital, Taloqan, was the main base of operations for Ahmad Shah Massoud and the Northern Alliance. But Taloqan fell in heavy fighting, and Massoud retreated to a village closer to the Tajik border, about twenty-five miles northeast of Dasht-i-Qala. He was there on September 9, when the two Arab suicide bombers, posing as journalists, set off a bomb while they were interviewing him. By then, the hills above Dasht-i-Qala were the last barrier between the Taliban and the border that provided the Northern Alliance with access to the outside world and supplies.

Dasht-i-Qala is near the confluence of two rivers—the Amu Dar'ya, which forms the border with Tajikistan, and the Kokcha, which runs into the Amu Dar'ya. The local Northern Alliance organization is called the Kokcha Union and is led by four commanders, each of whom represents a population center. They cooperate with the central Northern Alliance organization, which is nominally headed by Burhanuddin Rabbani, the president of the government formed by the mujahideen who took power in Kabul in 1992, when the Soviet-backed government fell.

The local commanders in the Northern Alliance negotiate with Rabbani's government for funds for their troops, but they have a great deal of autonomous authority in their districts. If an NGO wishes to build a school or an irrigation system or organize a food-for-work road-improvement project, it must make arrangements through the local commanders, whose bargaining power vis-à-vis the Northern Alliance as a whole derives from the fact that they have small armies of their own. The commanders supply troops in the war against the Taliban and coordinate their activities along the front with the Northern Alliance defense minister—formerly Ahmad Shah Massoud and now General Muhammad Fahim, who took Massoud's place after the assassination.

The commanders within a district have a rotating system of leadership. Last winter, the Dasht-i-Qala commander, Mamur Hassan, led the Kokcha Union troops for a four-month period and then relinquished his duties to one of the other district commanders. Hassan is a landowner, and his men are extremely deferential to him, as if he were a feudal lord. He says that he has been at war, more or less constantly, for the past twenty-four years. He is of Uzbek heritage, and he studied at an American-built high school in the province of Helmand, in southern Afghanistan, and at Kabul's agricultural university, but he came back home to Dasht-i-Qala to work on irrigation projects. Then the Soviets invaded. He laughed when I asked what he would do after the coming war. "I will farm," he said. "I have three hundred *jeribs*"—150 acres—"of land. I can be a rich man." For the time being, he supplies trucks to his nephews, who work the farm and split the harvest of wheat, corn, melons, and lentils with him.

Mamur Hassan is a small, sturdy-looking man, and light on his feet. He has a beard of medium length that is mostly gray, and short-cropped black hair running to gray as well. He usually wears a long-tailed tunic and matching pantaloon outfit—which is what most Pakistani and Afghan men wear—and, over it, a military-style multipocketed vest. He has a wide nose, and large brown eyes with crow's-feet at the corners. He listens attentively and speaks with a warm, reedy voice, full of inflection, in Uzbek or Dari, the Afghan variant of Farsi. Mamur Hassan appears to be in his late fifties. Like a lot of Afghans, he does not seem to have thought much about his age, and when we first met he told me that his father, who he said was 107 when he died two years ago, was thirty when he was born. I pointed out that if that was the case Mamur Hassan would be close to seventy. He hesitated and began counting on his fingers. He said that he was born in the Muslim year 1322—1943 in the Christian calendar—and, since it was now 1380, he agreed that it was possible that he was fifty-seven or fifty-eight.

Hassan lives with his two wives and five of his seven children in a brick-and-concrete house surrounded by orchards, at the end of a dirt drive that passes through a small glade of trees running from Dasht-i-Qala to the Kokcha River. The town itself is little more than a rambling spread of walled family compounds set around an intersection of dirt tracks fronted by little shops with wooden shutters, many of them made from ammunition boxes. On the other side of the river is the front line. Hassan's house is small but comfortable and modern by local standards. The garden is lush—because it is irrigated—with a green lawn and a large plane tree. There is a raised concrete area in a corner for afternoon prayers and for sleeping outdoors in the hot summers. Pink petunias and red and white roses grow next to a concrete bungalow that functions as his staff headquarters and guesthouse. It has a carpeted room that is used for meals and meetings and prayers, a radio room, a kitchen, and a sleeping room. Large white geese wander along the dirt path outside, near a muddy stream. Two pens house a number of pheasants, which occasionally break out in a peculiar song, a staccato clatter that ranges briefly through several tempos and then stops abruptly. There is an antiaircraft battery on one side of the house.

The first time I visited Hassan, he sat in a chair about twelve feet away from the one that had been placed on the lawn for me. He raised his arm in the direction of a soldier standing twenty feet behind him, and called for his worry beads. An aide came running with a set of amber beads, which Hassan began working with his left hand. I noticed that when he put the beads down his hands trembled. From time to time, he took out a small round tin case of *naswar,* the tobacco-spice-herb mixture—a mild stimulant—that many Afghan men are addicted to, and tapped a little onto his hand, then popped it into the gap between his teeth and his lower lip. Two bodyguards paced around us, and when I reached into my bag for a notepad, they looked especially alert. Later, after I had spent some time at the compound, they laughed and said that they thought I would understand their nervousness about journalists, since the men who killed Massoud had passed themselves off as reporters in search of an interview. When they were no longer suspicious, they greeted me with thermoses of tea and dishes of almonds and candies and tried out English phrases on me. Hassan invited me to stay at the compound when the air strikes became imminent.

It is not the custom in Afghanistan to invite guests into one's living quarters, since wives are not supposed to be seen. I never met the women in Hassan's household, but Hassan's youngest son, Babur Shah, a three-year-old toddler, played around our feet while we talked. Hassan occasionally called out to the little boy, remonstrating with him gently, but for the most part he just looked at him fondly. Babur Shah's older brother Ataullah, who is twenty, was also usually present, and took care of him. Ata, as he is called, has just received a scholarship to study journalism in China. Hassan has two other sons who live and study in Tehran, where one of his wives has a house. Hassan didn't want to send his sons away, but Ahmad Shah Massoud advised him to, so that he would not be distracted by having to look after them while fighting a war. He sent them to Iran because he could not afford to send them to Europe.

Mamur Hassan said that he was one of only two men still alive among the thirty from Dasht-i-Qala who took up arms as mujahideen against the Soviets in 1979. They had started out on their own, without any affiliations, he said, but later on, when Afghan Muslim leaders began receiving arms and funding from Pakistan, Saudi Arabia, and the United States, they threw in their lot with Gulbuddin Hekmatyar, the radical leader of an ethnic Pashtun mujahideen group. Hekmatyar was Massoud's rival. "At first, I was a member of Hekmatyar's party, and I fought against the Soviets but also against other Afghans," Hassan said. "We killed a lot of people and destroyed many places, and I regret this. I tell my sons not to have anything to do with political parties." He finally broke with Hekmatyar and joined Massoud, who offered to make a place for him when the mujahideen formed a government in Kabul in 1992. Hassan chose to return to Dasht-i-Qala instead. Now he helps out the Northern Alliance but maintains his independence. "I control a lot of men and a large area," he said. I asked whether the men he commanded owed their loyalties to him or to the Alliance, and he said, "To *me*."

There are apparently around five thousand soldiers in the Kokcha Union, with maybe a thousand in Dasht-i-Qala. "They are ready to fight for me whenever I order them to," Hassan said. The Alliance gave him two hundred Kalashnikovs, and he regularly receives food for six hundred soldiers, but he makes up the shortfalls and provides everything else that is needed, like clothing and medicine. "I pay for it myself," he told me, "out of my own pocket." He laughed. "My family was rich, but we spent it all in the jihad"—the war against the Soviets in the 1980s and then for four years against the Afghan Communist government.

I asked Hassan what Islamic state he admired, or could see as a model for Afghanistan, and he said that Islam, as he understood it, was a civilized religion and allowed for states in which, for example, Muslims and Christians could live together without problems: "This is the kind of Islamic state we want." He cited Egypt and Saudi Arabia as two nations that he thought had managed to balance the Muslim faith while retaining basic freedoms and also bringing modernization to their countries. I asked what he felt toward unbelievers. "I don't think anything," he said. "I don't mind what they are." I thought that perhaps he was telling me what he thought I wanted to hear, but Hassan does seem to enjoy a reputation locally for moderation and fairness. "He's not all that worked up about religion," Shahmurat, a hulking farmer who has known Hassan for most of his life, said to me. "He's a democrat." Massoud Aziz, an engineer who lives in Dasht-i-Qala, said that Hassan is highly regarded, especially by the middle-class intelligentsia. "He has evolved since his early mujahideen days," Aziz said. "He was not a democratic man then, but he is now."

ONE MORNING, MAMUR HASSAN TOOK ME WITH HIM ON AN IN-
spection tour of the front line. He sat next to the driver of his Russian
UAZ jeep and I sat between two of his bodyguards in the back seat. Two
more bodyguards were squeezed into the space behind us. We drove up
a huge dirty-yellow hill that housed a labyrinth of bunkers, dugouts,
sandbagged bivouacs with howitzers, and Russian T-55 tanks disguised
with straw matting, their cannons pointing toward the Taliban posi-

Mamur Hassan inspecting his troops on a hill overlooking the Amu Dar'ya River
and Ai Khanum, the site of an ancient city, October 2001.

THOMAS DWORZAK/MAGNUM PHOTOS

tions, which were barely visible through clouds of dust. We sped from
bivouac to bivouac, and Hassan popped out of the jeep at each stop,
dressed in a powder-blue tunic and green army fatigue jacket, a white
skullcap on his head. He poked around the soldiers' dugouts and asked
them what they had and what they needed, and jotted down what they
told him on a pad. I went with him into an underground bunker with
bare floors and Kalashnikovs and ammo clips hanging on the walls.
"Only two blankets for ten men," Hassan noted. "My mujahideen are
in bad shape."

The hill where Hassan's men were dug in overlooks the Amu Dar'ya,
near where the Kokcha meets it. The flat plain between the hill and the
river was honeycombed with large holes, and I realized later that this
was what was left of the archaeological excavation site of Ai Khanum,
where a great Hellenistic city flourished from the fourth to the second
centuries BC. The city had been surrounded by brick ramparts, with a
monumental gate and several square towers. It was a formidable citadel
with a palace, mansions, a theater, a temple, and an arsenal. There has
been widespread looting of antiquities in Afghanistan, not to mention
the destruction of ancient sites by bombs and religious zealots. Many of
the treasures from Ai Khanum were displayed in the Kabul Museum,
which was vandalized, its collections dispersed in bazaars and on the illicit art market. The pockmarked plain I saw had apparently been bulldozed to facilitate the looting. The site is one of the main transit points
for supplies and equipment coming into Northern Alliance territory
from Tajikistan, and we watched people landing on the Afghan side of
the river in what looked like a rubber raft. Trucks and other heavy items
are brought across by barge. One of the bases of the Russian border
guards who are still in charge of security in Tajikistan was visible on a
craggy promontory on the far side of the river.

Around four o'clock that day, when the sun was already beginning to descend, I found Mamur Hassan at prayers with some of his commanders in his garden. When they were finished, he called me over and said, in a hushed, edgy voice, that the Americans were supposed to have begun bombing at two p.m. that day, but, because there was a sandstorm and poor visibility, they hadn't. "Maybe they have already begun bombing Kandahar or Kabul, or will tonight," he said. The Alliance's front-line units had been ordered to cease shelling, he explained, so that they wouldn't be mistaken for Taliban positions and get bombed. Driving back to the compound where I had been living, thirty minutes or so from Hassan's home, I heard explosions in the distance. They didn't sound like the usual howitzers or rockets. I turned around and returned to Hassan's base, to stay there for the night.

Mamur Hassan inherited his position in Dasht-i-Qala. He said that his grandfather owned a lot of livestock, and that his father made the first irrigation canal in the area. "This was just a desert then," he said. The area still looks like a desert, but there is a series of irrigation ditches between Hassan's house and the river, and the land around them is fertile and tilled. Hassan's grandfather held the title of *arbob*—headman—which he passed down to his son, Hassan's father. Hassan explained that the title is no longer used. He is called Commander, he says, because of the war and because he leads soldiers, but he retains a social rank equivalent to or greater than that of his forefathers. "There are no more *arbobs*," he said.

Hassan explained that his duty as a commander is to provide security, and that during the years of jihad against the Soviets he also had to act as a judge. "Normally, there are courts, laws, and judges," he said, "but during the war, if someone killed someone else, then it was my responsibility to deal with these people. A commander must be educated and understand about courts and laws. Before the fighting, I didn't understand anything about courts, laws, or human rights, but later, after I took charge of Dasht-i-Qala, I sought out advice, and now I understand." His teacher, he says, was a Muslim priest who was killed in fighting among the mujahideen. "In those days, I rode around on a horse and we had no courts or anything, but now we have courts and laws."

There is, apparently, a good deal of overlap between the duties of a commander and those of the son of the district's former *arbob*. Once a month, Hassan and the three other commanders of the Kokcha Union meet with delegates from the villages and towns in their communities to discuss problems, hear proposals, and seek agreement on actions to be taken. "We try to see how we can help the people," he said, "and most of them give their sons to us to be soldiers."

As a child, Hassan listened to his father's stories about fighting the Russians in the 1920s, when the Central Asian republics were forced into the new USSR. There was a Tajik revolt against the Russian Communists. "The Russians forced the Tajiks into Afghanistan, and my father joined in their guerrilla raids. I wanted to grow up to be a fighter like that. But now I am tired of fighting." He says that when he was young Dasht-i-Qala was a very different kind of place. "We had everything we needed, even though we lived in a small village. We had schools, peace. There were several companies doing business here. But then the Russians crossed the Amu Dar'ya, and the people of Dasht-i-Qala took their children and fled into the mountains, and many of them died. At the time, I had only ten men with guns, and when I reached where the people were at sunrise the next morning, I found women and children there, dead under the snow. It is one of my most terrible memories."

During the jihad against the Soviets, Hassan and his men hid out in a forested section of the mountains east of Dasht-i-Qala, in the neighboring district of Rostaq, from which they carried out raids. "There were only animals there, goats and things," he said. "It is a hard place to get to—twelve hours by horse from Dasht-i-Qala. We had a big underground cave, several guns, and five Russian jeeps. I spent fourteen years there. The Soviets tried to attack us several times in the summer, but they were unable to get close to us. One winter, though, in the snow, they came right up, wearing white, and we didn't see them. They laid siege to us for three months and tried to starve us out, but even then we knew ways to obtain food. And in the end they weren't able to get us." After the Soviets withdrew from Afghanistan in 1989, leaving the puppet government of President Najibullah in place, Hassan helped lead the mujahideen's successful military campaign to reconquer Taloqan. This was managed with the collusion of two Najib commanders who decided to switch sides. In their joint offensive, they killed the top government commander in Taloqan and seized the city. From then until 1992, when Najibullah's government fell to the mujahideen, Takhar Province was one of the main mujahideen bases in Afghanistan.

Hassan has four brothers. Two of them, he said, were killed by the Soviets, along with his mother and five of his nephews. He said that his mother was killed in reprisal for his mujahideen activities. He was in the mountains, and one night he sneaked down to her house and she slaughtered a lamb and fed him and his men. Hassan said that the Russians heard about this and came to her and asked if he had been there. She said no, but they killed her anyway. Within two months, his two brothers were also dead. "The person who helped the Russians"—that is, the man who informed them about Hassan's visit to his mother's house—"was a relative who lived nearby," Hassan said. "The mujahideen had killed his father, and this was his way of taking vengeance. Later, we caught him and I said to him, 'We killed your father and you killed my mother and that's the end of it.' We ended things there." When I expressed surprise at his merciful gesture, he laughed. "Now I am amazed at what I did. But, because of it, this place is secure and no one threatens me or wants to kill me."

Hassan told me that he had also employed conciliatory tactics in 1992, when Dasht-i-Qala reverted to his control. He called an assembly, a *jalsa*, which lasted two or three days. The area had been bitterly divided between anti-Communists and pro-Communists. He proposed that they leave their rancor behind and rebuild their communities under a single commander—him. That is why, he repeated, "Dasht-i-Qala is a secure place and at peace and no one wants to kill me."

HASSAN'S WIVES WEAR BURKHAS, THE EXTREME, HEAD-TO-TOE coverings that the Taliban require and that are common in Northern Alliance territory also. "We must follow our customs," Hassan says. But he doesn't necessarily favor them. "Why is it that in Mecca, the holiest Islamic place, women go with their faces uncovered—and men, too, wear nothing on their heads? If that is the center of Islam, then why don't they wear burkhas?" He concluded, with a rueful smile, "I think the burkha is just an old-fashioned Afghan custom."

One afternoon in Dasht-i-Qala, two women, one in a deep-violet burkha and the other wearing emerald green, floated past, briefly enlivening the backdrop of beat-up olive-green military vehicles, brown desert, and dusty shop fronts. The sight of women, or at least discernibly human creatures in feminine clothes, is about the only thing that relieves the harshness of the landscape. The visible part of Afghan society is unremittingly male, as is the land, which is drab and muscular. There is nothing soft about anything here, none of the creature comforts a Westerner takes for granted. Dust clogs your throat and coats hair and skin, and the people, who cover their faces with scarves and turbans, have learned to live with it in much the same way the British have grown used to rain. Much of northern Afghanistan today is a preindustrial society, without electricity, running water, or telephones. There are not even toys for the children. Water is pumped by hand from wells that have been dug with shovels, and roads are made by crews who break rocks and produce gravel with sledgehammers. Barefoot boys walk back and forth through beds of harvested rice, turning the grains with their toes to dry them in the sun. In the bazaars, porters carry poles with reed baskets on the ends, filled with everything from water to rock salt, which is sold in pinkish-gray chunks before being ground down to powder. Lambs are tethered next to men with long knives who slaughter them and hang the carcasses from hooks, hacking them into a steadily diminishing mess of blood and meat and bone and fat by day's end. Grain and vegetables are weighed in tin scales that are balanced with stones. On market days, people walk from distant villages—some even cross Taliban lines—to buy livestock (donkeys, camels, cattle, and horses) and then they herd the animals back home. The flat horizon is dotted with robed men riding donkeys, others on camelback, and the odd motorbike spitting up clouds of dust.

There is a new primary school for boys and girls in the village of Nawabad, a couple of miles from Dasht-i-Qala. Six hundred boys study in the morning, and the girls, 430 of them, come to class in the afternoon. They study the Koran and Islamic religion, history, mathematics, and geography. Some of the older children are learning English. Most of them come from families who fled the Taliban's military advance last year, when they seized Taloqan and the area right up to the Kokcha River. A couple hundred displaced families still live in miserable little shacks on a scorching wasteland just outside the village, but some five thousand families have been resettled with host families by NGOs. The school is supported by UNICEF, which pays the salaries of the teachers, and Shelter Now International, which built the latrines and provides some of the classroom materials. The school opened in May; many of the girls had not been in a classroom since they fled their hometowns and villages, where the Taliban had closed all their schools.

I visited the school a half hour or so before the day's classes ended.

In twelve separate rooms off a mud courtyard, girls in headscarves sat on reed mats, reciting their lessons in unison. The teachers, mostly young women in their late teens and early twenties, stood in front of blackboards, their heads uncovered. Each of them held a twig switch, as a pointer, and as I entered classrooms or passed by doorways, many of them froze, or shifted their scarves. I asked Headmaster Muhamadi if one of the teachers might be willing to speak to me, and he said no, that was not a good idea. Not because of them, or him, but because of what people in the village would say.

The women teachers were beautiful, with large brown eyes and fair skin. They wore colorful tunics, some of which were decorated with flower patterns, and billowy pantaloons. One woman wore several gold bracelets, and most of the women had dark kohl painted around their eyes. When the classes ended and the students piled out from the school through the mud doorway, the teachers slipped silently down the dirt lane, garbed in white burkhas. They had become wraiths, stumbling along on foot or riding donkeys, bobbing away amid a throng of chattering, happy, barefaced girls.

THE DAY OF THE FIRST AIR STRIKES, MAMUR HASSAN WAS IN the nearby town of Khoja Bahauddin, where the Northern Alliance defense ministry has its headquarters. He returned around sunset and prayed with his lieutenants in the garden. Then everybody became somewhat frantic, and Hassan rushed around between his house and the radio room in the bungalow. When several men were getting ready to leave in their jeeps and began making a lot of noise, he shouted at them to be quiet and to remain on high alert at their bases. He told one man that if he wasn't prepared he would kill him. After they left, Hassan stood under the plane tree, watching the sky above and looking at his wristwatch, twitching with tension.

The men who stayed in the compound listened to Radio Tehran and the BBC's Farsi Service on shortwave radios. When reports of missile attacks began coming in, an exchange of tank and Katyusha rocket fire—baritone booms and clattery whooshes, respectively—could be heard in the distance. A dozen or so mujahideen stayed up most of the night, listening to the news and eavesdropping on enemy field-radio conversations. Hassan's personal secretary, Osman Muhammad, a twenty-four-year-old medical worker who had given up his job to fight the Taliban, had a long conversation on his radio with a Northern Alliance defector he knew. Osman explained to me that the man had had a misunderstanding with Qasi Qabir, Mamur Hassan's counterpart in Khoja Bahauddin, and had fled the district with his family. For the past two and a half years, he had been serving as an officer with the Taliban near Taloqan. Osman said that he had called the man when the bombing began to say, "Come back now or else you will die." The defector had replied that it was too late, that there was no going back, that Qasi Qabir would kill him. Osman said that he had given him his personal guarantee of safety if he returned, but he admitted to me that the promise was worthless, and that Qasi Qabir would have the final say about the defector's fate. "It would be a big problem if Qasi Qabir found out the man came back and stayed here with Mamur Hassan," he said. "He would ask, 'Why are you protecting my enemy?'" I asked Osman if the defector agreed with the Taliban. "No, that's what's so terrible about this," he said. "He doesn't understand why fate has driven him into the arms of his enemies."

The next morning, I asked Mamur Hassan how he had slept. He chuckled and said he had watched TV and listened to the news until one a.m. He has a satellite dish and an aerial, and is thus one of only a few people in Dasht-i-Qala who can watch television. He said that if the Americans kept up their missile strikes and bombing raids the Taliban would go to the mountains to wage a guerrilla campaign. This was not his speculation, he said, but a plan already outlined by the Taliban. He also said that the Northern Alliance had an agreement with the Americans to launch a military offensive in tandem with their raids. Without the air strikes, Hassan said, the Northern Alliance would be able to do very little. He refused to be drawn out on the question of how anyone was going to defeat the Taliban in a guerrilla war in the mountains, although as a veteran of fourteen years in similar mountains he seemed qualified to comment.

"So," I said, "all this talk about finishing off the Taliban in a week once the bombing started was just hot air?" He smiled. "It was to boost the morale of the mujahideen. You understand. The fact of the matter is that the Taliban are very powerful. We need the air strikes in order to make any headway." He claimed that the Taliban had recently increased their troop strength along the hundred or so kilometers of the Takhar Province front line from fifteen thousand to twenty-five thousand soldiers. "This will give you some idea of what we face." Hassan said that if the Americans were able to inflict real damage with the air strikes and if they and the Russians would give the Northern Alliance the military equipment they had promised, then the Taliban could be taken down in a couple of months. "General Fahim has told me to collect all my soldiers and to be at the ready. But it is very difficult for me. I have food for only six hundred men and I have one thousand to feed. So the conditions are not right for a sustained attack. The truth is this. In these conditions, it's impossible."

HASSAN HAD PROMISED TO INTRODUCE ME TO SADRUDDIN, the man who betrayed him and caused his mother's death during the years of the jihad. Sadruddin is forty-five, but he looks closer to sixty, a thin man with a goatee and a deeply furrowed, weather-beaten face. He arrived one morning a few days after the air strikes began. Sadruddin is

Mamur Hassan's second cousin, and he is married to Hassan's niece. I asked him to tell me his version of the story. Had Mamur Hassan killed his father? Yes, Sadruddin said, although Hassan did not give the order. The leader of the mujahideen group that Hassan belonged to at the time had ordered him to capture Sadruddin's father, a well-off landowner, and six others like him from the Dasht-i-Qala area. They took them back to their cave in the mountains of Rostaq, where the mujahideen commander executed them with a pistol. He killed them, Sadruddin says, not because they were pro-Soviet but because they were influential and wealthy people, and he was jealous and afraid of their power. "My father was a good man, and many people followed him. When he died, I was just a boy, and all the responsibility of my family fell upon me." He said that his desire for vengeance was so great that he joined the army of the Najibullah regime. "After I joined the Najib government, I told my soldiers to kill Mamur Hassan's mother." Had he been present at the execution? "Yes," he acknowledged. "But I stood some distance away. We killed her with guns."

Mamur Hassan had been unable to retaliate immediately, Sadruddin said, but "when Najib fell, and Ahmad Shah Massoud occupied this valley, Mamur Hassan became the mujahideen commander, and I fled with thirty-five soldiers to a village that we secured. Mamur Hassan laid siege to us. I held out for four days, until an assembly of *arbobs*, led by Mamur Hassan's father, who was the most respected of all of them, arranged a reconciliation between us. We resolved our differences then, and have been friends ever since. Afterward, all of my soldiers joined the mujahideen, under the command of Mamur Hassan, and later I married his niece." Sadruddin didn't think that this was all that anomalous. "In the Holy Koran it says that if someone kills someone in your family, then you must kill that person. It also preaches forgiveness." Sadruddin is a wheat farmer now. "No more war for me," he said.

# 3

## IN THE COURT OF
## THE PRETENDER

One afternoon in the crowded bazaar in Faizabad, a muddy town of about a hundred thousand people in the far northeastern corner of Afghanistan, I came upon a stall where weapons were being sold. A good submachine gun was available for the equivalent of $480, and there was a derringer in a shoulder holster, and ammunition. I was trying to have a conversation with the arms merchant when a worn-looking man appeared at my side and began to help translate. He spoke, with some effort, a curiously literary English with an Irish-sounding accent, and as we walked among the stalls of the bazaar he explained that he had been a journalist in Kabul until the Taliban closed down all the media. "Now I am jobless," he said, "and a displaced person." I was attracting quite a lot of attention by that time, as *kafirs*, or unbelievers—white-skinned non-Afghans—usually do. Dozens of children and men

This chapter was originally published as "In the Court of the Pretender," *The New Yorker*, October 28, 2001.

were crowding around, gaping and chattering. A soldier in a green jacket, camouflage pants, and black boots walked alongside us, wielding a short leather crop with which he whacked people who came too close to me. "The mujahideen are no different from the Taliban," my new companion said under his breath. He was referring to the soldier when he said "mujahideen," which is the general term for the Muslim fighters who participated in the jihad against the Soviets in the 1980s, and who are now fighting the Taliban. This particular mujahideen wore the uniform of the Islamic State of Afghanistan, the government that fled Kabul when the Taliban took over, in 1996. The members of the government-in-exile are now part of the Northern Alliance, the main anti-Taliban opposition. "The government is fundamentalist," the former journalist muttered. "The only difference is who is in power and who isn't. The problem is Islam, you know. It's like a drug." He told me that he would meet me the next day, that he had things he wanted to say, and he slipped into the crowd.

Faizabad is the capital of Badakhshan Province, which shares a mountainous border with Tajikistan on the north and Pakistan on the east. A panhandle of the province extends northeast for nearly two hundred miles, past the part of Kashmir controlled by Pakistan, and then on to the border with China. The Soviets seized Faizabad when they invaded Afghanistan in December 1979. They simply rolled their tanks across the Tajikistan border and established a base at the airstrip outside of town. Perhaps six thousand troops were stationed there. The mujahideen took control after the Soviets left, ten years later, and I was told that they went on a looting and burning rampage. The ruins of several government complexes are still visible.

Traders' caravans have passed through Faizabad for centuries. Smugglers still hawk their wares in the bazaar, a serpentine track lined with stalls of cloth merchants, shoemakers, and tailors working at old-fashioned hand-operated Butterfly sewing machines. The pelts of wolves, foxes, mink, lynx, and even snow leopards hang next to hand-wrought adzes, pickaxes, hatchets, and oxen plows. Money changers in the bazaar know with precision the current rates for American dollars, afghanis, and Iranian and Saudi rials. I met an eighteen-year-old boy there one day who had just arrived in town after walking over the mountains from Pakistan for a week. He was on the way, he said, to Germany, where an older brother lives. The boy was being helped by a network of relatives who had underworld contacts in Central Asia and Russia. Such people pass through Faizabad all the time, using the same routes by which arms and ammunition come into Afghanistan and by which opium and heroin flow out of it.

Burhanuddin Rabbani, the president of the Islamic State of Afghanistan—which still controls the country's seat in the UN, even though it hasn't controlled much else for some time—was born in Faizabad, and when the Taliban drove him out of Kabul he and his mujahideen fighters fled north, to Mazar-i-Sharif and Taloqan, and finally to his hometown. Faizabad seems like a medieval city, and Rabbani's place in it is similar to that of a theocratic vizier or khan. The streets—dirt lanes, actually—are full of refugees, pale children with running sores, beggars in rags, elderly Tajik and Uzbek men clad in long winter tunics, mujahideen with guns, and women concealed by burkhas. Cows, donkeys, and the occasional horse wander about. Many of the tradesmen have hooped wooden cages that contain partridges. They keep them for *kawk tangi* fights, an ancient sport that is played in the spring.

There is almost no modern urban infrastructure in Faizabad. Most vehicles belong to the government and the mujahideen or to foreign aid organizations, although there are a few traders' trucks with colorful wooden bulwarks. A tiny, Russian-built television station serves some five thousand TV sets, and a beat-up and out-of-date electrical generator produces a few hours of weak electricity every four days. An ancient windup-telephone system operates through a switchboard. Several men, working in a large shed, hand-set a biweekly government newspaper—one folded sheet printed in Farsi, with a circulation of five hundred. The printing machines, which are from India, East Germany, and Romania, are museum pieces from the age of steel and iron foundries. Water is produced by rudimentary waterwheels or hand-pumped from open wells and carried by men and boys with buckets hanging from poles resting on their shoulders. Rubbish is dumped pretty much everywhere, and, while some people have outhouse latrines, a great many people—men, at least—defecate out of doors. The stench in certain quarters of the city, particularly around ruined houses, vacant lots, and along stretches of the riverbank, is overwhelming.

PRESIDENT RABBANI'S HOME IS, BY FAIZABAD STANDARDS, LUX- urious. It is a two-story, tin-roofed house set behind a high stone-and-concrete wall on a back alleyway up the hill from the bazaar, in the Old City. The house is painted a pale blue, and there are iron railings on the verandas. Mujahideen sentinels are stationed outside. When Rabbani leaves the house, he travels in a convoy of two black Toyota Land Cruisers surrounded by gunmen. I interviewed him one afternoon in a bungalow called the Star Hotel, a few minutes from his house, where senior Northern Alliance officials work and live and which also serves as a kind of reception house for Rabbani. It was built on stone ramparts overlooking the Kokcha River, and you get to it on foot over a narrow concrete causeway. In the late afternoon, men fish from the causeway, and boys play games of volleyball on a nearby sandbar. Two soldiers carefully frisk visitors to the building and then inspect all their belongings. Items such as cigarette lighters, knives, and battery-operated flashlights are politely confiscated. Extra security precautions have been taken since September 9, when Massoud was assassinated. The assassins had interviewed Rabbani in the Panjshir Valley a few days before they traveled to Massoud's headquarters in Khoja Bahauddin.

A room in the Star Hotel has been set up for Rabbani's appearances. The floor is covered with a red carpet and the ceiling is draped with a cheap flowery fabric. Velvety armchairs are lined up against the walls, and at one end of the room, next to a flag stand with the banner of the Islamic State of Afghanistan, a chair has been placed for the president. Just in front, a low table is decorated with little vases filled with plastic flowers. The windows look out to the roiling, boulder-filled waters of the Kokcha, and the sound of rushing water penetrates the room.

The interview was scheduled for three o'clock, but Rabbani was an hour and a half late, and two of his senior minions—smooth young English-speaking men who wore Western clothes and had what looked like blow-dried hairdos—kept me company. Another aide began glancing pointedly at his watch after we had been standing in the room for more than an hour. "He must be busy with the Queen," the man said sarcastically. I was a little surprised, and asked him what people in Faizabad thought of Rabbani. "Except for a few commanders and these people"—he nodded his head toward the two minions with the hairdos—"he is hated by everyone." The man kept his voice low and watched to make sure that the loyalists were out of earshot. "People are fed up with him," he said. He explained that there had been no love lost between Rabbani and Massoud, and that there was a power struggle going on between Massoud's followers and Rabbani's. Massoud's official successor, General Fahim, had not yet managed to assume full command, and the situation was particularly tense because of the machinations involving the United States and the attempt to construct a "post-Taliban" government. Even some of Rabbani's relatives didn't want him to be president again. "Things have changed dramatically," the aide said, since Massoud's death, "and no one knows what will happen tomorrow." He then moved discreetly away to stand on the opposite side of the room.

Burhanuddin Rabbani leads a group of mujahideen in prayer at sunset in Faizabad.
October 2001.    THOMAS DWORZAK/MAGNUM PHOTOS

A few moments later, Rabbani entered the hallway leading to the room, his two aides scurrying along in half crouches in front of him, holding their hands on their hearts. Rabbani is in his early sixties. He has pale skin, and his beard is white and immaculately trimmed. He was wearing a pair of smart black leather loafers, a beige *shalwar kameez*— the tunic and loose pants that most Afghan men wear—and a camel-colored woolen waistcoat under a black-and-white herringbone blazer. His turban was white with black stripes. As he came into the room, he greeted me with a brief, friendly nod and said, in English, "Good afternoon." Then he sat in his armchair and awaited my questions. His responses consisted mostly of a litany of Taliban perfidies and a long soliloquy about his past good intentions, which had been sadly frustrated by the Taliban's seizure of power.

Rabbani said that the Taliban's radical and violent interpretation of Islam under the guise of Sharia law was in fact nothing but an extremist application of a tribal code. I asked him to explain for me the brand of Islam that he had tried to establish when he was president—from 1992, when the mujahideen ousted the Afghan government that the Soviets had installed, until 1996, when the Taliban came in. He was vague on details, and said, a little defensively, "As you know, while I was president, because of the constant infighting I was unable to enforce Islamic law in a way that could benefit and advance Afghan society." Rabbani talked about the things he had tried to do: He had signed an amnesty for his former Communist foes; allowed political parties and a diverse media to operate freely; he had promoted foreign investment; rebuilt the war-damaged Kabul University; encouraged female participation in teaching and banking jobs. Many other projects were still in the planning stages. "Unhappily, the ongoing civil war has not allowed us to take the practical steps to implement these projects," he said.

I asked Rabbani why, in the part of Afghanistan under his control, women wore the burkha. "The burkha is not a part of the Islamic tradition," he said. "When I was on the religious law faculty"—at Kabul University in the late sixties and early seventies—"I designed a new form of dress appropriate for female students that covered the head and shoulders, but left the face and hands exposed. Unfortunately, because of the coup, we were unable to take the matter further. Here the burkha is worn because of tradition. Because of the insecurity of the war situation, women are afraid not to wear it, but afterward they will be free not to use the burkha if they wish."

After about forty-five minutes of this sort of thing, Rabbani took his leave. The next day, I met with the man who had spoken about a rift between Massoud and Rabbani. "Massoud's people now suspect Rabbani and Abdul Rasul Sayyaf"—a mujahideen commander stationed in the Panjshir Valley—"of being behind the assassination," he said. Sayyaf has a bad reputation because in the 1980s he was closely allied with Arabs, particularly the Saudis. He gave the Arab assassins safe passage through Northern Alliance territory and helped them get an audience with Massoud, during which they set off a bomb hidden around one man's waist. Faizabad is full of conspiracy theories and skeptical glosses on events, and my informant, who told me that his name is Walid (a pseudonym, as are several other names here), was not the only person who gave me a version of the story of Rabbani's alleged complicity in Massoud's murder. Rabbani, on the other hand, told me that the assassins had wanted to kill him and Sayyaf as well as Massoud, and had tried to get all three of them together for a photograph.

IDRIS, THE FORMER JOURNALIST WHO SAID THAT ISLAM IS LIKE a drug, came to the government guesthouse where I was staying the day after we met in the bazaar. He suggested that we walk down by the river, and when we were out of earshot of the official minders, he said that we could sit next to the ruined concrete bridge, and that if anyone asked

what we were discussing we would say it was the history of the bridge.
So we sat on a pile of broken masonry and Idris talked about his despair.
He didn't care if he got into trouble for speaking to me. "I am tired of
this life," he said, "and I am willing to be sacrificed. I am against fundamentalism of all kinds. I am against Islam, and when the Soviets were
in Afghanistan I was also against Communism, which I think is a kind
of fundamentalism." I asked him about President Rabbani. "Rabbani is
a fundamentalist just like the Taliban," he said, and then he began to
whisper. "Rabbani is secretly trying to make a deal with the Taliban, except for the Arabs who are in Afghanistan." He meant excluding Osama
bin Laden's people. I asked Idris how he knew this, and he said that
someone who worked closely with Rabbani had told him that overtures
had taken place. Idris explained that Rabbani hoped to return to power
as the head of a "moderate" fundamentalist regime made up of his allies
and "acceptable" Taliban figures.

  This, again, was a version of a story I'd heard from others, some of
whom have more authoritative credentials than Idris does. In the public discussions about creating a coalition of factions that would form a
government if or when the Taliban are crushed, Rabbani has guardedly
supported the involvement of King Zahir Shah, whom the Americans
and the Pakistanis are encouraging to convene a Loya Jirga, a grand
national council that would choose a leader. But Walid said it is well
known that Rabbani would never be elected by the Loya Jirga, and that
he is secretly forming alliances to counter the king's coalition. The king
is an ethnic Pashtun—that is, a member of a group from which, historically, Afghanistan's rulers have been drawn. The Taliban and most people who live in the southern part of Afghanistan are also Pashtuns. The
mujahideen who formed a government in Kabul in 1992 and now make
up the Northern Alliance are mostly ethnic Tajiks, like Rabbani, and
Uzbeks.

A few days after our interview, President Rabbani went to Dushanbe, the capital of Tajikistan, to meet with the Russian president, Vladimir Putin, who was on his way home from Shanghai, where he had met with President Bush. Walid told me later that Putin had assured Rabbani that he was the most acceptable candidate for the presidency and had encouraged him not to support the king. "Of course, Rabbani does not need convincing about this," Walid said. According to Walid, Putin has been playing a double game with the Americans, as has Rabbani. But the meeting in Dushanbe clarified Putin's opposition to Taliban participation in a coalition government, and presumably Rabbani's gestures to the Taliban have ceased. Russia stepped up its military support for the Northern Alliance, and the first major shipment of new war matériel had just been handed over. "Russia provided the United Front"— the official name of the Northern Alliance—"with forty-five million dollars' worth of different weapons. Eight tanks, a remarkable amount of ammunition, and heavy and light weapons crossed the Tajik border into Afghanistan," Walid said. No helicopters were included in this package, he said, although Rabbani has been promised a further $75 million worth of hardware, including more tanks, helicopters, and new antiaircraft guns. The present understanding with Russia seems to be that Rabbani would lead a post-Taliban government that would include Afghan technocrats now living abroad—these presumably picked by the Americans, and perhaps including some of Zahir Shah's people. "Rabbani is very pleased," Walid said.


DURING OUR CHAT BY THE RIVER, IDRIS EXPLAINED WHY HE distrusted Rabbani. "When Rabbani was president," he said, "we had to wear beards, to pray all the time. Now he is weak, and so he is trying to put on a good face to the world, but if he becomes strong again he will do the same. He is a fundamentalist!" Idris is thirty-eight, although, like most Afghan men, he looks much older. He grew up in a rural district not far from Faizabad and studied journalism in Kabul in the 1980s. After he graduated, he served for three years in the military, during the government of Mohammad Najibullah, the Afghan Communist whom the Soviets made president in the late eighties, and who remained in power until he was ousted by the mujahideen in 1992. Idris wrote for army publications, and afterward worked for a newspaper that he describes as impartial. When Kabul fell to the mujahideen, however, he fled to Pakistan, fearing that he might be killed. He returned to Afghanistan two years ago. He has four children, ranging in age from three to thirteen. "How did you manage to have all those children if you were out of the country?" I asked him. He laughed, and explained that he had returned to Afghanistan several times, clandestinely, by walking over the border at Chitral—a timeworn smugglers' route—and sneaking back home. He would enter his village at night, he said, and not leave the house until it was time to go back to Pakistan. He came home to stay because after his last visit his wife had been beaten and interrogated by the local mujahideen commander. His family still lives in the village, and since he cannot get work he is finding it hard to spend time with them. He says they nearly died of hunger eight months ago. He came to Faizabad to see if he could find work as a translator for a Western journalist.

When I suggested to Idris that it must have been very hard for his wife all those years that he was away, he assured me that he had her total support, and that, like him, she is educated, and is in agreement with his views. He said that they have been teaching their children not to believe in Islam, although they understand that they must pay lip service to religion in school. He said that he had thought about naming his son Salman, after Salman Rushdie, "but some of my friends convinced me that this was not a good idea."

While he was in Pakistan, Idris survived by translating books from Urdu, which he learned while he was there, along with English. I ended up spending several days in Faizabad with him, and he always carried a Farsi-English dictionary and would ask me to explain the difference between similar terms—between "fornication" and "adultery," for instance. Idris said that Islam is like "a cave"—he pulled out the Farsi-English dictionary to find the word he wanted—which is "full of bacteria." I remarked that life must be extremely hard for him, being alone in a land such as this. "Well, you know, there are a lot of people in Afghanistan who hate Islam, but they cannot show their faces," he said. He described himself as a humanist, and said he had read a lot: "Goethe, Jean-Paul Sartre, Victor Hugo, Jean-Jacques Rousseau, and Albert Camus." Also American writers like Faulkner and Steinbeck, he added. "It helped me open my eyes and look at the sky of the world." He had written a book about Islam, unpublished, of course. It was critical of the Koran, and of the Prophet Muhammad, whom he described as an illiterate shepherd. The book was titled, he said, translating roughly from the Farsi, "The Crazy Dogs of Certain Centuries."

Idris is an iconoclast, and, for Afghanistan, an extraordinary man— brave to the point of foolhardiness. In this context, in fact, he could be regarded as half mad, and perhaps he is. He is well read, and an atheist, he understands that life can be different, and he is desperately clinging to his beliefs in a poverty-stricken charnel house that is ruled by illiterate gunmen, brutish warlords, and superstitious mullahs.

THERE IS A LARGE GRAFFITO ON A WALL ALONG THE MAIN ROAD into Faizabad that says, in English, "Production Sale and Use of Opium Is Strongly Forbidden by Islam." A similar declamation is painted on a ruined building at the airport. One can't help getting the impression that these are Potemkin-style diktats designed to please workers for

United Nations agencies and Western aid organizations who go in and out of town. Opium is the most important crop in Afghanistan, not least for the mujahideen, who got into the business in the eighties, during the jihad against the Soviets. Last year, according to the CIA, Afghanistan produced 70 percent of the world's opium. Much of it is said to go through Faizabad. After I had been in town for a few days, I met a man who works for one of the foreign aid organizations and who explained to me how some of the trafficking works. "A lot of opium is grown in Badakhshan Province," he said. "And some is purchased from local people on both sides of the front lines"—where the Taliban and the Northern Alliance are fighting. "It's mostly sent out in raw form and then refined in Tajikistan and sent to the West through Moscow." He said that in 2000, when he was helping distribute wheat to refugees near the front line on the Kokcha River, near the border with Tajikistan, he had seen donkeys ferrying opium between the Taliban and Northern Alliance sides. The Northern Alliance commanders and the Taliban arranged the exchanges by radio, he said. "Some of them had friendly contacts, even though they were fighting one another." Helicopters from Tajikistan picked up the opium at drop-off points near the border formed by the Amu Dar'ya River. The aid worker said that last year there was an official ban on opium trafficking, but that "no real practical steps have been taken." He smiled. The ban was a "nine-day wonder," good for public relations.

I also discussed the opium situation with Muhammad Nazir Shafiee, President Rabbani's foreign-relations adviser and a member of the President's Commission for the Fight Against Drugs and Narcotics. Nazir is twenty-seven years old. He was one of the aides who had held his hand over his heart as he escorted Rabbani into the room at the Star Hotel for our interview. He explained that Rabbani's government had been confiscating drugs, arresting traffickers, and destroying opium fields. But, he added, the Islamic State of Afghanistan also had to deal with drought, war, and the influx of displaced people from both plagues. The UN and other international aid organizations had not helped them much with crop-substitution programs for the affected farmers. Nazir blamed the opium trafficking and the heroin trade on ethnic Pashtuns, and on the Taliban. He was especially critical of Pakistan. "In Faizabad, there has only been one crime in the past twelve months—a theft from one shop. The people here are not familiar with international criminal activity—this comes from Pakistan. The Pakistanis, you know, will sell their own mothers for four thousand rupees."

Nazir also complained that whenever UN officials or foreign diplomats came to northern Afghanistan they were critical because women wore burkhas. "They don't have to wear burkhas," he said. "Women are free to do what they want here." He attributed the burkha-wearing phenomenon to social pressures. He denied claims that Rabbani first imposed the burkha when he became president. "At the beginning of the Islamic State of Afghanistan, we were weak and had to make compromises and accept the participation of Gulbuddin Hekmatyar, a fundamentalist. He had Pakistan behind him, and he was raining rockets on Kabul. He made women wear burkhas, but it was not the policy of the Islamic State of Afghanistan. The West thinks we are fundamentalists, and that because we started the Islamic revolution we are dangerous. But we are reasonable Muslims, I tell you!"

Nazir does not support the return of King Zahir Shah. "How can we accept this man who has spent the last twenty-eight years living a comfortable life in Rome? Did he come once to see the refugees in Pakistan during all the years of the jihad, even just to say hello? No, not once. Not for one day, not even one hour. He never came. And, before that, for forty years he was king of this country. He spent his time having a very good life, hunting, drinking, and playing with women. Did he make a road? Did he leave a factory that could make one of these?"— Nazir held up a ballpoint pen. "No! He left nothing." If there was any man qualified to run Afghanistan after the Taliban were thrown out, he said, it was Rabbani. And he hoped to go to Kabul and have a post—*inshallah*, God willing—in the future government with him.

Nazir explained that he owed his position and his rising influence in part to his late father, a religious scholar who had been chief justice for Rabbani's Jamiat-i-Islami Party and an old friend. His father was also Rabbani's law adviser during his presidency. Nazir is from an Afghan family of, as he put it, high standing. "We own twenty-four thousand acres of land," he said. "I have stamped documents from all the kings of Afghanistan over four centuries which says we are the owners." Under the Soviet-backed Communist regime, he said, the family's land was confiscated and split into many six-acre plots that were given to farmers. "We have recouped most of it." Four thousand people lived on the land as sharecroppers. The people in his district still treat him with deference and address him by the hereditary feudal title "Khan," but he doesn't like it. "I tell them not to, because I am a modern man, and I want to make my way with my own shoulders." If democracy returned to Afghanistan, he said, he hoped to go into politics himself, maybe by running for parliament. He would have a chance of winning, because of his family's influence. "We are not only economically powerful, you see; we have also been a very religious family, for centuries." So how high was he aiming? "First, parliament, and then who knows? I will see how far I can go."

ZARMEENA, AN AFGHAN WOMAN OF ABOUT THIRTY, WORKS FOR a foreign aid organization that has an office in the so-called New City, a spacious, dusty suburb of Faizabad where most of the NGOs have their compounds—although there are virtually no foreign workers left there. They fled the country after Massoud was killed and the World Trade Center was attacked. Zarmeena wears a burkha when she is in public, but inside her office she simply puts a scarf over her hair. She lived in Kabul through the years of Communist government and was there in 1992, when Najibullah fell and the mujahideen seized power. "The changes from Najib to Rabbani weren't so great," Zarmeena said, "except that the fighting went on, and every part of Kabul was controlled by a different mujahideen faction, and it was very difficult to move from one part of the city to the other. I lived in the area controlled by Rabbani and Massoud's men. When the Taliban came, I used to wear a big shawl with only my eyes showing. Then I heard that some women were being beaten in the city center for wearing the same kind of shawl, and so I put on the burkha. It is difficult to wear, especially for more than two or three hours; it is very hot inside, it is hard to walk, and you get a headache, because the top of it is so tight on your head."

Zarmeena was a medical student until that became no longer possible for women. "So then I got married," she said, with a laugh, "because I had nothing else to do, and a year after the Taliban took power we came here. When we arrived, it was more or less the same as Kabul. Women could be doctors and teachers, for instance, although they were not allowed to work with the Western NGOs. It was not looked well upon—that a woman would be working in an office together with men." Zarmeena was one of the first women to overcome that ban. As for the burkha, she believes that it is officially required in Northern Alliance territory. "I think it is a law." I told her that President Rabbani had said that Afghan women were free to go without it if they chose. Zarmeena smiled and raised her eyebrows. "I'd like to see him say that to a group of Afghan women," she said. Zarmeena was teaching English to some girls, and she had not yet got into trouble for that, although she knew people who had. "The way it works here, if I am very active—if I do things they don't like, like speaking out or participating in certain meetings—the mullahs will make remarks about me in the Friday prayers. The government supports the mullahs in this. It is a form of

social control. And this is why women here do not take off the burkha."
I asked her if she would go out without one. "It takes great courage to
be the first," she said. "It would be very hard."

SALAHUDDIN RABBANI, THE PRESIDENT'S ELDEST SON, IS MAR-
ried to a woman who does not wear a burkha, although he said he hoped
that I would not mention this. Salahuddin's wife and two children live
in London, as did he until September 15, when he returned to Afghanistan to be with his father. Salahuddin is thirty years old and is the third
of the president's ten children. He is a full-faced young man of medium
build and height, darker-skinned than his father, with a faint goatee and
dark hair parted in the middle. He wears frameless glasses, and has a
modest-seeming, intelligent demeanor.

Salahuddin studied at the King Fahd University of Petroleum and
Minerals in Dhahran from 1989 to 1995, and received a degree in mar-
keting. He went to Pakistan, married an Afghan girl from a Pashtun
family living in exile there, and moved to Dubai, where he started an
import-export business, which he didn't particularly enjoy. He and his
family then moved to London. He earned a degree in business manage-
ment and was going to continue his studies, but now he thinks he should
stay in Afghanistan. "I see my future here, as an Afghan trying to do
something for his country," he said to me, adding, with a chuckle, "Now
I just have to convince my wife."

Salahuddin came back, he said, because "the death of Massoud
placed a huge burden on my father." He confirmed that Massoud had
died when the bombs went off, but that his death was kept secret for almost a week because of the demoralizing effect it would have on the
Northern Alliance fighters. The Taliban immediately launched an offensive. "They intended to take northern Afghanistan," he said, "and
then Samarkand and Bukhara"—in Uzbekistan—and also advance

into Tajikistan. "And, you know, they might have succeeded, because the Central Asian states are very weak. If the Russian border guards weren't stationed there, they might have fallen already."

Salahuddin describes his father as a moderate political figure. He recalled that in the 1980s, during the jihad against the Soviets in Afghanistan, his father went to Washington at the invitation of President Reagan: "He went at the height of anti-American feeling in the Muslim world, and was opposed by many Arab states who had been backing the mujahideen, and he even laid a wreath at the Tomb of the Unknown Soldier." Afterward, Salahuddin said, "These wealthy Arabs stopped supporting us, and they began calling my father 'the American.'"

I said to Salahuddin that it seemed clear to me that his father, for all his careful language on the matter, was against the return of King Zahir Shah, and he agreed. "This government is the legitimate government and is made up of people who fought for the country for many years. If Zahir Shah comes back, which forces will pave the way for him and protect him—the UN?" He objected to the criticism of the Northern Alliance as a group of ethnic minorities. "There is no majority people in Afghanistan," he said. The notion that Afghanistan had to be led by an ethnic Pashtun was a Pakistani concoction.

Salahuddin made much of what he perceived as the dilemma the Pakistanis were now in because of their interference in Afghanistan's affairs. "With the Taliban and Osama bin Laden, the Pakistanis put all of their eggs in one basket. Now they are looking for another force to represent their interests. In a sense, before the missile strikes, by being the one country trying to legitimatize the Taliban in the eyes of the international community, they were trying to get a UN seat for bin Laden." Salahuddin laughed. "That would have been a real first. The first UN representation for an international terrorist."

Salahuddin, like Nazir, said that his father had not been responsible for the introduction of the burkha and other Islamic social restrictions.

"My wife is a dental hygienist," he said, "and currently a domestic engineer"—this was said lightheartedly, meaning she was raising their kids—"but if she wants to go to work I don't mind. My father did not impose the burkha. The burkha is an Afghan custom. No one is telling women they must wear it." He wouldn't let himself get drawn into a discussion of whether or not it would be appropriate for his wife to test this view of the situation if she came to Afghanistan, but when we said goodbye, amid the attendants and bodyguards, Salahuddin turned to me and said, "I hope when we next meet it will be in Kabul"—he smiled—"and that there you will see many women who are dressed only in scarves and loose clothing, not in burkhas."

I MET A MAN IN FAIZABAD, DR. ROSTUM, WHO IS WHAT HE DE-scribed as a member of Afghanistan's educated urban intelligentsia. He is more than a decade older than Salahuddin, and his experiences during the years that the Rabbani government was in power—years that Salahuddin was out of the country—did not conform with Salahuddin's recollections. Dr. Rostum came to Faizabad last year, when his hometown fell to the Taliban. It was the fifth time in the last six years that he had moved his family because of the advancing war. He came to see me at the guesthouse one afternoon just before sunset, and we went to the far end of the garden to talk. We sat at one of the stone tables overlooking the Kokcha, under a big walnut tree.

Dr. Rostum was a medical student in Kabul and had graduated during the Communist regime in the mid-eighties. He has a beard and wears a *shalwar kameez*, but he said that he used to be clean-shaven and wear Western clothes. Then, in the early nineties, when Rabbani took power, men were required to have beards and pray five times a day, and women were separated from men on public buses. "I am a Muslim," he said, "and sometimes I even go to the mosque to pray—but why should

I be forced to go five times a day?" The transformation of Afghanistan began when the mujahideen were in Kabul, he said. He described a mujahideen commander ordering the destruction of the electrical generator in the town where he lived in northern Afghanistan. It was an act of vengeance against the Communists. "The commander said, 'The Communists say that history can never be turned back. But I will turn it back.' And he destroyed the generator." Dr. Rostum clasped his hands together tightly when he told me this story, recalling what it meant for his country.

"In the seventies," Dr. Rostum said, "life for me was going to school and being well dressed and thinking about the future. A doctor was a well-regarded person then, with a secure job in a hospital. Every morning, he shaved and would dress in pants and a shirt, and then he would drive to work in his own vehicle, or go by government transport. There was a government, and the government paid him a salary. He didn't have to work in other jobs, like being a baker, a salesman, or a clerk. He only had to be a doctor. But now in Faizabad there are doctors and science teachers who are making bricks, working as clerks, selling food in the bazaar. I personally hoped that when the mujahideen came to power, since they had been backed by foreign countries, they would bring modernity with them. But it was exactly the opposite of what I hoped." And then, when the Taliban came, things got even worse.

"When we were younger, under Zahir Shah"—in the sixties—"and later under Daoud"—who overthrew the king in 1973—"there were cinemas and theaters in Kabul and Kandahar, Herat and Mazar-i-Sharif and Jalalabad, and for ladies there was no pressure to wear burkhas. In those days, maybe one to two percent of the girls wore burkhas—they were from very conservative religious families. And they were not like the burkhas of today, which have come from Iran or Pakistan; they were more like long veils. My father was a small trader who made trips to Kabul. My brothers and I begged him to bring us a radio, and, when he did, our house was like a wedding party for three months. All of our neighbors would come over to hear the news and listen to music." Dr. Rostum smiled as he recalled that the radio had played every morning from six to eight, then at lunchtime from twelve to one, and in the evenings from six to nine. "When Daoud came to power in Afghanistan, the education was great, it was the golden time for education. And at the end of his time he brought us a TV station. It was a very new thing for us, to see people announcing the news, watching films, and singing songs. And even after the Soviet invasion, in the cities that were controlled by the government, things continued mostly as usual. The educational system continued and received the support of the government. There were lots of books, as well, even if these came mostly from the Soviet bloc. The way things are today, it is as if Afghanistan had stepped back a hundred years in time."

I asked Dr. Rostum if he was depressed. "Yes," he said. "Very depressed. I want to live, to have a comfortable life. What is that? To have electricity, good sanitation, and to have time for oneself. For instance, now I have to spend a lot of my time—when I am not working—just in finding and preparing food for the family. There is no time for entertainment, or sports, or travel. It would be nice to have a TV satellite dish . . . or any of the things that are necessary for the enjoyment of modern life. The second reason I am depressed is that there is no possibility of a future for my children. My wife and I tutor them, but they still have to go to school for their accreditation. And the schools are very bad. My son, for instance, is in the eighth grade, and out of eleven subjects he has eight that have to do with religion or the Arabic language. It's very difficult for him—he is only twelve years old. All this started with the mujahideen.

"What I dream about for the future for Afghanistan is to have a stable government, to have electricity and paved roads, and good relations with our neighbors," Dr. Rostum said. "I hope that when the policy makers form their coalition they will not forget the educated people, the doctors and teachers and engineers who have been in Afghanistan during all these years of fighting. I say this because if Zahir Shah and his people come here from Europe to form a government and bring their aristocrats and their technocrats—they are of course welcome to include such qualified people—they should not forget those of us who were not with the Taliban or with the mujahideen. We have a right to have a voice in the future of our country."

# 4

## THE SURRENDER

Abdullah Gard lives in a run-down concrete-block house in Talo-qan, a city of about two hundred thousand people in a fertile valley in northern Afghanistan. The headquarters of Ahmad Shah Massoud was in Taloqan until September 2000, when the Taliban captured the city. Abdullah Gard helped the Northern Alliance defend Taloqan, and when Massoud retreated, he went with him. But early in 2001 Gard surprised many people who knew him by defecting, with his fighting force of several hundred men, to the Taliban. They fought against their former comrades in arms for months. Then, on November 11, as the Taliban abandoned one Afghan city after another, including Taloqan, Abdullah Gard and his men switched sides again.

I visited Abdullah Gard late one blustery afternoon a week after his most recent defection. Girls with brooms made of twigs were sweeping up autumn leaves under the plane trees outside his house. The gates in

This chapter was originally published as "The Surrender," *The New Yorker*, December 2, 2001.

front of the house were guarded by a dozen turbaned fighters, and in the
dusty yard children drew water from a well by hand. Several men escorted me into an upstairs room with red carpets on the floor and flat
red cushions around the sides. It was the third day of the Muslim holy
month of Ramadan, about an hour before sunset prayers and the end
of the day's fasting. A teakettle was set on a brazier in the corner, boiling water for the first tea to be drunk since sunrise. Through the window you could watch an American B-52 bomber flying slowly over
Taloqan, trailed by double jet streams. The plane was on its way back
from a bombing run over the nearby city of Kunduz, where thousands
of Afghan, Chechen, Pakistani, Uzbek, and Arab fighters were still
entrenched.

Abdullah Gard is a burly, bearded man in his late thirties. Three of
his officers lounged around the room, staring at me, and one of them, a
thin, gray-eyed man who played with plastic worry beads, glared suspiciously. Gard listened attentively as I explained my interest in understanding why he had switched sides twice in the war. Even one defection
seemed anomalous to a Westerner, and the Afghans' acceptance of such
things was puzzling. Gard replied that he was a special case, because—
and this was the first time he had discussed this, he said—he had been
acting secretly on orders from Massoud. He was a double agent. "I was
to find out how many foreign troops there were here with the Taliban,
their nationalities, who their commanders were, and their plans. And I
was supposed to help Massoud from inside Taloqan when he launched
an attack." Massoud was the only person who knew of the mission at
first, but after Massoud was assassinated, a few others were brought into
the picture. Most people still did not know why Abdullah Gard had
switched sides.

Gard said that the majority of foreign troops in the north were
"Punjabis," by which he meant Pakistanis; Uzbeks in the radical Islamic

Movement of Uzbekistan, led by Juma Namangani; Arabs of various nationalities; and Chechens. He said that they disagreed about strategy, although the common goal, of course, was the liberation of all of Afghanistan. But the Pakistanis argued that their country should be liberated next, and the Uzbeks insisted that it should be Uzbekistan. Not so long ago, Gard said, there was a rumor that Osama bin Laden had visited the north, but it was never confirmed, and he didn't see him.

Not all of the Taliban had been convinced by Gard's defection, and he was kept under surveillance. Once, he and his men were disarmed and he was told to stay in his home. During that period, he said, he refrained from contact with Massoud. Then, after a month, his command was returned to him. Just before the fall of Taloqan, he came under suspicion again. For most of his time with the Taliban, Gard said, he and his men operated as a mobile reserve battalion, and they were dispatched to places beyond Taloqan and Kunduz, such as Mazar-i-Sharif, Bamiyan, and Kabul.

I asked Gard how he had managed to persuade his fighters to go along with the ruse. He smiled. "That is my secret," he said affably. I pressed him. Surely, I said, he must have made an effort to avoid having his men on the forward lines, where they might kill his real allies? On the contrary, he replied. "I sent my men to the front line, and they were in some very bloody battles. Once, fifteen of them were captured, including five officers. One was taken prisoner and the other four were rearmed and returned to the battlefield as Northern Alliance fighters." Gard smiled, and shrugged. "They could not be told the truth, ever."

Gard said that he didn't particularly want to remain in the military. "If my country is secure, I would prefer not to continue being a commander." But how would he survive? "God is kind," he replied. "He will help us survive." He had three wives, with whom he had had two sons and two daughters. Maybe he would have time to make more children.

He laughed, and his officers laughed, too. It was sunset by then, and he left the room to pray.

IN THE FIRST WEEK OF ITS LIBERATION FROM TALIBAN CONtrol, Taloqan bustled and heaved with returning refugees and Northern Alliance fighters. Military vehicles, their horns blaring, careened around slow-moving donkey carts, darting children, and porters pulling handcarts loaded with goods. Jitneys drawn by horses adorned with ornamental red bobbles and jingling bells served as taxis. Occasionally, a helicopter clattered overhead, and several times a day B-52s added their dull roar to the din. Groups of boys hung out in front of newly opened kiosks where music blared and cassettes were sold. Under the Taliban, music was banned.

Taloqan is laid out in a geometrical grid of streets that are flanked by drainage ditches and lines of plane trees. Many houses are built of concrete rather than mud, and the main street is paved. The Taloqan River flows past the edge of town, and the land nearby is good for farming. Food stalls were stocked with fresh cauliflower, onions, radishes, red and yellow apples, pomegranates. Slaughtered lambs hung from meat hooks in butchers' stalls. There was plenty of the flat wheat bread, called naan, in the bakeries. The town has several *chaikhanas*, the traditional Afghan teahouses, where men gather to drink tea and eat kebab and rice with mutton. The *chaikhanas* provide space for sleeping, and at night large wooden platforms were filled with dozens of men lying willy-nilly alongside one another.

At the western end of town, the main street turns into the road to Kunduz, which lies forty miles away. The road snakes across a plain planted with wheat and dotted with small family farms. Mountains rise on all sides of the plain: A rumpled yellow, brown, and red anatomy of treeless hills ascend to great, snowcapped ridges. The new front line began at a bridge over a river near the village of Bangi, about twenty miles outside of Taloqan. The Taliban and the Northern Alliance were faced off at either end of a small valley, a half mile or so from each other. By mid-November, the fields were clipped stubble. As military trucks and tanks raced back and forth, children stood guard over husked wheat kernels that were spread out for drying in rectangular patches along the road.

One morning, I visited the military headquarters of Commander Daoud Khan, of the Northern Alliance, who was overseeing the reoccupation of Taloqan. There was a Toyota pickup truck smeared with mud outside the gate. Daoud's men told me that the truck had been driven across enemy lines and into town during the night by six Taliban field commanders who had defected, along with their three hundred fighters. I met two of the Taliban, dark men in disheveled black robes and turbans. They were surrounded by staring mujahideen. I asked one of the Taliban, who said his name was Muhammad Israel, why he had decided to defect, and he said that he had done so for the good of the country, in order to avoid unnecessary bloodshed. Given the fact that Kunduz was being bombed from the air and encircled by the Northern Alliance, I suggested, his decision appeared to have more to do with survival, but Israel pointed out that crossing Taliban lines with three hundred men, all of whom faced certain death if they were detected, had been very risky. He seemed to expect to be commended for his bravery, and when I moved away he and the other Taliban were regaling a group of mujahideen with the details of their nocturnal adventure.

Commander Daoud, a former Massoud aide, is a tall, strapping man in his late thirties. He said that since he had taken control of Taloqan, thirty local Taliban commanders had switched sides, bringing with them three thousand men. He was hoping that more would follow. "I don't want an attack to be launched on Kunduz," he said. "I want all the Taliban in Kunduz to surrender and be taken captive." He conceded that this was a faint prospect, given the large number of foreign fighters in the city, most of whom were thought to be ready to fight to the death. "If they don't accept this, then we have no recourse but to push forward, and to kill them."

DAOUD TOLD ME THAT THE FORMER TALIBAN COMMANDER IN Taloqan, Mullah Shabir Ahmed, was in "a safe location." My translator, Yama, the twenty-four-year-old son of the logistics chief for the Northern Alliance in this region, asked around and discovered that the safe location was Daoud's home, and he talked the guards there into letting us in. The mullah, a rather pale, wan man in his mid-thirties, with a long reddish beard, met me in an upstairs cubicle in a small building just inside the front gate. He sat near the room's sole window, an AK-47 assault rifle resting on the sill behind him. "I was studying at a madrasah in Pakistan," he said, in a reedy, tired-sounding voice, "and when the Taliban began I joined and entered Afghanistan with them, filled with pure Islamic feeling. In the beginning, this feeling we had was splendid, but, more recently, we have begun having doubts about some of the commanders who are with the Taliban"—he was alluding to the bin Laden crowd of foreigners—"and, following the martyrdom of Ahmad Shah Massoud, we realized that outside hands, terrorists, were involved in the movement. So, for the good of the country, we decided to come over to the Northern Alliance." He and the two commanders under him—both men were in the room and nodded to me as he pointed them out—and several hundred fighters remained behind in Taloqan and turned themselves over to Daoud. The rest of the Taliban retreated to Kunduz. Shabir Ahmed said that he had stayed on to ensure the security of the town, and he had personally called Daoud to tell him that the way into Taloqan was safe. That was how Taloqan had been reconquered by the Northern Alliance.

Shabir Ahmed had not revised his Muslim beliefs. "I am still proud of the name Taliban," he said. "As for those incidents in the West"—the attacks on the World Trade Center and the Pentagon—"those were not the actions of the Taliban, but of terrorists. It's hurtful to hear the Taliban name insulted, and to see it used by others who have their own purposes in mind." He said that he didn't agree with all of the Taliban edicts, like the ban on kite flying and the prohibition of music, "but there are aspects of Sharia"—Islamic law—"which we do think are important, such as the rule against rape, pederasty, and fornication, against gambling and drinking alcohol. And also the importance of beards. These are things commanded by the messenger of Islam." He didn't think that all Muslims necessarily had to wear beards, and he opposed the destruction of the giant Buddhas at Bamiyan. "They posed no danger to Islam, and they were part of Afghanistan's history," he said. Mullah Shabir Ahmed spoke in a chantlike monotone that gave him, whether by intention or practice, a priestlike quality. He swayed back and forth slightly. I noticed that he had very clean, white manicured fingernails and toenails.

THE NORTHERN ALLIANCE MOBILIZATION FOR THE ADVANCE on Kunduz began on November 22, Thanksgiving Day in the United States, amid conflicting rumors about negotiations for a surrender. Hundreds of mujahideen armed with rocket-propelled grenade launchers and Kalashnikovs began arriving in trucks and pickups at the Bangi front line. A large group of ethnic-Tajik Taliban had agreed to defect, and they were to rendezvous with representatives of the Northern Alliance at a village about a mile away. The sky was a deep and cloudless blue. A B-52 looped ponderously overhead, dropping bombs on the Taliban positions. B-52s are deceptively unthreatening. They drop their bombs while making banking curves, and there is a strange delay between

the curves and the explosions, which appear to occur far from the bombers' flight path. On its third or fourth run, the B-52 dropped a tremendous bomb on the summit of a Taliban ridge—perhaps a thousand feet
above the valley floor—sending a giant brown-gray cloud of dust and
dirt cascading down the mountainside and eventually covering it, like
an avalanche. Moments later, as the B-52 returned, men ran over the
sides of the next Taliban ridge—which was still receiving tank fire—
sending up their own dust clouds as they scrambled down the scree.

There was pandemonium at the Northern Alliance end of the valley, which looked like the scene of some kind of postmodern biblical
theatrical event. Few officers appeared to be present, and mujahideen
were swarming around aimlessly, their weapons pointing in all directions. Jeeps and trucks raced back and forth. Turbaned men wearing
blankets had spiky antitank rockets sticking out like arrows from quiv-
ers on their backs. Others wore bandoliers of shiny brass bullets, which
crisscrossed their torsos. There were flashes and booms from tanks and
Katyusha rocket launchers and, in the foreground, wheat fields and a
few flocks of longhaired black goats near the crumbling, fortresslike
mud compounds of peasant farmers. Here and there, in random soli-
tude, men knelt on their scarves, bending and rising in rhythmic prayer.

Sometime in the midafternoon, the mob of mujahideen began to
scatter, cocking their weapons as they scrambled down the road. You
could hear the sharp metallic clicks of their safeties snapping off. The
men were screaming "Talib! Talib!" and some of them were pointing
down the right side of the valley, where billowing dust clouds followed
several pickup trucks headed in our direction. The trucks were carrying
the defecting Taliban, and the panic subsided when the mujahideen realized that there was no hostile intent. Men who had run in the opposite direction came walking back, grinning as others teased them about
their mistake. Within a few minutes, several of the pickups had roared

across the bridge, and they came ripping through the crowd of mujahideen, who were still yelling "Talib," but smiling now. The Taliban were
all armed to the teeth.

A big Russian Kamaz truck with a howitzer mounted on the back
pulled up to great cheers. It was filled with Northern Alliance soldiers
from the group that had gone to the rendezvous with the Taliban. (It
turned out that during the rendezvous the defecting Taliban and the
Northern Alliance greeting party had come under fire from more stalwart Taliban, and had had to run for it.) A few minutes later, the truck
started off, heading toward Taloqan, and the mujahideen on the ground
became angry. All of a sudden, I found myself standing alone in the road
as the men on the truck pointed guns and half a dozen rocket-propelled
grenades at the men who had been congratulating them and who were
now screaming and pointing *their* guns. A battle seemed about to break
out among the mujahideen over who was to take possession of the truck,
and, indeed, as the truck pulled away, a soldier near me fired his gun, although the shot was high and in the air.

More pickups carrying Taliban appeared and parked on the road. I
asked one young Talib, a husky youth in his early twenties dressed all in
black, why he had defected, and he shrugged. "I came because my commander decided we should come," he said. He was from a province near
the Tajik border, and he was looking forward to going home. When I
asked him if he still considered himself a Talib, he said, "Yes, of course.
I am a student of the Koran, and tomorrow I will still be a Talib. It is a
holy thing to be."

Around three o'clock, the mujahideen began running or riding in
trucks down the road toward several copses of trees that marked the
Northern Alliance forward line. More tank, rocket, and machine-gun
fire could be heard. Word trickled back that somewhere down there
four Taliban had been killed. The B-52 bombed some more. The tanks

on the ridges fired continuously, and after a while I could see that the
Northern Alliance soldiers—their silhouettes clearly visible against the
sky—had moved one ridge closer to the Taliban.

The Taliban commanders who had led the defecting troops were
meeting with their Northern Alliance counterparts in a small room in
a farmhouse. The room was dank and full of people; it reminded me of
a photograph from the early days of the Russian Revolution. One of the
two Taliban, a man with a red beard and a concerned expression, was talking to General Nazir, a senior Northern Alliance commander. Nazir
was clicking worry beads and listening intently. The man was saying
that the Taliban positions on the hill and in the valley ahead were very

Anti-Taliban mujahideen warriors on the front line near Kunduz, November 2001.
THOMAS DWORZAK/MAGNUM PHOTOS

strong, and that the general should move his men out of their present positions and attack from the right side of the valley. The Taliban who were entrenched in the town of Khanabad, halfway between Bangi and Kunduz, had eighty tanks, and most of them were ready to resist to the death, he said. There were others who were willing to switch sides but had no one to help them. He advised Nazir to tell Commander Daoud that he should make contact with the Taliban commanders in Kunduz and Khanabad, and that many would defect if he could help arrange ways for them to do so. He criticized Nazir for the lax behavior of the mujahideen at the Bangi front line.

Back on the road, a scuffle was taking place between a mujahideen and a Talib. They were fighting over the Talib's jeep. I walked on, and about five minutes later I heard a bang, and once again people were running around and pointing their guns. Soon word came that a mujahideen had accidentally shot someone in the buttocks and grazed another man's head.

AS THE TALIBAN CONTINUED TO DEFECT DURING THE NEXT few days, I would often ask Yama, my translator, to identify the groups of fighters we saw near the Bangi front line. "Are they Talib or mujahideen?" There seemed to me to be precious little to distinguish them. Usually, the Taliban came across the front in vehicles covered in mud, to avoid detection from the air, but they wore virtually the same clothes as the mujahideen: pocketed vests, *patou* blankets, tunic and pantaloon outfits, a motley assortment of winter jackets, turbans, and scarves. They also carried the same weapons: Russian-made Kalashnikovs and anti-tank weapons. And they all drove Toyota pickups and Russian UAZ military jeeps and Kamaz trucks.

In general, the Taliban have fuller, longer beards than the mujahideen. The Taliban (though not all of them) wear black turbans, sometimes wrapped Tuareg style over their faces and necks against the wind and cold. Their commanders, who are often mullahs—although many of them are given the title simply out of respect—usually wear white turbans. The trademark headgear of the mujahideen is a flat-brimmed felt cap (brown, gray, beige, or white) called the *pakul*, which was worn by Massoud, and which became popular among the mujahideen during the anti-Soviet jihad of the 1980s. Not all mujahideen wear the *pakul*, however. Some merely wrap a striped or checked scarf over their heads or loop it around their necks. Or they wear a turban.

The Northern Alliance mujahideen are an unruly, noisy rabble much of the time, but the Taliban's fighters appear poised, watchful, and reserved. Those who defected to the Northern Alliance came in convoys, and at the handover points they usually stayed inside their vehicles, with the windows rolled up, or in the beds of trucks, sitting with their weapons next to piled-up gear. They would not speak, for the most part, unless given the OK to do so by a senior officer, and, when they did, they had an air of self-confidence. The mujahideen appeared to be in awe of them, and with good reason. Until the United States began making air strikes, the mujahideen were consistently defeated by the Taliban on the battlefield.

GHULAM SARWAR AKBARI OWNS A BOOKSTORE IN TALOQAN. HE is a thin man in his early fifties with a pockmarked face and a gentle manner. He has large, intelligent eyes, and speaks some English, shyly. I met him in his house, a modest two-story building near a soccer field where military helicopters now take off and land throughout the day. Two of his grandchildren, both toddlers, played at his feet in the common room of the house. One of them has vision problems, and he wore adult eyeglasses that frequently slipped off his face.

Akbari grew up in Taloqan and went to a technical high school in

Kabul, where he trained to become an air-traffic controller for the new Afghanistan that never came to be. He studied aviation and meteorology, and in the seventies, when the modernizing government of Mohammad Daoud was in power, he worked at different UN-sponsored weather stations around the country until returning to Taloqan, where he had a job at the airport. When the jihad against the Communist regime began, the airport and its facilities were destroyed. In the early eighties, the government of Babrak Karmal gave him the means to rebuild the weather station in Taloqan. This was a good time in his life, he says. "Government employees could survive on their salaries, and there were special coupon shops where we could buy things." Life continued in this fashion until the Soviet withdrawal from Afghanistan, in 1989, when Massoud's mujahideen took Taloqan. The new weather station was destroyed, and it was never rebuilt. Fearing for his life because of his affiliation with the Communist-backed government, Akbari fled with his family, along with the retreating government forces, to a village nearby. But the village fell to the mujahideen, and Akbari fled with his family again. In the early nineties, he moved to Kunduz, where he had a shop that sold items like shampoo and sugar and tea. When an amnesty was declared by the mujahideen government, he returned to Taloqan.

Akbari said that he had been a socialist, but that he didn't approve of many of the old government's ethnic policies, especially what he described as its partiality toward Pashtuns at the expense of other groups. Akbari is an Uzbek. "I believed, and still believe, that Afghan sovereignty should be preserved and the rights of all ethnic nationalities should be observed." I asked him whether he believed in the separation of church and state—a concept that is alien to most Afghans in the northern provinces—and he nodded.

Akbari described life in Taloqan under Massoud, when he first seized control, as difficult. "He seemed very strict; he tried to persuade people to pray and ordered women to wear Islamic coverings"—although not the burkha, which many rural women wore anyway. "Some people were imprisoned, and I felt in danger from Massoud's fighters. But this attitude became more moderate over time, especially after Najib"—President Najibullah, the Soviet-backed leader, who resigned in 1992—"was overthrown and the Islamic government decreed an amnesty." When the Taliban arrived in town, he was selling books of all kinds. His customers were most interested in history and fiction, he said, both foreign translations and books by Afghan and Iranian authors. Among their favorites were the works of Victor Hugo, Balzac, and John Reed, and books on politics and the military by the Najib-era Afghan general Azimi, as well as an Afghan history book by the late Mir Gholam Mohammad Ghobar, a classic.

"When the Taliban came to Taloqan, they always came to the shop," Akbari said, "looking for prohibited books, especially about politics and religion, and for any that might have images in them." He hid most of the books he thought they would find offensive. The only title they did confiscate, he says, was a songbook with the lyrics of the Afghan singer Ahmad Zahir. They didn't force him to sell religious books, but, since they were always asking for them, he and other booksellers tried to keep a good supply in stock. He gave me a look that said "Business is business." Now that the Taliban have left, he said, he has brought back out the books he'd hidden.

I asked him how he felt about seeing former Taliban walking, as it were, hand in hand with the Northern Alliance. What about the former Taliban commander of Taloqan, Mullah Shabir Ahmed? "I am at a loss about this merging of the two forces," he said. "Yesterday, Shabir Ahmed was a mullah wearing a turban and today he is living in Daoud Khan's house! And there are others who were wearing turbans and are now in *pakuls*, walking the streets." Akbari was appalled. "Every time a new government comes into power, the local strongmen change their disguises. They face up to no responsibility for the misfortune their wars cause to the civilians." He began to suggest that it was, as others had told me, the result of "foreign meddling." But Afghans were always blaming outsiders for their misfortunes, I said. He nodded, unperturbed. "Then it must be because of the poverty of the people. Need drives them to survive any way possible." A neighbor who had come in interjected, "It's all because of foreigners who want something from Afghanistan! Afghanistan is like a football kicked around between outsiders." Akbari concurred: "When there was fighting here between the government and the mujahideen, America helped the mujahideen in order to defeat the Soviets in Afghanistan. After the Soviets left, and the mujahideen were victorious, America, instead of helping them to create a good government, forgot about Afghanistan. America shouldn't have done this. It should have helped the mujahideen until there was a good government here. If that had been done, all this side-switching would never have happened."

ON SUNDAY, NOVEMBER 25, AFTER THE LAST LARGE DEFECTION of Taliban troops, Commander Daoud Khan took a convoy part of the way up the valley toward Kunduz. We drove there early Monday morning, and around five o'clock began seeing mujahideen walking in the direction of Kunduz, large groups and small, as shambolic as usual. We drove around a big bomb crater with a smashed military vehicle at the bottom of it, and just before dawn, at a fringe of trees some four or five miles outside Kunduz, we caught up with the Northern Alliance army as it gathered for the advance on the city.

Abdullah Gard, the commander who had, on Massoud's orders, engineered a fake defection to the Taliban in order to gather intelligence, was coordinating the advance. He wore a *pakul* and green military fatigues with a gold-white-and-black scarf around his neck, and he carried a field radio. The Taliban were supposed to be moving to an area near

the Kunduz airport, where they were to be disarmed and transported
by General Dostum's forces to a fort near Mazar-i-Sharif, a hundred
miles to the west—although since many prisoners had already been
killed in a battle at the fort the previous day, I wondered how cooperative the new group of prospective prisoners would be.

Abdullah Gard got out of his truck and began to walk, and so did
we, sticking close to him. When the outskirts of the town were just visible across a low bridge, he climbed into a muddy graveyard, where the
hummocks of graves were marked with flags on poles and metal plac-
ards with Koranic lettering, and listened to his radio. The front part
of the convoy, mostly troops on foot, massed between open fields and
walled family compounds. After about ten minutes, Gard walked back
to the road and vanished with a large group of men. He had been asked
to lead a flanking party toward a number of foreign Taliban who were
believed to be hiding at the edge of the city. We were left with the soldiers on the main road, and, without any high-ranking commander in
sight, we followed them as they crossed the low bridge and moved into
the suburbs and toward the center of Kunduz. We were still moving on
foot, with our jeep trailing behind.

There was some sporadic weapons fire and some rocket thumps, and
soon we were in a more densely populated area, where civilians stood
watching us pass. A mosque was at the end of the road, perhaps six
blocks ahead. In a few minutes, word came down the line that a gun battle was taking place in the center of town, and cars began whizzing past
us in wild retreat. Our driver was yelling for us to join the exodus, which
we did, and then we ordered him to stop so that we could find out what
had happened. We started and stopped two or three times over the next
hour or so. About four blocks from the mosque, a man appeared in the
center of the street, moving slowly toward us, and as he passed I saw that
he was covered with blood, and that one of his arms was loosely bound
with an olive-green bandage. He held the injured arm with his good

arm, and walked on, in a kind of determined trance, away from the center of town and whatever had happened there.

Around nine o'clock, Commander Daoud arrived from Taloqan with an entourage, and, as I waited to see him, I talked to friends of my translator, Yama, who is from Kunduz. They said that during the night there had been heavy bombing by American warplanes near the airport, and that there was a rumor that Pakistani planes had arrived, or tried to land, to evacuate Pakistani officers who were with the Taliban, and other foreign Taliban. Yama's friends spoke to one another in Dari, and I noticed that they used the English word "terrorist" (pronounced "tor-roh-riste"), which has evidently become part of the Afghan lexicon. No one knew whether the planes had been able to land or not, or what had happened, just as no one seemed to know what was happening in the city at that moment.

Someone told Yama that it was OK to go to the center of town, but when we got to the corner of the main street people were running, vehicles sped crazily past us, there was dust everywhere, and our driver beckoned frantically from the jeep, which was already moving. I climbed in, and once again we were leaving town without any clue about what was going on. Cars with fighters inside them roared by, but no one would stop. After about fifteen or twenty minutes, we began walking and driving back, and met a disheveled American journalist from the online magazine *Salon* who had been left behind by his driver. He said that there had been a fight between two rival Northern Alliance groups over Taliban cars.

In the bazaar area, several people were staring at the bodies of two Taliban fighters who lay dead in front of the shuttered shops. The bodies had been covered with robes, and people stopped to lift up the edges and peer at the corpses. The men had the gray, waxen look that even freshly dead people acquire. Blood coagulated in pools near their bodies. In one pool, a little plastic bag of *naswar*, the spicy chewing tobacco

Northern Alliance mujahideen on the advance to Kunduz, November 26, 2001.

that most Afghan men use, sat upright. Farther on, next to another shuttered shop, a wounded Talib lay on his side in a dusty, bleeding heap. He looked sideways at passersby above his outstretched arm. No one was tending to him or seemed very interested in him, except for a man who explained that the wounded soldier was a "Kandahari," meaning a Pashto-speaking Afghan from the south.

A group of soldiers appeared, leading five young, dark-skinned Taliban captives, their arms tied behind their backs with their turbans. They were dirty and looked terrified. The soldiers seemed not to have decided what to do with them and, trailed by curious onlookers, they led them up and down the main street and finally took them into a carter's yard, where one of the soldiers shut the yard's high metal gates behind them. Along with some other journalists, I followed them, our idea being to prevent the soldiers from executing their prisoners. The young men were Pashtuns, they said, from Helmand Province, in southern Afghanistan, and just six weeks earlier, a month before Ramadan, they had been forcibly conscripted and brought to Kunduz. They said that they didn't even know how to fight. Then, suddenly, their captors pushed them up some stairs and into a storage room. As we went up the stairs after them, the soldier who seemed to be in command stopped and said something to me in Dari. "He thinks you are an American military man," Yama explained, "and he wants you to give him a tip—*baksheesh*—because he has captured these Taliban." After some explanation about the difference between a journalist and a military man, which seemed to puzzle the soldier, he let me pass.

The prisoners sat on their knees on a floor covered with straw. The mujahideen who had asked me for a tip stood over them and yelled, and the photographers took pictures, and after a moment the soldier made everyone leave but me and a woman photographer. I asked the men why they hadn't surrendered, and they all answered at once. Their commander had left them behind when the shooting started, they said, and their comrades had run away. They had hidden, and when they saw Northern Alliance soldiers approaching, they gave themselves up and handed over their weapons. The soldiers had cocked their guns as if to shoot them, and then hit them with their gun butts, and tied their arms behind their backs and led them away. I told them that I would try to intercede with their captors, who had by now disappeared.

There was a lot of activity on the street. Many ordinary people, men and youths, were walking around, smiling and giving the thumbs-up sign. A group of Northern Alliance soldiers were taping posters of President Rabbani and Massoud on a cement booth in the middle of a traffic circle. An old man held aloft a poster of Massoud and yelled, "Down with blind Mullah Omar, long live Massoud!" Just then Commander Daoud drove up, and his car was surrounded by people, including the soldiers who had captured the five hapless Helmandi Talibs. The prisoners had been taken out of the carter's storage room and were being dragged around again. The man who had asked me for a tip was talking to Daoud. Then he led the prisoners away. I asked Yama, who had been within hearing range, what the soldier was saying. "He was asking Daoud for a tip because he had captured those men," Yama said.

Yama led me half a block from the traffic circle, to a building with a hand-painted sign: "Let's Learn English: Kunduz English Language Centre: American and British Systems." It was his language school. He and his brothers ran it. They had hired several teachers in other subjects, like physics and mathematics, and it had become a kind of private high school, he explained. They had more than seven hundred students. We went back to the traffic circle, looking for our driver, and saw that the soldiers were still wandering around aimlessly with their prisoners. A little farther along the road, a man pushed a handcart containing the wounded Taliban from the storefront.

A LARGE NUMBER OF VEHICLES WERE PARKED BESIDE A HUGE
field that stretched away from the walls of a factory on the edge of town.
A standoff was taking place, soldiers told us, with a group of a hundred
or so armed Taliban. We walked along the lane between the field and
the factory and saw several Taliban with machine guns, some of them
pointed toward us, on the perimeter wall of a small mosque, and in the
street just outside, facing them, several Northern Alliance soldiers.
About ten minutes after we arrived, there was a tremendous explosion,
apparently from an incoming antitank rocket, which landed somewhere behind us, followed by machine-gun fire. The shooting was coming not from the mosque but from a recess in the factory wall, where a
man in a black turban was aiming a rocket launcher. We all ran around
the corner and threw ourselves into a deep ditch. The shooting, and
more rocket explosions, continued for perhaps two minutes, and once
or twice I popped my head up to see what was happening. All I could
see was soldiers, lying prone or crouched in firing positions. Then it was
quiet, and we left the ditch to take shelter behind the thick pillar of
a house.

We took a circuitous route away from the factory, which was now
cordoned off by soldiers, and drove to Yama's house, a compound in a
pleasant working-class suburb of the city, with a well, a cookhouse, a
mud-walled toilet, and a cow tethered in the yard. His brothers and
cousins and little sisters (I never saw his mother, because it would have
been inappropriate for her to appear before a strange man) welcomed
him home, and, in spite of Ramadan, we were served a lunch of fried
eggs and vegetables.

That afternoon, back in Taloqan, I looked up a man named Shahmurat, whom I had met several weeks earlier, when the American air
campaign in Afghanistan began. Shahmurat is a big, irreverent man in his

early fifties. He is the son of a relatively well-off rural landowner (two hundred acres of land and some livestock) and the respected elder of his home village. Shahmurat studied at an agricultural school in Kabul, and when he returned home, as he tells it, he was unanimously named the *arbob*, or headman, of his village. He was *arbob* for six years. "My job was to make peace, and to be the intermediary between the government and the people," he explained. He did this until the Communist regime that overthrew President Daoud came to power and the rural Afghan feudal system—and, with it, his job—was abolished. He remembers those years, the waning years of Zahir Shah's monarchy and Daoud's brief stint in power, as a good time. "There was a government that the people respected," he said, "and no one complained about economic problems. There was peace."

Shahmurat was among those who opposed the new regime and the changes it brought. "Enlightened people gathered together and took up arms against the Communist government, and began to fight," he said. He eventually signed on with the Jamiat-i-Islami organization headed by Burhanuddin Rabbani and Ahmad Shah Massoud. He fought with Jamiat against the Communists for five years, until one day he had a change of heart.

"After five years, I realized that this war was meaningless to me, that East and West were both involved in Afghanistan for their own designs. I cashiered my troops, gave my weapons to other commanders, and returned to my family in my village." I asked whether something specific had happened to make him do this. "Our enemy was the Soviet invader," he explained. "But the mujahideen ended up fighting between themselves. So I went home. That was in 1983." He was also fed up, he said, with the increasingly radical Muslim character of the mujahideen organizations. "When they caught a government soldier, they killed him, and I disagreed with this practice. This was because of their fanaticism." Islam was supposed to preach tolerance and respect, he said. "The mujahideen became more and more fanatical during the war against the Soviets, and they remained so afterward, when they came to power. But they were powerless when they took over the government, because they fought with one another. And then came the Taliban."

Until a few weeks earlier, Shahmurat had stayed at home in his village since 1983, tending his family farm and living simply. It was the drought of the past three years that had brought him to Taloqan, where he hoped to find work. What did he hope to do? I asked. He shrugged. "Anything," he said. "Now there is no work. The whole country is poor. The money is all with the powerful commanders." Shahmurat seemed pessimistic and woeful.

I asked him to explain all the switching of sides that we had been witnessing recently. Why did Afghans change allegiances so easily? "In America and other places," Shahmurat said, tentatively, "people have the idea that their countries are important to them. But in Afghanistan the fighters don't have this notion, and the poverty here leads them to join whoever is powerful." Shahmurat, like Ghulam Sarwar Akbari, who is his friend, blamed the foreign powers that had armed and backed various Afghan factions. "These armed organizations have been supported by foreign countries who don't care whether Afghans are educated or not, and they have pushed the fighting men to kill the educated people and those with culture. And so now there are no educated, cultured people anymore. They are either dead or in exile, and if they are still in Afghanistan they are in their homes, and have no power to speak. The gun now governs Afghanistan. In other countries, the security of the people and the property of the nation is guaranteed, and this is also so within Islam. But here these things have been destroyed. How can we change this?" Shahmurat said that he hoped for a UN-sponsored political solution in Afghanistan. "Perhaps, through the UN, enlightened people can come to power in Afghanistan. When a person is thirsty, he wants water. Afghans are thirsty for unity and peace. We are sick of war."

# 5

## CITY OF DREAMS

The tomb of Ahmad Shah Massoud is in a shallow cave burrowed into a hill in the Panjshir Valley. The grave site, which is near the edge of a crude road cut along the steep valley slopes, is marked by a green sign with hand lettering that spells out "Chief of the Martyr's Hill" in Farsi and in English. The Panjshir Valley—a canyon some 120 miles long, stretching southwest from northern Afghanistan to the Shamali plain, just north of Kabul—is a bleakly rugged place. The road often falls away or is narrowed by mudslides, and ruined Soviet-era military tanks and armored personnel carriers litter the route, along with the twisted carcasses of trucks and jeeps that have slipped off the road onto the rocks below.

Massoud was born in Bazarak, a village less than a mile up the Panjshir River from Martyr's Hill. He was a national hero long before he was murdered, on September 9, 2001, and he has since become a figure

This chapter was originally published as "City of Dreams," *The New Yorker*, December 16, 2001.

of quasi-religious dimensions. Traveling down the valley toward Kabul
at the beginning of December with several other journalists, I noticed
that my driver, Enam, who is a native Panjshiri, had tied a black flag of
mourning to the antenna of our jeep. There was a Massoud poster plas-
tered to the windshield, practically obscuring it, and a small photograph
of Massoud taped onto the driver's-side window. We were part of a convoy of seventeen vehicles, many of which were decorated in a similar
fashion.

It had taken us four days to travel about 250 miles—south from the
city of Taloqan, over the Hindu Kush, and into the Panjshir Valley—
across an isolated, edgy region where the Northern Alliance seemed to
have only a tenuous presence. On the fourth day, the sun was setting on
Massoud's grave as we made our way toward the paved road that crosses
the plain to Kabul. Once we were on the road, our headlights illumi-
nated blasted vehicles, ruined tanks, collapsed houses, and broken walls
covered with starbursts from shell fire and pocked by bullets. After the
Taliban took Kabul, in 1996, they destroyed all the villages in the Shamali, emptying the area of civilians and creating a buffer zone for their
front line with the Northern Alliance, which forayed out from the Panjshir. In the weeks leading up to the Taliban's retreat from Kabul, in
mid-November, the frontline positions had been heavily pounded by
American bombers and warplanes, and the road was gouged and cra-
tered. Enam drove slowly and weaved around the holes, but was careful
not to get too close to the edge of the road. Newly posted signs warned
of land mines.

Kabul appeared out of the night, shockingly, as we reached the top
of a small cluster of hills that rose from the plain. There was light everywhere. Glowing squares and rectangles of white, blue, and yellow crossed
the valley. It was the first Afghan city I had seen with a functioning electrical system.

WITH THE TALIBAN GONE, KABUL HAS REVERTED TO BEING the one city in Afghanistan where, in relative terms, almost anything goes. Liquor is still forbidden and scarce, but it's available. Street vendors sell postcards of sultry Indian screen idols, and cockfights have resumed. Metalworkers are doing a brisk business in satellite dishes, which are hand-beaten from scrap; the finished products are covered with the logos and brand names of canned goods, making them look like pop art. The cult of Massoud is also flourishing. Throngs of young men scuffled for tickets to the premiere of a French documentary, *Massoud l'Afghan*, and an official morning of homage was held recently at several of Kabul's main mosques. Northern Alliance soldiers laden with Massoud posters tucked them under the windshield wipers of cars, like parking tickets.

Yet there seems to be an underlying uncertainty about the changes that have taken place so suddenly. A British reporter and I were walking around downtown one morning, and we stopped on a street where there were several washing-machine and appliance-repair shops. My companion decided to interview a twelve-year-old boy who was working as a repairman. A group of curious men and boys soon surrounded us, and I noticed that four women in blue burkhas had paused to watch as well, from a short distance away. After a few minutes, the women came forward, and one of them, who said her name was Shahkoko and that she was forty-five years old, asked if we knew of any foreign aid agencies or NGOs that needed English-speaking Afghan personnel. She had once been a teacher, she said, and under the Taliban had continued teaching, clandestinely, in her home, to help her family survive. But she had been discovered, and the Taliban had detained her teenage son, beaten him, and cut him with knives. So she had stopped giving her illegal classes. Now she was desperate to find real, paying work again. I took down her name, and two men who were listening helped me sort out some confusion over her street address.

Suddenly, we were interrupted by an irascible bearded man who owned one of the shops. He yelled at Yama, my translator, who is from northern Afghanistan. The bearded man was a Pashtun—a member of the tribal group that most of the Taliban are also from—and he excoriated Yama for helping foreigners talk to Afghan women. Yama was a yokel from Badakhshan Province, he said, which was an insulting reference to Yama's Tajik heritage. This upset Yama, who tried to pull me away, but by then I was angry, and I cursed the man and called him a "Talib." Shahkoko, the former teacher, nodded her head vigorously. "Thank you," she whispered. "You are right, he is a Talib." Then she and her friends moved quickly down the street, away from us and the little mob scene. My companions and I went in the opposite direction, leaving the shopkeeper blustering on the pavement. Yama chastised me for my outburst. "You cannot talk this way in Kabul yet," he said. "It is not safe for you. There are still many people here who think like the Taliban do."

It must be strange for many of the citizens of Kabul to be dealing with Western expectations when until only a few weeks ago the only foreigners in the city—or in the country, for that matter—were the Pakistanis, Chechens, Uzbeks, and Arabs fighting alongside the Taliban and Osama bin Laden's Al Qaeda organization. They have all vanished, and in their place are several hundred journalists from all over the world, who have packed the city's few hotels, rented scores of cars, and hired numerous translators. On the curb outside the Herat Restaurant, a kebab-and-pilaf place whose walls are adorned with old black-and-white photographs of Afghanistan's principal ancient sites (except for the destroyed Bamiyan Buddhas, which are curiously absent, as if they had never existed), a contingent of beggar boys and women in dirty burkhas are on permanent stakeout. The Herat is said to have been the favorite dining spot of the foreign Taliban in the capital, before the journalists came.

In the residential district of Wazir Akbar Khan, where carefully laid out tree-lined streets and public parks recall a time when Kabul was almost a modern city, workmen are busy repainting and restoring dilapidated houses for media organizations. There is a *Newsweek* house, a *New York Times* house, and an ABC and CBS house. A British journalist who is setting up a Kabul office for his television news agency has rented a house in which one of Osama bin Laden's wives used to live. The United Nations has resumed its operations, as have a number of international relief agencies, and foreign embassies are reopening. The Russians, British, Iranians, Turks, French, and Germans were among the first to come back, and in mid-December a group of American marines went into the US embassy compound, which had been closed since 1989. The marines swept the grounds for unexploded ordnance and set up machine-gun nests behind sandbags on the roof.

A single concrete office tower rises some eighteen stories above the city center. It is the Telecommunications Ministry, Kabul's tallest building, and perhaps the last vestige of the days when Afghanistan seemed to have some kind of future. Architecturally, it is as though time had stopped in Kabul in the late seventies. Nothing much appears to have been constructed since then, except for dingy Soviet-built apartment blocks, and one half-finished bank building and a mosque, both begun under the Taliban.

A GREAT DEAL HAS BEEN DESTROYED. ONE DAY WHILE I WAS driving around the city with Fridoun, an affable twenty-three-year-old medical student, I remarked that he was born just about the time that the war against the Communists began—the jihad that was followed by civil war. "Yes," he said. "All I know is war. For me, rockets and

War-devastated southern Kabul, December 2001.   THOMAS DWORZAK/MAGNUM PHOTOS

bombings—all these things are normal." He shrugged. He was eager for Kabul's medical school to reopen, so that he could finish his studies and become a doctor. As we drove along the Kabul River, which has for several years been nearly bone-dry because of a drought, and began to circle the city, the scale of the destruction was overwhelming. Entire sections of Kabul have been obliterated. Block after block of buildings is a dismal ruin of bricks and twisted concrete; roofs have caved in, façades are full of bullet holes or have been pierced by tank shells. Fridoun explained what had caused each piece of devastation, and after a while it seemed as though we were examining the city the way one assesses the age of a dead tree by counting the rings in its stump.

Fridoun pointed out the beat-up tomb of King Nadir Shah—the father of Zahir Shah, who is now in exile in Rome—on a large dirt hill not far away. The hill was honeycombed with abandoned dugouts and fortifications, and sparsely adorned with martyrs' flags. It had been one of the front lines in the fighting over Kabul that began in 1992, when President Burhanuddin Rabbani and Massoud took power. The ruined buildings, lone walls, and solitary columns below the hill resembled giant sand castles or sections of an archaeological dig. "This area used to be very famous as a place of business for people coming in from the provinces," Fridoun said. "There were many hotels and shops." Now several ragged men and children were selling scrap metal and recycled spare parts for cars; bicycle repairmen sat on boxes at the roadside next to inner tubes, waiting for customers.

Fridoun said that Gulbuddin Hekmatyar, a Pashtun Muslim fundamentalist backed by Pakistan and Saudi Arabia (and, during the anti-Soviet jihad in the 1980s, by the CIA), had established a base in the mountains fringing the city beyond the hill, and from there he was able to rain rockets on the population, which he did with vicious abandon—even though he was officially the prime minister of the mujahideen government during this period. Massoud was at first assisted in the defense

of the city by the Uzbek warlord Abdul Rashid Dostum, who had
fought with the Soviets against the mujahideen until 1992, when he
switched sides, thereby facilitating Massoud's seizure of Kabul. Dostum
switched sides again in 1994. From the same hill where he had fought
with Massoud against Hekmatyar, Dostum now turned his guns against
Massoud. Then the Taliban attacked Hekmatyar and Dostum from behind. They retreated, and Massoud faced the Taliban and another mujahideen faction, the Hazaras—ethnic Shias—who were entrenched in
western Kabul, around the university. "What people say," Fridoun explained, "is that Massoud told the Taliban, 'Let's join together and finish the Hazaras.'" In any case, he said, the Taliban began fighting with
the Hazaras, killed their leader, and Massoud chased them out of the
city. "Then," Fridoun continued, "Massoud attacked the Taliban."

Fridoun went on in this manner as we drove into the devastated
western suburbs, and I stopped trying to keep track of the precise chronology of what destruction was caused when and by whom. The result,
in the end, was the same. All of the devastation had a name attached to
it, and most of the names were still key figures in Afghanistan's politics.
As we passed the former Soviet Cultural Center, Fridoun pointed across
the road to a large building that had been peppered by gunfire. "This
was where the Hazaras killed their prisoners when they were in control
here. They killed them by shooting, by *halal*, as we say"—Fridoun drew
an imaginary knife across his throat—"by fire, by boiling water, and
even by driving nails into heads."

I asked Fridoun how he felt about showing me the ruins. "I feel
ashamed," he replied. "I feel ashamed that a foreign person sees this and
thinks: This was destroyed by Afghans themselves." Then what did he
think about the men who had done this, men who were still wielding
power? "We know this is their last chance to be here with guns," he said
softly. "If there are elections in Afghanistan for a new government, none
of these people will be voted for. The people are very angry with these

men. Right now, I know, if I say 'Massoud is bad' in Kabul, I will go to prison. But if democracy comes I can say who is bad and who is good, and I can vote for whoever I want to lead Afghanistan."

PROFESSOR MUHAMMAD KAZEM AHUNG IS A WRITER AND IN-tellectual who stayed in the city during most of the years of turmoil. He received me in his home, a drab, two-story concrete-and-glass house with a walled garden. It must have been a comfortable, upper-middle-class residence once, but now it was freezing cold inside, and there seemed to be no furniture. Ahung apologized for this, indicating that I should sit on some cushions arranged around a frayed carpet. There was nothing on the walls of the house, either upstairs or downstairs. It seemed to have been stripped bare except for the floor coverings.

Professor Ahung is a robust man of sixty-eight, but—unusual for an Afghan—he appears younger. He has a neatly trimmed salt-and-pepper beard, and on the day we met he was wearing a woolen waistcoat over a traditional Afghan long shirt and pantaloons. He speaks excellent English, and since he was clearly uncomfortable in the presence of the translator I had brought—a young Panjshiri named Qais, who has relatives who are officers in the Northern Alliance—I asked Qais to go to the bazaar to buy some fruit. Professor Ahung relaxed and brought me tea and biscuits, even though he was observing Ramadan.

Ahung grew up on a farm on the Shamali plain, where his father, who was an army officer, had retired to live on the land and grow grapes. He went to Kabul University and graduated from the Academy of Let-ters in 1958, then began working in the Ministry of Information and Culture. He became chief of the reporting staff of the government's official daily gazette, and in 1963 he went to East Lansing, Michigan, where he earned an MA in journalism at Michigan State. When he re-turned to Kabul, he was promoted to assistant chief editor, but in 1966 he was fired, he says, because he had been accused of being a member of the Afghan Communist Party. "I am a socialist by inclination, not an extremist," Ahung said. "Not like these people"—he motioned to the world outside the windows of his house. He spoke with warmth of his two years in the United States, and of the time immediately afterward, back home in Kabul, when he was an avid visitor at the United States Information Service library. "In those days, the Western press was very well represented here," he said. "The library had copies of *Time, Life, Ladies' Home Journal*, the *London Illustrated News*. We read everything, and I translated many articles for Afghan readers."

Ahung continued to work as a writer for the Ministry of Information, and he also began teaching journalism classes at Kabul University: "I taught reporting, and English as a second language, a course designed for journalists." In 1973, the king was overthrown in a bloodless coup by his cousin, Mohammad Daoud, and five years later Daoud was killed by Marxist military officers and replaced by Nur Muhammad Taraki. At this point, Ahung's journalistic career took off again. "Since I had some really close personal friends who were involved in the revolution," he said, "they proposed to Taraki that I become head of *The Kabul Times*." Taraki agreed, and Ahung stayed on as editor when Taraki was executed by Hafizullah Amin, his deputy. Amin was murdered soon afterward, and Babrak Karmal, the leader of a rival Communist faction, became president.

Babrak Karmal came to power in 1979, when the Soviets invaded Afghanistan, and he fired Ahung from *The Kabul Times*. Ahung retreated, once again, to Kabul University, where he taught and wrote articles and books. He was the dean of the journalism school for twelve years. He had written more than twenty books, he said, although most were no longer in print. He remained at the university until the Taliban purged the school of those who were not appropriately Islamicized. Since then, he had tried to keep busy. He had even written a number of short stories. He showed me a book that was published this year in Pakistan. I barely recognized him in the photograph on the jacket. He had a long beard, grown to appease the Taliban.

I asked Ahung what had kept him going. "I'll tell you," he said. "Whenever the regime in power thought I felt this way or that, contrary to their way of thinking, they usually just fired me and I went home and said nothing. I shut up. I became a conservative! That is how I survived." Hadn't this self-censorship been difficult? I asked him. He pondered a moment. "Well, no," he said. "If I had shouted, they would have put me in jail, and what would have been the use of that? If I was ousted from my country, what could I do? Who could I help in places where the people are better educated than myself? I could have gone to Iran or Pakistan, but the Iranians look down on Afghans for reasons of language and culture. And the Pakistanis, they are businessmen, in every sense of the word—you know what I mean." Ahung blames the Communists for having begun the destruction of Afghanistan. "Before, economically and culturally, and in terms of social equality, we were making progress. But this was destroyed by the Communists. I was among them, but I did not want that."

Ahung seemed to have few illusions about his pragmatism and its costs. "Spiritually and intellectually, I did not feel particularly proud about things," he said. "Materially, I was just able to sustain myself and my family. Meanwhile, I encouraged others not to be conservative like me. I encouraged them, my students and my sons, to fight for their beliefs. But I had students who spied upon me. They have called me treacherous," he said indignantly. "They have."

Professor Ahung and his wife live alone in the house in Kabul. "I'm getting old," he said. "I have five sons and three daughters and twenty-four grandchildren. They are all independent and live away from here." His three daughters are married and live in Herat with their husbands. Three of his five sons went to the former Soviet Union to study and have not returned. A fourth son followed them there, and the fifth works for an international relief agency in Herat. Ahung's wife—whom I never saw, although I heard her rustling around in an adjacent room occasionally—missed the children, and he tried not to be away from the house for long, so that she wouldn't be alone. "Of course I feel sorrow," he said. "But what I do is I sit with myself, and I say, 'Throw it out of your mind.' And it works, you know, it does." He had not yet been asked to resume his duties when the university reopens next spring. "With all due respect," he said, "I am not going to ask. I am not going to sacrifice my pride. I have no money. I have sold all of my carpets, my dishes, and my wife's gold in order to survive these past six years. My house and farm in Shamali, which used to give us some small income, was burned down. They should come to see me, for my pride."

I asked Ahung how he felt about things now, with the Taliban gone and political change in the air. "I am disturbed," he said. The previous evening he had listened to the fundamentalist mujahideen leader Abdul Rasul Sayyaf speak at a nearby mosque. The Afghan delegates who had met in Bonn to establish an interim government in Kabul had just announced who would be in the new administration, and Sayyaf and other conservative Afghan leaders were angry at not being given posts. "Sayyaf said that if the US-supported interim government came and the king returned, guerrilla war would begin again in Afghanistan," Professor Ahung said. "This disturbs me."

The Bonn agreement was a victory for the Massoud loyalists. Muhammad Fahim, who became the Northern Alliance's defense minister after Massoud's assassination, kept his job in the new government, as did Massoud's close friend Abdullah Abdullah, the foreign minister, and Yunis Qanouni, the interior minister. All of them, like Massoud, grew up in the Panjshir Valley. President Rabbani, who is an ethnic Tajik from a northeastern province, had to relinquish his office to Hamid Karzai, a Pashtun from a prominent family in Kandahar. In a few months, a Loya Jirga, a traditional assembly of various Afghan groups, was to meet and choose a more permanent government. "We all know that if the US had not bombed this country looking for Osama bin Laden," Professor Ahung said, "we would not have an interim government. As an American, you should feel responsible for this whole thing, and for Afghanistan, because if you leave there will be a civil war, and it will be worse than ever before."

THE AFGHAN PRESIDENTIAL PALACE IS IN THE SPRAWLING, parklike nineteenth-century royal compound in downtown Kabul. The grounds of the complex are unkempt now, and the roofs of several buildings have caved in, apparently because they were hit by rockets, or perhaps tank fire. I went there to speak to President Rabbani's eldest son, Salahuddin, whom I had met several weeks earlier in Faizabad. He had accompanied his father to Kabul when the Taliban left. I waited for Salahuddin in a room that had a huge gray metal Soviet-era intercom system clumsily inscribed with Cyrillic lettering. It clashed with the crystal chandelier, heavy curtains, Persian carpets, and gilded furniture. Salahuddin greeted me in the private presidential meeting room. It was the first time, he said, he had talked to someone there, and he seemed to be enjoying himself. The room was dark and cold, but there was a small, Russian-made electric heater in the corner that made it bearable.

Salahuddin said that he had not been back to London since September, and that he hoped his family would join him in Afghanistan, perhaps next summer. He was diplomatic about the new government and about his father's position. "I'd say that my father is not angry," he said, "but that he is not entirely happy, either." They approved of Hamid Karzai as the new leader, but would have liked what Salahuddin described as broader representation for other members of the Northern Alliance. He shrugged and smiled. "I think there was pressure for a quick fix in Afghanistan, and you know that no such thing is possible here."

I asked Salahuddin what he thought was going to happen. "All I can tell you is that my father is ready to hand over power," he said. "But as for the rest I cannot say." A Northern Alliance security official who had been close to Massoud had told me privately that the day after the Bonn agreement was announced, General Fahim became so angry about Rabbani's complaints that he threatened to arrest him. Fahim backed down, but he told Rabbani to stay in his residence and to shut up. Fahim had also issued some kind of ultimatum to General Dostum, and, coincidentally or not, several days later Dostum told reporters that he had no intention of spilling blood over his differences with the new government.

Salahuddin said he had hoped that the UN would not attempt to impose a disarmament process, and in fact that possibility had been left out of the final text of the Bonn agreement. "What do you think," Salahuddin said, "that the Blue Helmets would be able to come and say to the people, 'Give me your gun'? The gun is more than about power and survival; to Afghans having a gun is a source of pride. You can't just take them away. So this is impossible in Afghanistan." He had also been troubled by the preliminary language for one of the clauses of the agreement, which he described as calling for justice against perpetrators of past atrocities. "This is a real problem," he said. "How to define atrocities. There are many commanders who have killed people who might fear that they could now be considered war criminals. Our soldiers have killed a lot of Taliban. Does that constitute an atrocity?" This argument prevailed in Bonn, and the final version of the pact didn't address retribution.

After we had chatted awhile, Salahuddin said, rather abruptly, "Now I have a question for you. What is your opinion of my prospects for a political future here in Afghanistan?" In Faizabad, people had referred to Salahuddin—although not in his presence—as "the Vice President," and I had once told him so. He had laughed then, and looked pleased. Now it was less of a joke.

I told Salahuddin that I thought that Afghanistan's older generation of political leaders had failed abysmally, and that his country needed the ideas of a new generation of people who were educated and knowledgeable about the modern world but were also in touch with their own culture.

"That is what I have been thinking, too," Salahuddin said.

As he was showing me out, Salahuddin introduced me to the palace's oldest employee, a bearded man in his late sixties who wore a coat with shiny buttons and who stood at attention as we passed. He had been at the palace since the time of King Zahir Shah, Salahuddin said, although he had been dismissed by the Taliban. The Rabbanis had asked him to return. He and Salahuddin bantered about presidential secrets, and Salahuddin described one of the important events that the old retainer had witnessed: the moment in 1959 when Queen Homaira, King Zahir Shah's wife and the leader of a movement to liberate modern Afghan women, threw off her veil. The old man nodded, confirming this, but kept silent.

# 6

## HOLY AND OTHER WARRIORS

The road from Kabul to Jalalabad follows the Kabul River east for about eighty miles. Fifty miles outside of Kabul, it begins winding through the Sarobi Gorge, where, in January 1842, sixteen thousand British and Indian soldiers and their families were massacred by Afghan tribesmen. The gorge is a dismal, Stygian place, all gray scree and brown dust. The road through it was paved once, but now it is just a narrow dirt-and-rock passageway cut into a mountainside. A mess of giant tumbled boulders and landslides, it falls away on one side to the gray-green river torrent below.

The Sarobi Gorge is one of the most dangerous places in Afghanistan. Bandits and gunmen lie in wait to ambush hapless travelers, whom they rob and sometimes kill. In November, after the fall of Kabul, four journalists who were traveling from Jalalabad were murdered there. In

This chapter was originally published as "Holy and Other Warriors" in *The Lion's Grave* (Grove Press, 2002), pp. 127–49.

early December, a bus from Jalalabad was said to have been stopped by renegade Taliban who cut off the noses and ears of the male passengers who weren't wearing beards. I wasn't particularly keen to drive through the gorge, a trip that takes six or seven hours, but I wanted to get to Kandahar, three hundred miles southwest of Kabul, and the direct route was more or less suicidal for Westerners. The Taliban cleared out of Kandahar on December 7, and the next day in Kabul I met a young man who said his name was Nasruddin and that he had just come from Kandahar in a taxi. Nasruddin had seen truckloads of heavily armed Arab Al Qaeda fighters heading in the direction of Khost, near the Pakistan border. The taxi had been stopped several times by Pashtun gunmen dressed in black. Nasruddin, who is a Tajik, assumed that they were Taliban, and he was terrified. He agreed that the only way for me to get to Kandahar was to go to Jalalabad, then cross the border into Pakistan, and reenter Afghanistan farther south, from Quetta, which is linked to Kandahar by a well-traveled road.

The Taliban had vanished from Afghanistan's cities by then, but in much of the countryside, vague new front lines had emerged where the anti-Taliban forces had halted their forward advances. The areas beyond these front lines were no-man's-lands controlled by militias still loyal to the Taliban and by gangs of common bandits, and sometimes by both. This provided an opportunity for enterprising security services, like the one run by Jack, a stocky American in his mid-forties who assembled the convoy to Jalalabad that I joined. Jack—which is not his real name—put together a party of seven journalists who were accompanied by seventeen Afghan fighters from three militias: two from Kabul and one from Sarobi. We each paid him $800. Jack had a mustache and short hair and always wore dark sunglasses and military clothing. A revolver was strapped to his leg in a special holster and he carried an assault rifle. He described himself as a former Green Beret who was working with the new Afghan government as a civilian adviser. Jack wouldn't say whether or not he had any official links to the US armed forces, but he hinted that he enjoyed a cooperative relationship of sorts with the army's counterterrorism task force. He had, he said, been in Afghanistan since September, moving around with the Northern Alliance as they seized territory from the Taliban. Participating in an armed convoy to Jalalabad, he told me, was good training for the Afghans. He hoped to recruit the best of them to become part of an elite Afghan Army security corps. "You know," he said, "I'm half hoping we run into some of the bad guys along the way, and that they try to fuck with us, because I'd love nothing better than to let these guys loose on 'em, and kill 'em all."

We saw a few gunmen lurking along the road as we drove through the gorge, their faces shrouded with brown *patou* blankets, and there were others on a crude hilltop bivouac, but none of them interfered with us. They behaved like wild dogs circling a passing herd, hanging back but ready to strike if the opportunity arose. In the end, our convoy made it through to Jalalabad unscathed except for frayed nerves and two flat tires.

JALALABAD IS A BUSTLING, PROSPEROUS CITY OF FARMERS, merchants, and smugglers situated in a fertile river valley two hours by car from the Khyber Pass and the Pakistan border. Snowcapped mountains, including the Tora Bora range to the southeast, surround the valley. Jalalabad is an overwhelmingly Pashtun city, heavily influenced by its proximity to Pakistan, and is distinctly different in style and atmosphere from the provincial Tajik and Uzbek cities of northern Afghanistan, or, for that matter, from the relatively cosmopolitan capital of Kabul, where Tajiks, Uzbeks, and Hazaras, as well as Pashtuns, live in close proximity to one another. Jalalabad's streets are noisy with motorized rickshaws (abundant in Pakistan, scarce in Kabul) and garishly decorated trucks. The signboards of the shop fronts are louder, the bazaar smells spicier. The people have darker skin, wear different clothes, and seem more self-possessed and clannish. Jalalabad's Pashtuns gather around to stare at Westerners—as people do everywhere in Afghanistan— but instead of calling out greetings, they stand quietly, commenting softly among themselves.

Posters of Ahmad Shah Massoud are ubiquitous in northern Afghanistan and in Kabul, but they weren't much in evidence in Jalalabad. Instead of Massoud's image, photographs of a local Pashtun hero, Abdul Haq, hung on electrical poles and on the walls of public buildings. Haq was a mujahideen commander in the anti-Soviet jihad and then became a businessman in Dubai. In October, he returned covertly to Afghanistan with the support of the CIA and began recruiting an anti-Taliban fighting force in his old stomping grounds near Jalalabad, but the Taliban soon captured him and hung him from a chestnut tree just outside of Kabul. The particularly high public esteem held for him may perhaps be explained by the fact that one of his brothers, Haji Abdul Qadir, is the current governor of Nangarhar Province, of which Jalalabad is the capital. Until 1996, when the Taliban seized Jalalabad and he fled into exile in Pakistan, Haji Abdul Qadir was Nangarhar's strongman and head of the so-called Eastern *shura*, a cooperative council of regional mujahideen factions. A wealthy man, he has long been accused of being a major player in the province's flourishing opium trade. Nangarhar is one of Afghanistan's main opium-growing provinces, and it is strategically located next to the heroin refineries that operate just across the border inside Pakistan's freebooting North-West Frontier Province. The Taliban cracked down on opium cultivation in the summer of 2000, and production was cut drastically.

I had been in Jalalabad during the spring and early summer of 1989, when opium was growing everywhere—entire fields of it, and rectangular patches tucked in among rows of wheat. Jalalabad was then under siege. The Soviets had withdrawn their troops from Afghanistan, but they continued to support the regime of Mohammad Najibullah in

Kabul with military aid and advisers, and Soviet pilots still flew bombing missions over Afghanistan. Several mujahideen factions—backed by the United States, Saudi Arabia, and Pakistan—were attempting to gain control of Jalalabad and planned to proclaim themselves the legitimate Afghan government. I was driven through the Khyber Pass by a plainclothes Pakistani agent from Inter-Services Intelligence. He was assisting the mujahideen, and a few days earlier some of them had captured eighty-odd government soldiers and executed them—not a tactic designed to encourage surrender. The front lines nearest the enemy positions—around the Jalalabad airport at the eastern edge of the city—were exposed to enemy fire and manned for the most part by untrained fourteen- and fifteen-year-old boys who had been recruited only weeks earlier from madrasahs in Pakistan's Afghan refugee camps, and they were dying in droves. Occasionally, big white Scud missiles—fired all the way from Kabul—flew in and exploded. Shells, mortars, bullets, bombs, and rockets were landing all over the place, here and there setting the harvest-ready fields of opium and wheat ablaze, sending up great crackling orange curtains of flame and clouds of black smoke.

A group of Arabs were fighting alongside the mujahideen. They had their own camp next to the road that led to the airport. I had not yet heard of Osama bin Laden, but he was apparently there that summer, and those fighters were his men—volunteers for the Islamic crusade against the atheistic regime in Kabul from countries like Egypt, Saudi Arabia, Palestine, Yemen, and Algeria. I drove past a group of them one day when I visited a frontline mujahideen position in an old mud-walled fortress that overlooked Jalalabad's airstrip from a small hill. They were dug into trenches and behind sandbags by the road, weapons pointed, and stared with open hostility as we passed. A couple of hours later, when I was in the fortress, the man we had left with our vehicle came urgently to fetch us: Some Arabs had asked if there were any Western *kafirs* in our party. He had told them no, and they had left, but he didn't think they believed him. It was a hunting party, he explained, and we should leave the area immediately because they were likely to come back. We drove past the Arab encampment again. The fighters bristled and glared, but they didn't open fire, probably because I was with a mujahideen escort. The next day, just up the road, an Australian friend was nearly killed by some Arabs who were annoyed that he was witnessing the burial of mujahideen martyrs. Later, I heard stories of other journalists who had encountered the Arabs and had gotten into trouble.

Osama bin Laden and his men, of course, flourished during the Taliban's tenure, only to retreat to their old haunts in the mountains near Jalalabad when the Taliban collapsed. They holed up in caves and bunkers in the Tora Bora mountain range and for more than two weeks fought off several ground offensives by local Afghan mujahideen. They were bombed by US warplanes and hunted down by American, Australian, Canadian, and British commandos. Then, suddenly, the Al Qaeda men had stopped fighting back, and vanished, presumably fleeing through the high mountains into Pakistan. The American bombing campaign was suspended, and, together with their mujahideen allies, US Special Forces soldiers began a ground search in Tora Bora's snowy ridges for enemy survivors.

OSAMA BIN LADEN HAD SEVERAL WIVES AND SEVERAL HOUSES that, for security reasons, among others, he moved in and out of. One of the houses is in the village of Naji Mujahid, on a desert plain just south of Jalalabad. The house has high mud walls and metal gates. It and a gaggle of similar compounds form a dusty, trash-strewn pit stop strategically located on the jeep track leading to the Tora Bora foothills. Bin Laden's compound is nondescript, a haphazard welter of mud patios and small square houses with spartan rooms and alleyways leading to other cubicles. There were no flower beds, no decorations, and no furniture by the time I arrived. All that had been looted by the local mujahideen. Bin Laden had evidently had plenty of time to gather up his more valuable possessions before he left, and also to burn things he didn't want left lying around. In several places there were blackened swatches of ground and heaps of charred paper.

There were also some unburned papers, and I picked up a page from an English-language Turkish defense magazine with the specifications for an electronic siren and public address system sold by Military Electronics Industries, Inc., of Turkey; an advertisement from the Swedish arms company FFV Ordnance for a tank-busting rocket warhead; an

American military privateer Jack Idema with his hired mujahideen gunmen at Tora Bora, December 2001.   THOMAS DWORZAK/MAGNUM PHOTOS

operator's manual for a portable radio transceiver made by Kachina
Communications, Inc.; a tax-free shopping receipt for several digital
multimeters that cost 173 deutsche marks, purchased from Conrad
Electronic in Munich on May 6, 2000. I also found an article from the
November 1989 edition of *Modern Electronics*, entitled "More on How
to Detect Ultraviolet, Visible Light and Infrared," the second of two
articles on the subject of radiation.

While I was poking around the compound, accompanied by Jack
and a platoon of mujahideen, a sharp-faced young Afghan man and several children wandered in to watch. The man, whose name was Redwarullah, said that he was a neighbor, and he confirmed that until a few
weeks earlier the village had been the home of a community of Arab
families including that of Osama bin Laden. I asked Redwarullah if
he thought bin Laden had masterminded the attacks on the World
Trade Center in New York. He said that he didn't think so. "People here
thought he was a very nice Muslim," he said. My mujahideen escorts interrupted our chat and led me out of Osama bin Laden's house. They explained that the inhabitants of Naji Mujahid were Al Qaeda supporters,
and that it was best not to stay there too long. The next day, we drove up
the jeep track beyond the village into a dramatic panorama of ravines
and steep, rocky hills covered with scrub oaks and fir trees. Trails led
through the diminishing tree line toward the jagged, snow-covered peaks
of Tora Bora. It was there that bin Laden's trail had gone cold.

The Afghan mujahideen militias who had been enlisted by the
United States to launch the ground attacks at Tora Bora drove their
pickups and Russian tanks purposefully around the flanks of the mountains, but there was no action taking place. The Western journalists who
had come to witness the much-hyped last stand of Al Qaeda were beginning to pull out of the area. Geraldo Rivera had moved on. The tent
city erected for the press on a windblown lower ridge of the mountain was littered with satellite dishes, plastic bottles, cans, and wrappers

of imported foodstuffs. It looked like a climbers' base camp in the Himalayas, but it was shrinking, a process that had been hastened by a number of assaults and robberies perpetrated by the increasingly unruly mujahideen.

Up in the mountains, some Afghan fighters and a handful of reporters wandered cautiously around the site of a bomb-blasted Al Qaeda training camp. There were still Al Qaeda men in the vicinity, by all accounts. Some had attacked this very spot in broad daylight a couple of days earlier, sending mujahideen and journalists scattering for cover. Most of the trees that were still standing had been literally peeled, their branches shorn of twigs and bark by explosions, and what had been caves and underground bunkers was now an uncertain welter of mounds and holes. There was also the confused refuse left behind by human beings: pieces of ripped camouflage clothing, sleeping bags, hundreds of tin ammunition boxes with Chinese lettering, the yellow tags of unexploded cluster bomblets, and bits of paper. Here and there lay sections—huge ones—of American bomb casings. In the distance I could see an Afghan man chopping up the ravaged trees with an ax, preparing to cart the kindling away. The next day, a scavenger was blown in half by a partially buried bomblet.

I picked up a bull's-eye that had been used for target shooting; some handwritten notes about ammunition supplies; an instruction sheet for Negram, a medicine for urinary and intestinal infections; and an English-language phrasebook for Arabic speakers. The phrasebook was illustrated with cartoonlike scenes peopled with men wearing suits and homburgs. Their faces had been inked out. Looking through the book, I wondered about the utility of some of the phrases bin Laden's warriors had learned: "It is nice to listen to good music on the radio"; "Plenty of brushing improves your hair"; "I am trying to keep the room clean, but he keeps putting things on the piano"; "Please don't speak to my dog unkindly." It was hard to imagine an Al Qaeda volunteer living up in this bleak mountainscape, praying devoutly five times daily, medicating himself against stomach ailments while learning how to shoot properly, and, in his free moments, boning up on his English so that, presumably, he would at some future date be able to negotiate his way into a Western country like England or the United States to carry out an atrocious mission in which he would most likely die.

On the way down the mountain, Jack, who was armed and wearing full combat regalia, clambered onto one of the mujahideen tanks with a tin of white paint and a brush. He wrote "N.Y.P.D." on the tank's green steel carapace. The mujahideen smiled obligingly and asked to borrow his paint. In lacy Farsi script they added the words "Dear Massoud, we will follow your way."

THE HOTEL SPINGHAR IN JALALABAD IS A FADED LATE-DECO place surrounded by a grove of orange trees. The image of a Kalashnikov with a red X over it, like a no-smoking sign, has been pasted onto the wall outside the front door. A portrait of a regional warlord, Hazrat Ali, a wiry man with a graying beard, hangs inside, next to the reception desk. Hazrat Ali is said to be the Spinghar's owner, though how he acquired the hotel is something of a mystery. He was the leader of a band of anti-Taliban guerrillas in the hills outside Jalalabad, and when the Taliban and their Al Qaeda allies fled town in the middle of November, he led his fighters into the city. In the subsequent division of political spoils, Hazrat Ali, who is a member of the Northern Alliance, became the security chief for the Eastern *shura*, which controls Nangarhar Province in loose cooperation with the Karzai regime in Kabul. Hazrat Ali was the favorite local proxy fighter of the US Special Forces advisers in the fighting at Tora Bora.

I met Commander Ali the day he gave an impromptu press conference in a banquet room of the hotel. He wore a waxed hunting jacket with a gray fleece lining and was surrounded by a retinue of gunmen. He spoke with bluff bravado, declaring that Al Qaeda was "no longer a problem," then seemed to hedge, admitting that terrorists might be able to infiltrate the ranks of his own fighting force. "This is a danger we must be on the alert for." Hazrat Ali may well have been preempting the rumors that were already beginning to circulate that some of his men had assisted the escape of hundreds of Al Qaeda terrorists from Tora Bora into Pakistan. "God only knows where Osama bin Laden is now," he said, lamely.

Hazrat Ali ended the press conference with what sounded like a backhanded warning to his new sponsors. "If the US tries to take over the suppression of all the Al Qaeda activities in Afghanistan by itself, in my view this will bring it problems similar to the ones experienced by the Soviets in Afghanistan. But if the United States supports the popular resistance forces who have been fighting terrorism in Afghanistan for many years, then I am sure the people will be happy with that."

That night I met Hazrat Ali's eldest son, Samiullah, a handsome and self-possessed twenty-two-year-old who is a military commander in his own right, with two hundred fighters and a crew of bodyguards. "Osama and his troops were so well entrenched that it was not easy rooting them out," he said. "We were fighting them on the ground, but their deep caves made it difficult. The American air support helped a lot." Samiullah insisted that American soldiers had not done the real fighting for the caves. "The US Special Forces are only here as target spotters, not fighters," he said, "and even so they have caused many casualties from their bombs among the mujahideen—even more than those caused by Al Qaeda." Like his father, Samiullah was unenthusiastic about more overt American involvement on the ground. "My forces are sensitive about the presence of foreigners," he said. "If big numbers of Americans come here, I think the people will react against them."

Hazrat Ali gave Jack and me permission to visit some Al Qaeda prisoners in the Jalalabad jail. The mujahideen guarding the door at the jail didn't want to let us in but finally said we could stay for fifteen minutes. The day before, news had reached Jalalabad that a group of Al Qaeda fighters who had been caught on the other side of the border with Pakistan had overpowered the guards on a bus that was transporting them to Peshawar. They had seized their guns, killed several of them, and caused the bus to crash. A number of these Al Qaeda fighters had escaped and were still at large.

It was a brilliant winter day. Birds sang in the trees. We entered an unkempt garden planted with ratty rosebushes and shaded by large mulberry trees with orange leaves. At the end of the garden, armed sentries stood in front of a fortresslike brick building with big gray gates and crenellated parapets. Several mujahideen officials came up to us and laid out ground rules for our visit. They explained that the prisoners were dangerous. "They have already tried to take away our guns," one official said. They would select a couple of prisoners to speak to us, and bring them out in handcuffs and ankle chains.

While we waited for the prisoners to appear, a man approached me and asked me, slyly, if I wanted to see something. He showed me a passport. It belonged to one of the terrorists, he said, and he wished to sell it. It was a brand-new Algerian passport, issued in 2001, with a picture of a neat young man of Arab appearance named Salim Yahiaqui who had been born in 1979. It described his profession as "photographer." The man snatched it back after I had noted down these details. He stuffed it into his jacket pocket and moved away. A few minutes later the doors of the prison opened, and a dozen or so men came out. We were told to walk toward them, and our two groups met on the footpath of the garden and formed a large circle. Someone pointed out the two prisoners for me. One was a short, stocky man with a black beard and pitted olive skin. He wore a dirty black anorak, a gray *shalwar kameez*, camouflage fatigue trousers, and new black leather boots. A stocking cap partially covered his thick black hair, which was uncombed and dirty. He stared intently at us. The other prisoner was taller and thinner and older looking, with a vague expression. Neither man was handcuffed or wore ankle chains, which I found alarming, since they were only a few feet away from us and right next to mujahideen who were armed but who seemed less than attentive about their duties as guards. The younger prisoner was watchful and self-confident; he had a half smile that was not quite a sneer, but almost.

One of the Afghans began speaking to the prisoners in Arabic, explaining who we were, and telling them that we wanted to hear their stories. The younger man said his name was Faiz Muhammad Ahmed, that he was twenty-six years old, and was from Kuwait. He spoke in Arabic, but it soon became evident that he understood English as well, because he occasionally corrected the interpreter. "The international community is mistaken about Arabs in Afghanistan," he said. "Not all are here for Osama bin Laden." He was a businessman. "I have a lot of money, and I came to Afghanistan to help Muslims. I came to dig wells." When Jalalabad fell he had met some Arabs. "These Arabs, who I didn't know, said I should go to the mountains with them, and so I did and that's when I was caught." The interpreter laughed as he translated this, and put his hand on the Kuwaiti's shoulder in a matey kind of way. Faiz Muhammad Ahmed stared at us with his half smile.

"This is hardly credible," I said.

"But it is a big mistake to say all Arabs in Afghanistan are with Osama bin Laden and are terrorists," Faiz Muhammad Ahmed replied. "It would be as if we said, 'All Westerners in Afghanistan are CIA.'" He glanced toward Jack, and added, "Maybe you are."

If he was a businessman, as he claimed, I asked, why was he dressed as he was? "My normal clothes were blown up by the American bombing," he explained. What was his opinion of Osama bin Laden and Al

Qaeda? "I personally do not agree with Osama bin Laden's policy; it is against the Koran," he said. "But I also think that the US is at fault for attacking Muslims. I am an eyewitness of American bombing against civilians in Afghanistan." Then he said that he would like to send a message through us.

Jack interrupted, angrily: "No! You sent a message to us on September eleventh!" I argued with Jack about letting the man speak, and he relented. Given his opportunity, Faiz Muhammad Ahmed made a statement: "I want to say that I am from Kuwait and that I have been to the United States. My background should be checked out and I should be sent to Kuwait for trial."

The second prisoner said that his name was Nassir Abdel Latif. He was from Casablanca, Morocco, and was thirty-six years old. He wore a camouflage jacket and US Special Forces combat boots and a gray *pakul* cap. He spoke in a neutral and matter-of-fact tone of voice. "I came to Afghanistan because of Afghanistan's strict Islamic rule and because it was full of Islamic scholars," he said. He had come to live, not fight, in Afghanistan, he stressed, but he happened to be in Kabul when it fell, and then he escaped to Jalalabad, and when it also fell he had to flee to the mountains.

We asked if he had been fighting when he was caught. "Yes," he said. "By then I was carrying a gun. I was a military man." But, he added, unconvincingly, he didn't know the identity of the group he was with in the mountains. "We not only condemn Osama bin Laden," he said, "but Israel too. You people should remember that there are some actions which made Osama bin Laden carry out *his* action."

Faiz Muhammad Ahmed interrupted. "The Al Qaeda didn't keep their people with us," he said. "Al Qaeda takes its people to a big secret place in the mountains. There are a lot of secret things in Al Qaeda."

The guards were listening, but they didn't seem to notice that Faiz

Muhammad Ahmed had inched forward. He moved forward slightly all the time we were talking, and I kept stepping back from him. The whole circle of men moved perhaps two feet during our forty-minute encounter.

I asked Nassir Abdel Latif if he was a member of Al Qaeda. "I was in military training camps," he said. "First in Casablanca, and then in Kabul. Then I was a businessman, and when I came to Kabul I was living in a training camp, but not actually training." When I asked him what kind of business he was involved in, he replied, vaguely, that he had been doing business between Libya and Sudan, and had then gone to Yemen and from there to Pakistan, and finally had arrived in Afghanistan. Nassir Abdel Latif then acknowledged that he had received military training in Kabul after all, and told us that the place he had been living was called the Libyan Jihadi Military Training Camp. He *had* been a businessman once, he said, but in the end had wanted to be a fighter.

Jack asked to see the palms of the men's hands and concluded that they both were fighters. "This is from holding a Kalashnikov," he said, pointing to Faiz Muhammad Ahmed's calluses.

I asked if either of them had seen Osama bin Laden. Faiz Muhammad Ahmed said no, but Nassir Abdel Latif said that he had: "He was in Tora Bora for a long time and he was receiving a lot of visitors. Osama bin Laden told us: 'Believe in us, believe in Allah, believe in me, in this jihad, we will win in the end.'" Nassir Abdel Latif stared at me directly with his pale brown eyes. "We did not come here to fight Afghans, we came here to fight Americans, and we will keep fighting until we destroy them totally."

That seemed to make Jack happy, and Faiz Muhammad Ahmed tried to qualify things. "Most of us who were on Tora Bora wanted to fight Americans," he said, "but not all Americans. Just those who are fighting Muslims." I asked him if Osama bin Laden was still alive. "God only knows," he said. And then our meeting was at an end. Jack raised his hand and wagged a finger at them. "America will come and get you," he said. They didn't reply.


JACK'S CORPS OF AFGHAN BODYGUARDS WAS AN UNRULY GROUP. They squabbled among themselves or with Jack over food and money, and once some of them threatened to kill Jack's irritating young interpreter for trying to order them around. Jack told the boy to keep his mouth shut and to stick to translating what he said. But problems cropped up every day, and after some altercation with the fighters Jack turned to me and remarked, "Compared with the Afghans, the Haitians were fuckin' easy. You just told 'em, 'Do this, motherfucker!' And they said 'OK!' But not these guys." He shook his head.

Jack was extremely critical of the way the US military had handled things at Tora Bora. They had allowed undisciplined, untrained, and ill-equipped Afghans to carry out the bulk of the fighting while they remained in the background. "If we don't fucking send in some American advisers here quick, we're gonna be right back to where we were five years from now," he said. "We failed the Afghans after the Russians left. We didn't do any demobilization and normalization. There's tens of thousands of soldiers and commanders with guns in this country! What're you gonna do with 'em? Instead of sending in five thousand British peacekeepers, we should send in a hundred instructors to teach them how to do it themselves. All these guys need is professional training. The less training an army has, the more dangerous it is."

Jack said that he was born in upstate New York and that he lived now in Fayetteville, North Carolina. He was forty-six and had joined the Green Berets in 1974, when he was nineteen. "I spent twenty-five years in Special Operations in one form or another," he said. "Except for a brief period in which I was trying to be a cop." Was he still active duty, or was he retired? "I have no official relationship to the US government," he said, as if by rote. We played cat and mouse on this question, but Jack told me some of the places he had been as a US military adviser. "I trained the US Marine security mission in Haiti in 1980," he said. He had spent time in El Salvador, as well. "I was in Vilnius, Lithuania, during the coup in January ninety-one; also at the Moscow coup in August ninety-one. I was just there as assistance to pro-US forces—with the Alpha group teams in Moscow. They were on the good guys' side, the anti-Communists." He had been involved in the Gulf War, as well. A couple of years ago, he'd resigned his Special Forces commission. "I was getting too old to carry a rucksack, and I had broken my back and my neck."

So why was he in Afghanistan? "I just said I was goin' one way or another, to some people in DOD"—the Department of Defense—he replied. His first mission was to provide ground assistance to the air drops of US humanitarian aid rations. He had also conducted an investigation into the rumors circulating among Afghans that the rations were poisoned.

"I found out who did it," Jack said, "and it was not Al Qaeda or the Taliban. And there wasn't any poison. The people were eating the desiccant"—the preservative drying agent—"that comes in little packets in each ration pack. It says 'Do Not Eat' in English, French, Spanish, and Chinese. But not in Farsi or Pashto. They thought it was spices! So there were some severe injuries and several presumed deaths. One guy who died ate the Handi Wipes, the desiccant—everything. These people, I mean, they don't even have napkins, how do they know what a Handi Wipe is? I gather he thought it smelled good, so he ate it." Other people had become ill, Jack found, because many of the ration packs had exploded on impact, and the food inside had been exposed and become contaminated. Jack said that he wrote a report that was sent to DOD, and about a week later the problems were sorted out.

"When that was over," Jack said, "I went back to doing what I normally do, which is to advise foreign armies."

# 7

## MULLAH OMAR'S FAVORITE SONGS

In the winter of 1988–89, I spent a month in a mujahideen camp in the Arghandab Valley, a few miles north of Kandahar. The Soviets had begun to withdraw their troops from Afghanistan, but MiG warplanes were still carrying out daily bombing and strafing runs, and in the slummy southern suburbs of Kandahar there was a front line where both sides were dug in. The commander of the camp, Mullah Naquibullah, known as Naquib, was a tall, beefy fellow, the chief of Kandahar's second-largest tribe, the Alokozai. He had installed about thirty of his fighters on the outskirts of his home village of Charqulba. The village itself was mostly destroyed and abandoned; nearly all the inhabitants had fled to refugee camps in Pakistan. The only civilians in the area were a few Kutchi nomad families who wandered around with their camels and herds of goats. The desert was pocked from years of Soviet bombardment, and unexploded rockets stuck out of the earth at odd angles

This chapter was originally published as "After the Revolution," *The New Yorker*, January 20, 2002.

here and there, like children's arrows. Naquib's camp consisted of half a dozen flat-roofed mud huts and a prayer ground in the midst of vineyards. The day before I arrived, a bomb had landed nearby, leaving a huge crater in which a beautiful black stallion lay dead, its hooves in the air.

The war, such as it was, was fairly abstract by then. You could see bombs exploding in the distance most days, but there was no real threat of ground attacks from the besieged government garrison, and Mullah Naquib pretty much had the run of the Arghandab Valley. His mujahideen prayed diligently five times a day, and, given their devotion and their abstinent way of life, I began to think of them as warrior monks.

One day Naquib sent me off to observe a court session led by two elderly Islamic scholars who were charged with imposing Sharia, religious law, in the region. I was driven at breakneck speed along a bombed-out road by a young man who played tapes of wailing Kandahari love songs at high volume on the cassette deck of a Toyota pickup truck. The court was set up out-of-doors, in the shade of a raisin-storage silo. The judges leaned on pillows propped up against the silo walls and told me how they followed the Koran in reaching verdicts about territorial rights, adultery, theft, and so forth. After some bickering over numbers, they agreed that they had put eighteen murderers to death. Their discourse on justice went on for some time, and then the younger of the two produced a piece of paper and announced that a new edict was being sent to all the mujahideen commanders in the region. Crime had increased, and this was due, they believed, to the playing of recorded music, which was banned from now on.

The ban obviously came as a shock to the mujahideen who had accompanied me. They looked embarrassed but didn't say much, and we left as soon as the court broke for lunch. Driving back to Naquib's camp, the young driver pointedly inserted a tape into the cassette deck and turned the volume up even louder than it had been before. I learned later that Naquib told his men that he was not going to make a big issue of the new edict. He said that they could continue to play music, but only when they were in camp, and that they should keep it low. Meanwhile, he told the judges that he would comply with their order. Naquib's pragmatic way of dealing with the situation seemed to me admirable.

I thought of that rustic court recently when I visited Mullah Naquib in Kandahar, where he has been living on and off since 1992, when the Communist-backed Afghan regime was finally defeated. Naquib is a controversial figure in Kandahar because of his relationship with the Taliban. When Burhanuddin Rabbani was president of Afghanistan, Naquib was made the supreme military commander of Kandahar, but in 1994 he turned the city over to the Taliban. Many people believe that he was also involved in the recent, unexplained disappearance of the Taliban from Kandahar, and they blame him especially for the escape of Mullah Omar.

Naquib didn't remember me at first, but when he did he seemed pleased, and he began introducing me as a friend from the old days of the jihad against the Soviets. Naquib has aged badly; although he is only forty-seven, he looks much older. He wears glasses now, and his long black beard is streaked with gray. He has a bad cough. We reminisced for a while, and he offered to take me back to the Arghandab Valley to revisit the mujahideen camp where we had met more than a decade earlier. The next day, followed by a dozen or so bodyguards, he led me to the carport in his living compound, where two late-model SUVs were parked. We got into a pearl-colored VX Limited Edition Toyota Land Cruiser, and several small boys, the youngest of Naquib's eleven children, climbed into the back. The Toyota had a sunroof and a luxurious tan leather interior and a CD player with an LCD display. It was a fine car, I said to Naquib. He chuckled. "It was Mullah Omar's," he said. "I have ten of his cars."

We took off, and I asked Naquib how he had come to own Mullah

Omar's cars. "They were just parked, so I took them," he replied, somewhat glibly. We came to a gate on the security perimeter of Mullah
Omar's property, which turned out to be more or less next door. The
sentries at the gate saluted Naquib. Mullah Omar apparently owned a
hundred acres or so on the edge of town, with about ten acres given over
to a compound of living quarters and guesthouses that were surrounded
by a maze of walls. We drove down a dirt road that runs through Omar's
property, and soon came to the paved road to the Arghandab Valley, a
rural fastness where dusty tracks lead off in all directions into the desert and the mountain ranges beyond. Omar's house was well placed for
a getaway.

I asked Naquib if he had met Mullah Omar. "Lots of times," he said.
He described him as "a very quiet man who never spoke to people."

As we drove through a pass between the mountains just behind
Omar's land, Naquib turned on the CD player, and the Toyota was filled
with Afghan music. I asked if the CD was his or had come with the car.

"It was here when I got it," Naquib said, opening the CD storage
container on the armrest between the front seats. We looked for secu-
lar music among the discs of keening prayers, and fiddled with the sound
system for a while.

"Are you telling me," I said, when we had made a selection, "that this
stuff belonged to the man who put people in prison for listening to
music?" Naquib shrugged. "It seems so." The song that was playing, he
said, was a popular Afghan tune that vilified General Rashid Dostum,
the Uzbek warlord from Mazar-i-Sharif. Its chief refrain was "O murderer of the Afghan people."

"What is life without music?" Mullah Naquib said.


MANY VESTIGES OF THE TALIBAN ERA REMAIN UNTOUCHED IN
the beat-up, dusty center of Kandahar, where the ruins of buildings that

collapsed during the recent American bombing campaign lie among the ruins of older battles. Vendors with carts sell "Super Osama bin Laden Kulfa Balls"—coconut candy manufactured in Pakistan and packaged in pink-and-purple boxes covered with images of bin Laden surrounded by tanks, cruise missiles, and jet fighters. The chaotic streets are full of men who look like Taliban, with white or black turbans and big, bushy beards. They roar around in Toyota pickups adorned with flags with green, black, and red stripes—the old royalist flag of Afghanistan, which has been revived by the followers of Hamid Karzai, the interim prime minister—and there is no way, really, to know their past affiliations. In Kandahar, as in most other parts of Afghanistan, the Taliban didn't surrender so much as melt away. The leaders vanished, but most rank-and-file members simply returned to their homes. Karzai promised not to persecute former Taliban who stopped fighting, and he has kept his word. Kandahar is officially Taliban-free, but it has an unreconciled atmosphere. The past has not quite been overcome, and the future is unresolved.

The mausoleum that adjoins the Ahmed Shah Mosque, which is across the street from the governor's palace, has a special subterranean chamber that *kafirs* cannot enter. It houses the cloak that is believed to have belonged to the Prophet Muhammad. On April 4, 1996, when Mullah Omar was declared the Keeper of the Faithful, he took the cloak out of the chamber and, in a dramatic display of hubris, donned it before a crowd of spectators. It was one of the few times that Omar appeared in public. I met only one person in Kandahar, besides Mullah Naquib, who had ever seen him. This was a young man named Popal, who worked at the governor's palace. Popal kept me company one evening as I waited for an interview with Gul Agha Shirzai, who had been appointed governor of Kandahar in mid-December. Popal brought me tea, and we sat together on the floor of a large office. He apologized for the lack of chairs, and explained that the Taliban had taken virtually everything when they left—even the carpets. The cheap imitation Persian we were sitting on, he said, had been bought in the bazaar. "And those"—he pointed to some computer monitors, keyboards, and printers—"we got from some of the Arabs' houses." He was referring to members of Al Qaeda, several hundred of whom had lived in Kandahar. I noticed that none of the computers had towers. "The Americans who have a base here, just behind the palace," Popal said, "are checking the hard drives for information, and when they are done they will give them to us."

The city was crawling with Americans, mostly marines, who drove around in heavily armed convoys of sand-colored Humvees, their guns pointed and their faces masked by black balaclavas. There were also small groups of weather-beaten Special Forces commandos, who wore Afghan clothes and drove Toyota four-wheel-drive pickups. From a distance, they were hard to distinguish from the many mujahideen fighters in town. They kept to themselves.

Popal had worked at the palace under the Taliban, too. It was hard to find a job in Kandahar. His long-term goal, he said, was to improve his English, so that he could become an English-Pashto translator, and also to learn computer programming. These were both things that had been nearly impossible to do under the Taliban. "The Taliban wanted us to learn Arabic. They let us work with computers, but we could not use CDs or any programs that showed human images." He said that once, a few years back, he had been stopped by the Taliban's religious police, who said that his beard was too short. They had taken him to a building and told him that his head was going to be shaved as punishment. "The building had no running water, but there was a drainage ditch outside, full of sewage, and they made me wet my hair from it and they used a razor to shave my head. It was very dirty water."

Popal said that many Taliban officials had fled to the nearby Paki-

stani city of Quetta, and a few days earlier several of them, including the
Taliban minister of justice, had dispatched representatives to Kandahar
to meet with the new governor. "You see, the Pakistani authorities are
now bothering them, saying they must leave Pakistan. So they sent their
people to meet with Mr. Gul Agha Shirzai and they told him where they
had hidden weapons and vehicles in Kandahar. And they asked Mr. Gul
Agha Shirzai to ask the Pakistani authorities, on their behalf, to allow
them to stay there. He has sent those letters today, I believe." This was a
couple of weeks before the Taliban minister of justice and other Taliban
officials turned up in Kandahar and were sent home by Gul Agha, much
to the dismay of the Americans.

Popal had met Mullah Omar at the governor's palace. "I remember
he arrived in a Toyota Corolla that belonged to someone else," Popal
said. "A normal car. He came here because the father of one of the officials was ill and he wanted to wish him well. He was very quiet, gentle.
He seemed to me like a good man, not like those other Taliban who
shaved my head with the drainage water."


THE AUSTERITY OF THE TALIBAN WAS PARTICULARLY ANOMA-
lous in the Pashtun homelands of eastern and southern Afghanistan, of
which Kandahar is the principal city. Mosques, for instance, are more
architecturally ornate in the Pashtun region than they are in the north.
The streets are filled with motorized rickshaws covered with fanciful
bronze embossing and shiny decals. Trucks are decorated with painted
tin panels and wooden bulwarks like the prows of old-fashioned schoo-
ners. Metal gewgaws dangling from their fenders tinkle as the trucks
lumber along.

Pashtun men, Kandaharis in particular, are very conscious of their
personal appearance. Many of them line their eyes with black kohl and

color their toenails, and sometimes their fingernails, with henna. Some also dye their hair. It is quite common to see otherwise sober-seeming older men with long beards that are a flaming, almost punklike orange color. Burly, bearded men who carry weapons also wear *chaplis*, colorful high-heeled sandals. I noticed that to be really chic in Kandahar you wear your *chaplis* a size or so too small, which means that you mince and wobble as you walk.

Afghans from other regions joke about the high incidence of pederasty among Kandahari men. They say that when crows fly over Kandahar they clamp one wing over their bottoms, just in case. One of the first things the Taliban did—a popular move—was to punish mujahideen commanders who were accused of rape or pederasty. Homosexuals who were sentenced to death faced a particularly grisly end. Tanks or bulldozers crushed them and buried them under mud walls. Pederasty was evidently a continuing source of concern to Mullah Omar, who decreed that Taliban commanders couldn't have beardless boys in their ranks.

In downtown Kandahar, directly across from a row of small bakeries and the run-down Noor Jehan hotel, Kandahar's finest, there are several hole-in-the-wall photo shops. After the exodus of the Taliban from the city in early December, the proprietors hung portraits of their clients in the windows, along with photographs of famous people like Bruce Lee, Leonardo DiCaprio, Ahmad Shah Massoud, and King Zahir Shah. There are many portraits of Taliban fighters posing in front of curtains or painted backdrops. They hold guns and bouquets of plastic flowers. Some are alone, others are with a friend. Some sit rigidly side by side and a few have their arms draped over one another, and some even clasp their hands together affectionately.

Said Kamal, the proprietor of the Photo Shah Zada shop, did a brisk business in Taliban portraits. He specializes in retouched photos. Kamal's artful brushwork removes blemishes and adds color. The backdrops of his portraits are vivid greens or blues with halos of red and orange, and clothing has been transformed from the drab to the garish. Many of the Taliban sat for their portraits with heavily kohled eyes, which made them look like silent-movie stars.

Taliban portraits lie under the glass of Said Kamal's front counter and hang on the wall in tin frames. He said that they belong to Taliban who fled the city, and he doesn't expect them to be picked up. I found this confusing, since Mullah Omar had enforced the Koranic prohibition on representations of the human image, but Said Kamal explained that after the ban on images was announced, and the Taliban forced the photo shops to shut down, they realized that even they needed passport

Portraits of Taliban fighters who had posed for pictures in a Kandahar photo studio.

THOMAS DWORZAK/MAGNUM PHOTOS (ORIGINAL IN COLOR)

pictures. There was no way around it, if they wanted to travel. So an exception was made to Mullah Omar's edict. Officially, Said Kamal made passport photographs, and he formally complied with the rules, displaying no pictures of human beings in his shop window. But the rules were never fully obeyed by everyone. Said Kamal continued to make portraits of the Taliban, just as he continued to take clandestine wedding pictures at the request of ordinary Kandaharis.

I VISITED MULLAH OMAR'S COMPOUND BY MYSELF ONE DAY after Mullah Naquib had pointed it out. It had been heavily bombed and strafed and rocketed, and untidy piles of bricks and masonry lay everywhere, but the section in which Mullah Omar lived with his wives and children was mostly still intact, thanks to twelve-foot-thick bombproof roofs. Construction materials for future additions and improvements lay alongside the debris. Mullah Omar had had plans. He wanted to make the desert bloom. Scores of young shade saplings were planted along the driveways, and there were several flower gardens inside the compound. At one of the guesthouses, a tanker truck pumped water onto a bed of geraniums. The words "Donated by UNICEF to Kandahar Water Supply Department" were written on the side of the truck. The men holding the hose told me that they had been coming to water Omar's gardens for some time.

A pickup truck came by. Several RPG antitank rockets stood upright on either side of the cab, and an armed American wearing a black turban was sitting in the back. A US soldier who appeared to be in his late thirties told me that the part of the compound in front of me was off-limits but that I could walk around the part where Mullah Omar's living quarters were. "You can't miss it," he said. "It's the place that looks like Motel 6."

In front of Omar's house there is a small concrete mosque with several minarets, domed cupolas, and pillars with huge flowers painted on them. A sculpture of a fallen tree and boulders, painted black and green, serves as a kind of traffic island between the mosque and the house. Two or three faux date palms jut up around the sculpture, which seems to serve also as a fountain, although it was dry on the day I visited. The outer walls of the house are covered with murals depicting lakes and ornamental gardens and more flowers. Omar lived with his favorite wife in a private apartment on one side of the house, painted, for the most part, pink and green. The floor is covered with plastic terrazzo tiles. The bedroom, which is small and dank, has a ceiling fan, a double bed, and two white and faux gilt mini-chandeliers. Several mujahideen were resting on Omar's bed when I poked my head in; they got up quickly and adjusted their turbans. On the other side of the house, I was told, three more wives had lived with their several children. These rooms were much plainer, and there was only one rather crude flower painted on a wall of the common hallway.

Down the road, at Mullah Naquib's house, one of his bodyguards, a sun-darkened and rough-hewn man in black, showed me Naquib's flower garden in an inner courtyard. There were clumps of carefully tended roses, daffodils, and dahlias, and I complimented him on their beauty. The bodyguard smiled. "This is what we've grown with hardly any water, but you should see it when we have rain."

THE DAY NAQUIB DROVE ME TO THE ARGHANDAB VALLEY TO visit the old mujahideen camp, I recognized landmarks such as the tomb of Baba Wali—a holy man whose shrine is on top of a hill that during the jihad was part of Naquib's domain—but there were many more trees than I remembered, and cultivated fields, and more people, too. Naquib said that most of the people who had fled to Pakistan during the war had returned. Now it was drought, not war, that was the problem.

We drove along dirt tracks between vineyards, and then walked across fields to where the camp had been. "We've plowed it all under to grow grapes," Naquib said. The only house left standing was the one where he had slept. In the intervening years, he had bought more land. He had inherited only ten *jeribs* from his father, but now he owned 250, about 125 acres. He was growing wheat, grapes, almonds, and pomegranates.

Naquib's grandfather, and his father, too, had been the head of the Alokozai tribe, but during Zahir Shah's reign a *malek*, a government administrator, was appointed. Then, after the anti-Soviet jihad began, things reverted to the way they had been. Naquib said that a man named Azizullah Wasfi, who had moved to the United States, is the official tribal elder, but that in his absence Naquib was put in charge.

I asked Naquib to whom the tribal authority would pass when Azizullah Wasfi died. "Well, when the tribe appoints a leader, it chooses someone who can serve them," he said. "I am not so interested in doing this, because of health problems, but I will help if I am asked." Naquib said that his duties were "resolving disputes and grievances." For example, he said, "when Mullah Omar decided to leave Kandahar, he came to me as leader of the Alokozai." Almost as an afterthought, Naquib added, "The tribal chief also can call up the men for war." There were Alokozai all over the place, not only in Arghandab but in the neighboring provinces of Uruzgan, Helmand, and even, he said, as far away as Herat.

For a couple of hours, we walked from one sharecropper's home to another. Invariably, the peasants kissed Naquib's hand deferentially. He inspected irrigation systems and asked questions and gave orders. Then we drove to his house, near the village of Charqulba, and sat on large mats and cushions that his men fetched for us. His bodyguards fanned out vigilantly, and we talked about what had happened to him after I left Afghanistan. Apparently everything had gone well at first. "But then the civil war started, and during the chaos the Taliban appeared.

When the Taliban movement started, Hamid Karzai came to see me and told me not to fight against them. And Rabbani also called me and told me not to fight. At the time, we all thought the Talib were fighting for the king"—for the restoration of Zahir Shah to the throne—"and they told me, 'You should surrender the garrison and your guns.' Rabbani wasn't sending money or ammunition to me. How could anyone fight against the Taliban under those conditions?"

After he handed over Kandahar, Naquib said, the Taliban ordered him to go back to Charqulba to live. "I stayed here for a few years, and then I was wounded in an assassination attempt, and went to Islamabad for treatment." Naquib pulled up a sleeve and a trouser leg to show me his scars. He'd been hit by a bullet in his left leg and another in his left elbow, and he pointed to his chest, where, he said, he'd received a rocket fragment. The six men traveling with him had been killed; he was the only survivor. The attackers had been apprehended, he told me. "They claimed that it had been a case of mistaken identity. They said they thought I was a Taliban official." Naquib shrugged, and continued with his story: "I stayed in Islamabad for about two years, and Hamid Karzai and I met with some American officials there. The Americans wanted to know about Al Qaeda, so that they could act against it. We also met with the Italian ambassador. They all told us they would not let Pakistan interfere anymore in our country. And afterward, when I returned home to Kandahar, Hamid Karzai stayed in touch with me."

Naquib lived in Kandahar for about two years after his return from Pakistan, he said. "But then when September eleventh happened, and the Americans started bombing, I came to this house in the village, and I was in touch with Hamid Karzai. He gave me a satellite phone." In early December, Naquib said, when Karzai was chosen as Afghanistan's interim leader, "Mullah Omar and the Taliban agreed to leave, and Karzai agreed that the Taliban would transfer power in Kandahar to me. But by the morning after the night the BBC announced the transfer, the

Taliban had all left. Gul Agha entered the city, and Karzai appointed him governor and myself corps commander. I have some health problems, so I refused the job, and gave it to my deputy, Khan Muhammad."

The competition between Mullah Naquib and Gul Agha had been intense, and many people had expected fighting to break out between them in the days after the Taliban left the city, but Naquib insisted that he had no bad feelings toward Gul Agha, and I didn't press him, because he seemed to like his version of events and wasn't about to change it. He was more candid about his health problems, which were "mental." He had been to two hospitals in Germany for treatment. "I was crazy," he said, and laughed, and all the men who were gathered around now, listening to us, laughed, too, evidently at the memory of his behavior. "I was not myself. I would get tense and have headaches. The doctors told me that I had a heavy workload and it had damaged some of my brain cells." Naquib's symptoms had appeared after the Taliban took over Kandahar, but he said that the problems might have been caused by the explosion of a Russian mortar shell near him during the jihad. "A piece of the shell hit me here," he said, pointing to his forehead. "It was just a small piece, but maybe it had something to do with it." He pulled out a strip of capsules. He had been given a prescription for Risperdal, an antipsychotic. "Each pill costs three hundred rupees," he said, or about four and a half dollars.

EARLY ONE MORNING, A GUNFIGHT BROKE OUT IN A RESIDEN-tial neighborhood in Kandahar, not far from my hotel. At first, people said that it was a confrontation between Mullah Naquib and Gul Agha, but it turned out that one of Gul Agha's commanders, who claimed that he hadn't been paid his salary, had led his soldiers on a robbery expedition, and the local police chief had foiled it. Things had been resolved by sunset, when I stopped by the governor's palace. The commander had barricaded himself in a police station and threatened to blow himself up with grenades, but he had finally surrendered. He and his men had been beaten and put in jail, a guard at the palace told me.

Gul Agha was receiving visitors in a long room that had a red carpet and chandeliers. A framed portrait of King Zahir Shah was propped on a desk at one end of the room. Four or five uniformed soldiers carrying rifles stood around, and a couple dozen venerable-looking petitioners sat attentively on red sofas awaiting their turn to speak with the governor.

Gul Agha is a squat, bushy-haired man with a big belly and a rubbery face. He wore a brown *shalwar kameez* and sandals, and I noticed that his toenails were long and untidy. He was sitting in a chair next to the door, talking to a group of Noorzai tribal elders from the western province of Farah, an eight-hour drive from Kandahar. They had come to see him because they were having problems with mujahideen who had recently arrived from Iran. Gul Agha smoked a Benson & Hedges Special Filter cigarette and listened to the elders, and when they had finished he told them that he was aware of what he termed, darkly, "the Iranian interference" in their province, and that President Karzai was also aware of it. The problem would be dealt with soon. Gul Agha lisps clumsily, as if his tongue were too big for his mouth. "Before now," he said loudly, "there were commanders with autonomous power. But now I am the overall commander of the whole area."

While Gul Agha was speaking, a soldier passed out cold cans of Pepsi to some of the guests. I took one and sipped it and then placed the can on the floor next to my feet, but almost immediately someone stuck his hand under my chair and grabbed it. I turned around and saw a soldier sitting on the carpet behind me, holding the Pepsi and snickering to a friend. I reached over and swiped it back.

When it was my turn to speak with the governor, I asked him to describe his role in recent events. He had been governor of Kandahar during Rabbani's tenure, although Mullah Naquib, as military commander, had more power than he did then. When the Taliban took over Kandahar in 1994, Gul Agha moved to Quetta, across the border in Pakistan. "I went into business," he said, "trading goods between Pakistan, Japan, the United Arab Emirates, and other countries. When the Taliban and Al Qaeda became strong in Afghanistan, I wrote three separate letters to Mullah Omar, advising him not to do what he was doing, because he'd bring disaster upon Afghanistan. When he didn't listen to us, we began to fight against him, just as we fought against the Russians. The Afghan people have a long history, more than five thousand years old, and they have never accepted foreign invaders and have always fought to resist them. We have told the UN and US troops at the airport that they are here to stop the foreign interference."

Gul Agha then complained at length about how some foreign powers, namely Iran and Russia, were still meddling in Afghanistan by backing fundamentalist warlords, including former President Rabbani. "These men all have the ideology of the Muslim Brotherhood," Gul Agha said. They were trying to sabotage the interim government of Hamid Karzai by disseminating propaganda, sending their gunmen to his territory, and generally stirring up trouble. "We want an end to foreign interference in Afghanistan," he repeated. "We want peace in Afghanistan and we ask Allah to help us have honest government. We want rights for women, and we are against drugs and terrorism. My greatest hope and wish is that there will be a broad-based government in Afghanistan without friction between different groups."

The governor sat back in his chair, apparently satisfied with his oration.

Since he had brought up the subject of friction, I said, what was his current relationship with Mullah Naquib? "Mullah Naquib himself agreed to leave the government," Gul Agha replied, "and he has no duties now." He said that he had told Hamid Karzai that he did not want to work with Naquib. "It was he who brought the Taliban and Al Qaeda to Kandahar," Gul Agha said, and he had helped the Taliban leaders escape. "The world is not happy with him, and the Americans are not happy with him. So maybe he will be brought to justice."

AHMED WALI KARZAI, ONE OF THE PRESIDENT'S YOUNGER brothers, lives in Kandahar, in a heavily guarded house a few miles from the governor's palace. He speaks fluent American-accented English. "I spent ten years in Chicago," he explained. "I opened the first Afghan restaurant there." His Chicago restaurant was one of a family-owned chain of Afghan restaurants in the United States, all of them called the Helmand, after Afghanistan's longest river.

"We're trying to get things functioning here again," Karzai said. "Our main concern is security. We want to get the gunmen off the streets, and we've asked the commanders to have no more than one or two bodyguards." Karzai was reasonably sanguine about the town rivals, Mullah Naquib and Gul Agha. It was just a matter of keeping a lid on things until international peacekeeping forces took over and an Afghan National Army was in place.

Karzai was less circumspect about Naquib's relationship with the Taliban. "In the early days, we did kind of help the Taliban," he said. "But you have to understand that in the beginning they were mostly commanders who had fought against the Russians. There weren't any Arabs and only a few Pakistanis." The Karzais began campaigning against the Taliban a little over three years ago. "In July 1998, my brother and I talked to Mullah Naquib and asked him to go to Bonn"—for a meeting of Afghan opposition leaders—"and even gave him a ticket and a passport, but he didn't go," Karzai said. "He didn't want to leave his land,

and he said that if he were to go to Bonn he would not be safe in Kandahar afterward. And I think this was the truth. But the fact is Naquib never took any action against the Taliban."

In November, when Gul Agha was approaching Kandahar from the south and Hamid Karzai was north of the city, Mullah Naquib was given the satellite phone to help him get involved. "But he said he was under too much surveillance," Ahmed Wali Karzai recalled. "All he did in the end was arrange for the talks between the Taliban and my brother. Mullah Naquib called me in Quetta to say that Mullah Omar was ready to talk." Karzai said that it was the Taliban's idea to hand the city over to Naquib. "But it didn't happen the way it had been agreed. We expected them to stay in the city, although we never expected Mullah Omar to remain."

Karzai said that the assassination attempt that had almost killed Naquib in 1998 had been ordered by the Taliban security chief. They had done an investigation and had evidence to prove it. An influential businessman in Kandahar told me the same thing and claimed that the Taliban flew Naquib to Pakistan for medical treatment in one of their own helicopters to cover up their complicity in the attempted murder. Why, I asked the businessman, would the Taliban have wanted to kill Naquib? "Because Naquib was the only powerful figure remaining in Kandahar from the time before the Taliban came," he said. "In Arghandab, the people consider him their tribal leader. He represented a potential threat to the Taliban."

The Taliban may have had reservations about Mullah Naquib, but in December, when they realized they had to leave the city, they turned to him to make the arrangements. A man named Khairullah, an intellectual in his sixties who is a distinguished elder in one of the city's tribal councils, told me that the Taliban had bequeathed Naquib many of their weapons when they left. Naquib had complained to me that Rabbani had withheld weapons from him, yet he seemed to have them now, and was vague about where they came from, just as he was vague about the acquisition of the ten Toyota Land Cruisers. Khairullah also said that, as far as he knew, Naquib didn't have any serious health problems, mental or otherwise—certainly nothing incapacitating.

ONE AFTERNOON, A MAN WAITING OUTSIDE GUL AGHA'S PAL-ace approached my translator, Qais, and said he had an Al Qaeda prisoner to sell. He was holding him in his house and would hand him over for $2,000. Qais came back to our hotel to give me the news. He was excited. "What do you think?" he said. "What should I tell him? Will you pay the two thousand dollars?" I reminded Qais that I was not a Green Beret or a CIA agent. Where would I keep an Al Qaeda prisoner? But I was curious, so I told Qais to tell the man to come see me. He showed up a couple of hours later, and Qais went downstairs to talk to him. It turned out that the man's story had been a lie, bait to see if we were interested. He didn't actually have a prisoner in his house. He had come from a village in eastern Afghanistan about a day's drive away, where, he claimed, there were a hundred or so Al Qaeda fighters hiding in a nearby cave. The villagers sympathized with them and took turns taking them food and other supplies. He had delivered food to the cave himself a few days earlier. But he was willing to betray the men for $2,000. He would guide us to the exact spot, so we could capture them, he said.

Qais invited the man up to my room, but when Qais said that I was a journalist, the deal was off. The man didn't want to talk to a journalist. He wanted to do business. In that case, Qais said, the best thing for him to do was to go out to the Kandahar airport and approach the Americans stationed there, who ran a detention camp for Al Qaeda members. The man thanked Qais and left.

I had been offered purloined Al Qaeda documents in Kabul and

Jalalabad, and it didn't seem odd that an enterprising man from a village in eastern Afghanistan had raised the level of entrepreneurship. He must have assumed that if the Americans would pay $25 million for Osama bin Laden they would pay a fair price for lesser souls.

Afghanistan was teeming with opportunists. It was not the country I had visited more than a decade earlier, when Mullah Naquib and his men were fighting a rather simple war over ideas of faith and nationhood. Or perhaps it just seemed simple then. Perhaps the jockeying for power, the hypocrisy and naked ambition and mendacity, had just not had a chance to flower.

I asked Qais what it would take for me to set myself up as a warlord in Afghanistan. "It would be easy," he said. "You hire a hundred gunmen for a month, get a few Toyota pickups, and you're in business." He estimated that it would cost about $10,000. Gunmen came cheap, and most of them had their own Kalashnikovs already. In any case, Kalashnikovs were cheap, too. We might, he suggested, spend a bit more to add some muscle. We could buy a few RPG rocket launchers and a heavy PK machine gun or two, for instance.

OK, I said. But once I have this army, what do I do? It is cheap enough to get going, but how do you sustain it?

This was also easy, Qais said. "In the first month, you find ways to make money so that it doesn't cost you anything more." You went to wealthy local people, merchants and traders, and asked them for money, and they paid.

Qais seemed to be talking about setting up a protection racket. Extortion was only the beginning, of course, he explained. Most of the mujahideen commanders in the Northern Alliance, for instance, were also involved in the opium and heroin trade.

Qais is young, maybe twenty-two, and his enthusiasm for whatever enterprise presents itself to him will serve him well in the new Afghanistan, just as Naquib's pragmatism and canny methods of dealing with the authorities have enabled him to prosper and to survive sudden and dangerous shifts in power. I even began to wonder about Naquib's illness, which conveniently removed him from a confrontation with Gul Agha that he probably wouldn't have won. His Risperdal capsules reminded me of Vincent (the Chin) Gigante, shuffling around Greenwich Village in his bathrobe and pajamas, trying to avoid racketeering charges. But then perhaps I had been in Afghanistan too long.

# 8

## THE ASSASSINS

Ahmad Shah Massoud was a wiry, thin-boned man with a long, handsome face that was distinguished by an aquiline nose and by deep furrows in the cheeks and around the eyes. He had a patchy beard at the edge of his jawline. He usually wore a *pakul*, a kind of flat-topped, soft wool hat, which he and his mujahideen had adopted from the Nuristani, a tribe that claims to have descended from Alexander the Great's army. In the fall of last year, Massoud was forty-nine years old, and dramatic white streaks had appeared in his dark hair, above his temples.

Massoud had been at war pretty much steadily since 1975, when he and several other anti-Communist Islamist students made a series of botched attacks on outposts of the government of Mohammad Daoud. In the fall of 2001, he had been fighting the Taliban for more than five years, and his front line by then extended from the edge of the Shamali plain, which lies between the Panjshir Valley and Kabul, for about

---

This chapter was originally published as "The Assassins," *The New Yorker*, June 10, 2002.

180 miles, up to the Tajik border, where he had his headquarters in Khoja Bahauddin, a little smugglers' town.

That summer, Massoud had begun receiving intelligence reports that a large number of Taliban and Al Qaeda fighters, as many as sixteen thousand, were massing along his northernmost front, among them many Arabs, Pakistanis, Chinese, Uzbeks, and Tajiks. These numbers seemed preposterously inflated, and he dismissed them. Early in September, he and several of his commanders flew over the front line in a helicopter. Massoud sat in the cockpit with binoculars. It was a dangerous trip, one of the men who was with him recalled recently, "but we knew that Allah would help us and that Amur Sahib"—a phrase meaning, more or less, Big Boss, which is what Massoud's men called him—"was with us." They photographed the area, and Massoud instructed his commanders where to position their men.

Massoud stayed up reading Persian poetry aloud with several colleagues until three in the morning on September 9. A few minutes after he went to sleep, his personal secretary—a young man named Jamshid, who was also his nephew and his brother-in-law—received a call from a Northern Alliance commander, Bismillah Khan, saying that the Taliban had attacked the Shamali front. Jamshid woke Massoud up, and Massoud and Bismillah Khan talked on the phone until daybreak. Then Massoud went back to bed. Around seven thirty, Jamshid learned that the Taliban were in retreat, and he let his uncle sleep until nine.

After breakfast, Massoud was about to leave on a reconnaissance trip when he decided to see two Arab journalists who had come to Khoja Bahauddin from the Panjshir Valley nine days earlier and had been waiting to interview him. They had sent word that they had to leave Khoja Bahauddin that day. The Arabs had arrived with a letter of introduction from the director of an organization called the Islamic Observation Centre, in London. Jamshid says that he was also contacted by a man who worked for Abdul Rasul Sayyaf, one of the founders of the Afghan Islamist movement, who now commanded a thousand-odd anti-Taliban fighters from a base in the Panjshir. Jamshid was told that the Arabs were friends of Sayyaf's.

I asked Jamshid if he had noticed anything unusual about the Arabs, since most Arabs in Afghanistan at the time were associated with Al Qaeda.

"No," he said. And his uncle thought they could be of use. "He wanted to say through them to the Muslim world, 'We are not *kafirs*. We are Muslims, and we don't have Russians and Iranians fighting here.'" Massoud was religious. He prayed five times a day, in the orthodox fashion, and his wife wore a burkha. But he was a Sunni Muslim at war with other Sunni Muslims—the Taliban—and they professed to be righteous and incorruptible, while he had accepted support from Iranian Shiites and from non-Muslim governments.

Fahim Dashty, a slender young man who is now the editor of a multilingual newspaper in Kabul, was also in Khoja Bahauddin on September 9. Dashty had known Massoud since he was a small boy. In the fall of 1996, when the Taliban took Kabul, Dashty joined Massoud's retreat to the Panjshir Valley. He stayed in Northern Alliance territory and formed a small film company, Ariana, with one of Massoud's commanders. They made documentaries about Massoud's war with the Taliban. Dashty had just come back from a two-month stay in Paris, where he participated in a workshop on film editing sponsored by the group Reporters Without Borders. He stayed in the same guesthouse as the two Arabs. He remembers thinking that it was odd to see Arabs in Northern Alliance territory, but that these two didn't seem suspicious. "They had gone to refugee camps, and to visit prisoners—all the things journalists do," he said. One of them spoke a little French and English, the other only Arabic.

A few weeks earlier, I was shown a rough cut of Ariana's most recent film about Massoud. The two Arabs are in some of the scenes. In footage shot in August, they are interviewing Burhanuddin Rabbani. The putative reporter is a fair-skinned, muscular man who appears to be in his mid-thirties. He is clean-shaven and has a crew cut. He wears Western clothes—a brown shirt and slacks—and glasses. He has two odd brownish marks, like round scars, on his forehead. The cameraman isn't visible in this scene, but later in the film there is a still shot of him in the doorway of the guesthouse. He is tall and dark-skinned. He is wearing a black shirt and is glaring at the camera, with what one can easily imagine is both hatred and fear.

The Ariana team usually filmed Massoud's interviews, and around noon on September 9 Fahim Dashty and the two Arabs and their translator drove over to Massoud's headquarters. Massoud and Jamshid were there with the chief of security, whose office was being used for the interview, and Massoud Khalili, the Northern Alliance's ambassador to India. Ahmad Shah Massoud was sitting on a sofa, using an orthopedic cushion that helped alleviate his chronic back pain. He said hello to the Arabs. "He asked them where they were from," Dashty said. "One of them said they were Belgian but were born in Morocco, and that they had come from Pakistan to Kabul and from there to Khoja Bahauddin."

Ambassador Khalili recalled that Massoud told the Arab who was to conduct the interview that he would like to hear the list of questions first, and the man began to read them out in English. Khalili translated into Persian for Massoud. He said that he was rather surprised that most of the questions had to do with Osama bin Laden—for example, "What will you do with Osama bin Laden if you take power?" and "Why do you call him a fundamentalist?" The ambassador found the questions tendentious, and he asked the Arab what paper he worked for. "I am not a journalist," the man replied. "I am from the Islamic centers. We have offices in London and Paris and all over the world." Khalili turned to Massoud and whispered, "Commander, they are from those guys"—meaning Al Qaeda. Massoud nodded, and said, tersely, "Let's just get through with it."

The Arabs had moved a table and some chairs that were between Massoud and their camera, which they had positioned on the lowest level of the tripod. Dashty, who had set up his camera behind theirs, was adjusting his backlight when the room exploded. Ambassador Khalili said that he saw a thick blue fire coming toward him.

"I felt I was burning," Dashty said. He went outside and saw Jamshid, who had left the room with the chief of security a few minutes earlier. "I asked him to take me to the hospital, and he asked me where Mr. Massoud was, and I went back inside and saw him. He was very badly injured all over his body, his face, his hands and legs." An Afghan intelligence officer told me recently that Massoud must have died within thirty seconds. Two pieces of metal were lodged in his heart. Most of the fingers of his right hand had been blown off. I was shown a photograph of his body. Every other inch of his skin was ruptured in open wounds. White gauze had been stuffed into his eye sockets.

The cameraman's battery belt had been packed with explosives. The sofa that Massoud had been sitting on was charred, and a hole had been blasted through the back. In the Ariana film, there is a shot of the cameraman's body on a stretcher. His legs are scorched and bloody and the upper part of his body seems to have been blown apart. The Afghan translator was also killed.

Two bodyguards carried Massoud to his car. Dashty, who was badly burned, got in, and they drove to the helicopter pad. Ambassador Khalili, who was also burned and had been hit heavily by shrapnel, followed in another car. They were all flown to a hospital across the border in Tajikistan, where General Fahim, Massoud's second-in-command, soon arrived. Fahim conferred with other Northern Alliance officials, and they agreed that the assassination should be kept a secret for the time being.

The Arab who did the interviewing had survived the blast, and while Massoud's body was being taken to Tajikistan, he was held in a room near where the explosion had taken place. He tore the wire-mesh screen from a small window and wriggled through, then ran across a graveyard to a steep river embankment a few hundred yards away. A man who worked for a local warlord chased him and killed him.

I asked Dashty if he believed that Massoud had been betrayed. "Yes," he said. "It would have been impossible otherwise. Somehow, I think, there was contact between Al Qaeda and our guys."

ON SEPTEMBER 11, AT AROUND EIGHT P.M. IN AFGHANISTAN, Mullah Omar, who was in Kandahar, called the Taliban foreign minister in Kabul. According to Afghan intelligence sources, who intercepted the call, Mullah Omar said, "Things have gone much further than expected." It was eleven thirty a.m. in New York, less than three hours after American Airlines Flight 11 had crashed into the north tower of the World Trade Center, and an hour and a half after the south tower had collapsed. Mullah Omar told the foreign minister to call a press conference to say that the Taliban had not been involved in the attack. The press conference took place at nine thirty p.m. in Kabul. The foreign minister assured reporters that Afghanistan had not attacked the United States, and he read a statement by Mullah Omar saying that Osama bin Laden was not involved: "This type of terrorism is too great for one man."

Among the calls intercepted that night was one from Kabul to Kandahar. "Where's the Sheikh?" the caller asked. Sheikh was the code name that senior Taliban officials used for Osama bin Laden. Again according to Afghan intelligence sources, someone in Mullah Omar's house told the caller that bin Laden was there. "Then, afterward," an intelligence officer said to me, "there was a chaos of phone calls back and forth between Kandahar and Kabul."

It seemed obvious during those early days in September that the assassination of Massoud on the ninth and the attack on the World Trade Center two days later were somehow related, but exactly how they were related and who was involved continues to be the subject of speculation. Massoud's younger brother, Wali, who was the chargé d'affaires at the Afghan embassy in London when Massoud was killed, is now in Kabul, and has been nominated to lead a Massoudist party, the National Movement of Afghanistan. He believes that the assassination of his brother was the first step in a larger plot, and that the attacks on September 11 were the second step. "Look at the logic," he says. "They wanted to do what they wanted to do on the eleventh, but provided there was no Massoud." The people who killed Massoud assumed that his death would destroy the Northern Alliance, and that if the Americans retaliated for the attacks on the World Trade Center they would have no Afghan allies on the ground. The buildup of troops on the front lines in the late summer and early fall was, then, preparation for Massoud's assassination. "They were waiting for something," an Afghan intelligence official said. The foreign troops that were prepared to overrun a demoralized Northern Alliance were, it appears, to have marched into Central Asia. In the ensuing chaos, reprisals against Osama bin Laden and the Taliban would have been difficult. But since the official story was, at first, that Massoud had only been wounded, the Northern Alliance held its ground. And, of course, as can be seen from Mullah Omar's phone conversation, the operation against the United States was not expected to be as spectacular as it turned out to be. "They were expecting a reaction," the intelligence official said. "But they thought it would be a Clinton-type reaction. They didn't anticipate the kind of revenge that occurred."

The "terrorists," which is the word that Afghans commonly use to refer to Al Qaeda, had strategic as well as tactical reasons for wanting to kill Massoud. Their most stalwart enemy had begun to gain support outside the country. In April 2001, Massoud had been invited to speak to the European Parliament in Strasbourg. He gave a press conference in Paris and met with European officials there and in Brussels. "He behaved like a statesman and was received as a statesman," Wali says. "The media took an interest in him—except for the American media. I think this was a turning point. He warned the international community that Al Qaeda was dangerous, not only to Afghanistan but to the world." In July, in London, Wali organized a conference of Afghan intellectuals in exile. They passed a resolution endorsing Massoud and various motions in support of democracy, human rights, and women's rights. "This spurred his enemies against him," Wali said. "On the one side there was Osama, saying, 'We represent Muslims,' and on the other Massoud, who stood for moderate Islam. That trip to Europe, in which he outlined his vision, cost him his life."

Wali and other Afghans I talked to insisted that Pakistan was also involved in Massoud's murder. Massoud had never established close links with the Pakistanis, even in the seventies and eighties, when many Afghan Islamists went into exile in Pakistan. (He was legendary as a fighter in part because he stayed in Afghanistan, in the field.) The ISI, the Pakistani security services, had supported the Taliban early on, and many people suspect that the remnants of the Taliban and Al Qaeda are still getting assistance from Pakistan. An intelligence officer who was close to Massoud said that on the night of September 9 the president of Pakistan, Pervez Musharraf, held a party to celebrate the assassination. He said that this information came from General Fahim, who is now minister of defense in the interim Afghan government headed by Hamid Karzai. I asked Fahim if there had been such a party, and he was evasive. "Maybe," he said. But he confirmed that Musharraf was at ISI headquarters that evening, meeting with Hamid Gul, the former head of the ISI, who had just returned from northern Afghanistan. I asked Fahim what he felt when he met Musharraf recently in Kabul. He had shaken his hand. "Sometimes, for the sake of the greater interest," Fahim said, "one has to take a cup of poison."

MASSOUD'S ASSASSINS WERE TUNISIANS, NOT MOROCCANS, AS they had claimed. They had been in Belgium, and they carried Belgian passports and letters of introduction with the signature of Yassir al-Sirri, the director of the Islamic Observation Centre. The stamps on the passports indicated that the Arabs had arrived in Islamabad, Pakistan, on July 25, where they were given visas by the Taliban embassy, and that they went from there to Kabul. But the passports and visas were forged. Both of the assassins had been living for several months in an Al Qaeda training camp near Jalalabad.

The assassins entered the Panjshir Valley under the auspices of the Northern Alliance leader Abdul Rasul Sayyaf, who says that in mid-August he was contacted by an Egyptian who had fought with him in the jihad against the Soviets. The man said that he was calling from Bosnia. (Although an Afghan intelligence officer told me that the call had, in fact, come from Kandahar.) The man asked Sayyaf to help two Arab journalists who wanted to interview him and Massoud and President Rabbani. Engineer Muhammad Aref ("engineer" is a common Afghan honorific, indicating that someone is educated and has studied engineering), who is now the head of the Afghan intelligence services, was Massoud's chief of security; it was in his office that the assassination took place. Aref says that Sayyaf's imprimatur permitted the Arabs to bypass normal security procedures. "They came not as journalists but as guests," Aref says. "Sayyaf and Bismillah Khan"—the commander of the Shamali front line—"sent their men and cars to pick them up. Everybody helped them, and they met lots of people."

Maulana Attah Rahman Salim, a deputy minister in Karzai's interim government, is a respected Muslim scholar and cleric. He had an office in Khoja Bahauddin last fall and traveled to the Panjshir Valley with Massoud a week before the assassination. Rahman says that recriminations were voiced almost immediately after Massoud was killed. "Everyone began saying, 'Why weren't the terrorists searched more carefully? Why didn't people do their jobs better?' The accusations focused on Sayyaf more than anyone else, and an Iranian newspaper published the suspicions."

Sayyaf is an Islamic fundamentalist and is closely associated with the global terrorists who were nurtured during the Afghan jihad in the eighties. He and Rabbani studied at al-Azhar University in Cairo, where they were influenced by the Muslim Brotherhood, and they both taught Islamic studies at Kabul University in the early seventies. They were among the founders of the Islamist movement that became the principal opposition to the Soviets. Sayyaf, who is a Pashtun, spoke Arabic fluently, and he became close to the Saudis. Like the Saudi royal family, he is a member of the severe Wahhabi sect, and after the Communist takeover of Afghanistan in the late seventies, when the Saudis began to fund various Afghan resistance movements, Sayyaf received an inordinate share of the largesse. He formed a political party, the Ittihad-i-Islami, or Islamic Union, in 1981, and four years later founded a university in an Afghan refugee camp near Peshawar. He was allied politically with Massoud and Rabbani, but in many ways he has more in common ideologically with the Islamists who became the Taliban.

Sayyaf's university was called Dawa'a al-Jihad, which means Convert and Struggle, and it became known as the preeminent "school for terrorism." Ramzi Ahmed Yousef, who is serving a life sentence in a federal prison in Colorado for masterminding the bombing of the World Trade Center in 1993, attended Dawa'a al-Jihad and fought with Sayyaf's mujahideen. Sheikh Omar Abdel-Rahman, the blind Egyptian cleric who is in the same prison, serving a life sentence for seditious conspiracy to blow up various New York City landmarks (not including the World Trade Center, although he is suspected of having been involved in the first bombing of that, too), lectured in the camps around Peshawar in the mid-eighties. Osama bin Laden supported Sayyaf financially and led a brigade of Arab fighters who used Sayyaf's base in Afghanistan. The ISI provided military and intelligence expertise. When the Soviets withdrew from Afghanistan in 1989 and many of the foreign jihadis moved on, a group of Ittihad members—some of them native Filipinos and some of them Arabs—formed the Abu Sayyaf terrorist organization in the Philippines.

In October 2001, Yassir al-Sirri, of the Islamic Observation Centre, was arrested in London for his alleged role in the preparation of the letters of introduction for the two Arab assassins. In April 2002, in New York, Ahmed Abdel Sattar, a US Postal Service employee who lives on Staten Island, was arrested and charged with being a "surrogate" for Sheikh Omar Abdel-Rahman. Sattar had worked for the sheikh as a paralegal during his conspiracy trial in New York in the mid-nineties. The indictment said that Sattar was serving as a "communications facility" for the sheikh—that is, passing on his orders from jail. Sattar's phone had been tapped for some time, and among the calls scrutinized were several between him and Yassir al-Sirri in London. In May, a British judge dismissed the charges against al-Sirri.

ABDUL RASUL SAYYAF IS A BIG, BEEFY MAN WITH FAIR SKIN AND a thick gray beard. He must be about six foot three and weighs probably 250 pounds. He usually wears a white skullcap or a large turban and a *shalwar kameez*. Wali Massoud is slight and clean-shaven. He usually wears slacks and a sports jacket. His dark hair is parted on one side, and it often flops about boyishly. On April 28, during a parade in Kabul to commemorate the tenth anniversary of the mujahideen's entry into the city and their victory over the Soviet-backed government there, Wali and Sayyaf were sitting together on a VIP viewing stand across the street from the Eid Mosque, a long, low, pale-yellow-and-green building with a yellow dome.

The VIPs looked out over a Daliesque panorama of wholesale destruction. Southern Kabul is a desolate expanse of collapsed and gouged buildings, and most of the jihadi leaders on the viewing stand had participated in the destruction. Tens of thousands of people were slaughtered in the internecine battles that took place between April 1992, when Ahmad Shah Massoud triumphantly entered Kabul, and September 1996, when Massoud's forces retreated to the north and the Taliban took over. Most of the men on the viewing stand were also now maneuvering for positions in the new government in Kabul, which would be chosen at the Loya Jirga, the tribal council to be held six weeks later. It was assumed that the Loya Jirga would ratify Hamid Karzai as head of state. Wali could become prime minister or vice president, which might appeal to Karzai, since that arrangement would assure him the continued support of the Three Panjshiris—Defense Minister Fahim, Foreign Minister Abdullah Abdullah, and Interior Minister Yunis Qanouni— who grew up in the Panjshir Valley and were close to Massoud, and are the leading figures in the new configuration of the old Northern Alliance faction of ethnic Tajiks.

Karzai sat at the center of the front row of dignitaries, in a gray silk collarless shirt and a gray *chapan*, a finely woven Afghan robe. General Fahim was on his right, resplendent in a medal-bedecked uniform and peaked cap. General Fahim was now officially Marshal Fahim, having received a sudden promotion the night before. A number of other mujahideen commanders loyal to Fahim had also been promoted. (A few days later, I asked one of President Karzai's Afghan American advisers if the promotions were Karzai's idea. "They forced him to do it," the man said. "He had no choice." We were talking in a parking lot, because, the adviser explained to me, the Intercontinental Hotel, where he and several other members of Karzai's government live, is bugged: "They're in the curtains.")

Wali Massoud sat between Karzai and Sayyaf, and ex-president Rabbani was on Sayyaf's other side, next to several other of the surviving jihadis. Among the missing figures in the national drama were Gulbuddin Hekmatyar, Massoud's archenemy, who had shelled the city mercilessly in the early nineties. Hekmatyar's whereabouts are unknown, although two weeks after the parade there were reports that the CIA had fired a missile at him from an unmanned Predator spy plane, somewhere near Kabul. The Uzbek warlord Rashid Dostum, who liberated much of the northern part of the country from the Taliban, did not attend. To do so would have been inappropriate, since Dostum fought on the Soviet side during the jihad. It had been thought that Zahir Shah, the former king, who had not been seen in public since his arrival in Kabul a week earlier, would make an appearance, but he didn't.

Patriotic music began blaring from loudspeakers, and Karzai and Fahim left the viewing stand and got into two convertible Russian military jeeps. The jeeps were driven past squads of soldiers who stood at attention in the great plaza in front of the mosque. Karzai waved at the soldiers and Fahim saluted stiffly, the tips of his fingers almost touching the beak of his outsized marshal's hat. Meanwhile, a master of ceremonies and a poet took turns at the microphone. "Whoever attacks Afghanistan will weep, just as Britain and Russia did," the master of ceremonies said. Karzai and Fahim returned to the viewing stand, and Fahim made a speech about how the mujahideen had vanquished the Soviets and the Taliban. He didn't mention the American bombing campaign. A float moved slowly down the avenue, bearing a huge portrait of Massoud in white safari clothes, his arms thoughtfully folded.

Mujahideen holding Kalashnikovs stood at attention. Some of them wore Massoud T-shirts. Karzai announced that Massoud was henceforth Afghanistan's official National Hero.

Scores of Russian tanks and armored personnel carriers rumbled past, bearing framed portraits of Massoud and Karzai. They were followed by disabled jihadi veterans in blue-gray tunics, on crutches and in wheelchairs. Behind the veterans came one marching platoon after another of mujahideen, organized according to their home provinces, with Massoud's Panjshiris in the lead. A parachutist floated down from a helicopter, intending to land in front of the mosque, but he missed his target and drifted off into the ruins in the distance. Fifteen minutes later, he showed up on the back of a motorbike, his parachute billowing behind him. A second parachutist, a woman this time, headed for the plaza, and she, too, disappeared into the ruins but soon reappeared, marching by to applause, and carrying a carpet decorated with Massoud's image.

As the parade ended, I made my way past the front of the viewing stand, close enough to see Sayyaf lean over and say something to Wali Massoud. Wali sat bolt upright in his chair. He nodded his head and smiled unconvincingly.

AFTER THE MEETING OF AFGHAN DELEGATIONS IN BONN IN DE-cember 2001, at which Karzai's interim government was set up, two of Sayyaf's deputies were given minor ministerial positions. Apparently, Sayyaf was reasonably happy with this arrangement, and he agreed to withdraw his gunmen from Kabul and to establish a command base in his hometown of Paghman, an hour's drive into the mountains northwest of the city. His militia controls all the territory between Paghman and the suburbs of Kabul, ending just a few hundred meters from the Intercontinental Hotel.

In March, the ISAF, the international security force in Afghanistan, accused Sayyaf's militiamen of carrying out several robberies and killings in the western suburbs, where many of the city's minority ethnic Shia Muslims, the Hazaras, live. Sayyaf denied the accusations. As with most such incidents in Afghanistan, the investigation of this one appears to have fizzled away inconclusively. There is a lot of bad history between Sayyaf and the Hazaras. In the mid-nineties, Sayyaf's troops massacred perhaps thousands of Hazara civilians in Kabul. According to Human Rights Watch, his militia became renowned for a particularly gruesome method of dispatching its enemies—herding them into metal shipping containers and then setting fires beneath them, to roast them alive.

A medical student told me that he had studied under Sayyaf at Kabul University in 1996, before the Taliban took the city. Sayyaf taught a required course in Islamic thought. "He would arrive in a convoy of two or three cars with sixteen to twenty armed bodyguards," the young man recalled. "Some of the bodyguards would stay with the cars, others would stand at the doors, and two or three would stand next to him on the stage of a large hall. Sometimes, we could hear the sound of bombs and Kalashnikovs and RPGs while he was teaching us. We all knew that his men were fighting with the Hazaras and that their positions were nearby. Sayyaf would say to us: 'In Islam it's forbidden to kill a Muslim, and it's forbidden to destroy and loot houses,' and then just a day or two later we would hear that his men had looted and destroyed a lot of houses and taken Hazara girls to their barracks. I heard that Sayyaf's men cut off women's breasts. None of us ever asked him about this, because we knew if we did, we'd be taken out of the classroom and killed.

"There were boys and girls in our classes," the young man said, "but they put up a curtain between us. The girls especially hated Sayyaf. One day he gave us some papers that talked about how in all the Muslim countries there were demonstrations in favor of Palestine and against Israel. 'Demonstrating cannot help Palestinians,' he said, 'because Palestinians cannot make weapons from our demonstrations to fight against Israel. Palestinians cannot make food from our demonstrations to eat, and Palestinians cannot use our demonstrations as a house to live in. We must help them directly, not just by demonstrating and shouting.' He never talked about the fighting that was going on then in Kabul.

"At that time, his Dawa'a al-Jihad university was in Kabul. He had brought it from Pakistan. It was in a building next to the Kabul Polytechnic, behind the Intercontinental Hotel. They had engineering, medical, and Sharia departments, and also a veterinary school, and they had more Islamic courses than Kabul University did. Fights would break out between the students of the two universities. The students of Dawa'a al-Jihad thought that the students at Kabul University were Communists, and we thought that they were fucking jihadis who had destroyed our country."

I had met Sayyaf for the first time a little more than a week before the parade, in his headquarters in Paghman. We sat on a red carpet under a walnut tree on a grassy, terraced hillside. He had a couple of friends with him, and a dozen or so armed bodyguards stood a short distance away. The view was pastoral and majestic. Tilled land dropped away into a patchwork of earth-colored hamlets, and in the distance stony, brown mountains fronted a long, jagged range of blue mountains capped with white snow.

King Zahir Shah had returned to Afghanistan that morning, and Sayyaf was dismissive about the whole thing. "Afghanistan, you know, is a destroyed country," he said, "and it needs strong and able people to rebuild it. But as far as I know, the king needs help from two people just to stand up. He's an old man." Sayyaf said that Karzai had a good chance of being ratified by the Loya Jirga, and he also tossed out the names of Fahim and Yunis Qanouni as possible leaders: the Panjshiris.

I told Sayyaf that I had been in Jalalabad in 1989, when the mujahideen—among them hundreds of Arab Wahhabi fighters re-cruited by Sayyaf—had laid siege to the city. He asked me why I had not come to his camp, which was off the road leading to Jalalabad from the Pakistani border, in the Khyber Pass. I didn't remind him that in those days his virulently anti-Western views had made him off-limits to most foreign journalists, many of whom had been terrorized by his Wahhabi friends. I just said that I had not had very good contacts. He nodded.

When I got up to leave, I saw a group of men walking toward me. One of them, who was surrounded by gunmen, was then-General Fahim's brother.

The day after the parade, I met Sayyaf at his house in the northwestern suburbs of Kabul, in a neighborhood that had been devastated in the fighting between his men and the Hazaras in the mid-nineties. Sayyaf was in a meeting in an upstairs room, and as it broke up I saw that one of the men with him was a mujahideen commander whose forces had helped take Kunduz from the Taliban in November. Sayyaf introduced him to me as the new governor of Kabul Province. When the other men left, we sat in the living room and he talked about himself. His father died when he was six, and he attended a madrasah in Paghman, and then Kabul University, where Burhanuddin Rabbani had been his teacher. Sayyaf was lecturing in Islamic studies in 1973, when Daoud overthrew the king and the Communists began to take over the government. He was in prison for nearly six years because of his Islamist activities, and then in exile in Pakistan. He claimed that he had spent most of the war years in Afghanistan, which gave him more legitimacy as a leader than some others had. And he said that he had been unjustly accused of being abusive: "Islam taught me to be kind to people."

After I had seen Sayyaf a few times, he became unavailable. He was ill or busy or I should call back tomorrow. And then the phone was switched off. So one hot Sunday morning in the middle of May I drove up to Paghman with one of Sayyaf's Ittihad fighters, a number of whom are bivouacked at a villa he owns in the Wazir Akbar Khan neighborhood in Kabul. It would have been difficult to get anywhere near Sayyaf without one of his men as an escort. The road between Paghman and Kabul is considered unsafe by late afternoon; several armed robberies and murders have occurred along it in recent months.

We stopped at a junction in the track where there was a sentry hut and a dozen or so fighters. I gave one of them my business card with a note scribbled on the back of it, addressed to Sayyaf, and the man took it and walked off toward an orchard a hundred meters or so in front of us. He came back in a few minutes and motioned us to drive on. Sayyaf was seated with several other men under the walnut tree where we had had our first conversation. One of the men was General Bismillah Khan, the Northern Alliance commander who had escorted the Arab assassins on excursions to the front lines when they were in the Panjshir Valley in August, posing as journalists. Bismillah Khan is now in charge of Kabul's military defenses.

I apologized for my intrusion, and said it was good that both Sayyaf and Bismillah Khan were there, since I wished to talk to them both. "As I am sure you know," I said to Sayyaf, "there are those who have expressed doubts about your relationship with Massoud's assassins, because they first came into the Northern Alliance territory through you." Sayyaf's eyes narrowed, and he stared hard at me. He translated what I had said to Bismillah Khan, who speaks no English, and then he turned and said to me, in English that seemed much more halting than during our previous meetings, that they had let the Arabs in so they could see that they were good Muslims, and that their forces had not been tainted by Westerners.

Bismillah Khan began speaking in Persian, and Sayyaf translated. Khan said that in retrospect the two Arabs behaved suspiciously, but he had not noticed this at the time. "Now, when I think about them, I re-member that they had had beards but had recently shaved them off. The marks of the beards were still there." He moved his hands along his jaw-line to show what he meant. Sayyaf chuckled and said that the Arabs had been very nervous whenever they were in a car. "If they went with our people to the bunkers"—at the Shamali front line—"they would say, 'Please go slowly, because of our cameras; we don't want them to be damaged.' Before the car moved, they always put the cameras on their knees and told the driver to be careful."

I asked Sayyaf how the two Arabs had come to be with him in the first place. He described the phone call from the former jihadi—"an Arab from Egypt, Abu Hani"—who said he was in Bosnia and wanted Sayyaf to help the two journalists get an interview with Massoud. Sayyaf also described a meeting of most of the Northern Alliance leadership that took place in the Panjshir Valley while the Arabs were there. He said that the Arabs had tried to come into the meeting room but had been stopped by guards. "They wanted to carry out their plan there," he said. "They wanted to eliminate all the leaders of the resistance." Bismil-lah Khan said something in Persian, and Sayyaf translated it as a com-ment about Sayyaf telling Massoud and Bismillah Khan that he had doubts about the Arabs and warning Massoud not to see them. Sayyaf threw up his hands to indicate that he had done all he could.

My final meeting with Sayyaf took place three days later, in another of his houses, off the road leading from Kabul to Paghman. He wasn't there when I arrived, but he soon drove up, in a convoy of Land Cruis-ers full of armed men. We sat in the living room with several aides and a general from Paktia Province who was visiting. I asked Sayyaf to de-scribe his vision of the future of Afghanistan, and he spoke about the importance of an Islamic state, and about closely following the teach-ings of the Koran and not trying to introduce new ideas—the funda-mentalist line. Then he brought up the betrayal of Afghanistan by the

West in the early nineties, after the Soviets had retreated. "Once the
Afghans kicked out the Red Army, the Western countries cut their
backing," he said. "They had been supporting us only for their own
interests."

I asked him about Osama bin Laden and the other Arabs whom he
had known well and who had fought alongside him against the Russians. Osama had regarded Sayyaf as a father figure, had he not? Sayyaf
smiled, and took off his turban and placed it on the sofa next to him.
His hands were trembling. "I want to tell you frankly about those who
became extremists," he said. "No one can name one example of harm
done by those men when they were with us in the jihad. We were not
extremists, and neither were they. But later, when Osama and his friends
were brought to help the Taliban, who were extremists, they began to
harm the world. I want to ask you, who brought Osama?"

Sayyaf was agitated. He sat on the edge of the sofa and leaned forward. He was expressing a conspiracy theory that is not uncommon in
Kabul, even among reasonably sophisticated Afghans who have visited
the West: that the Americans, with the aid of Pakistan, supported the
Taliban and Osama bin Laden so that they could justify an invasion and
take over the country. "The extremists backed by the foreigners were
able to attack us," Sayyaf said. "We were the victims." His aides and the
general from Paktia nodded in agreement. "I know that Osama and
the Taliban did the assassination," Sayyaf said. "But who was behind
them? All of those who were trying to help the Taliban were behind the
assassination."

ABDULLAH ABDULLAH, THE FOREIGN MINISTER OF AFGHANI-
stan, is a sophisticated man with a great deal of charm, and he was a familiar figure on Western television as a spokesman for the Northern
Alliance during the American bombing campaign that led to the defeat

of the Taliban. I met him in a sitting room in his office in Kabul. The room had a blue carpet and plush blue chairs. There was a vase of freshly cut carnations on a side table. Abdullah was one of Massoud's best friends. "I was with him since 1985, during victories and defeats and the withdrawal from Kabul. I was ready to die for him ten times," he said. "He was extremely important for our country. He was exceptional. He was so humble, and so alive—the most alive creature I've ever met."

Abdullah was in New Delhi when Massoud was assassinated, and he was one of the few people who were told that Massoud had died. "When I heard the news," he said, "I was one hundred percent certain that the United Front"—the official name of the Northern Alliance—"would collapse. There was no doubt in my mind. I'm sure we would have failed if the news had not been withheld." On September 11, Abdullah was trying to get back into Afghanistan. "I heard the news on the BBC," he said. "I was trying to focus on what was happening when the second plane hit. And then I thought, 'It's Al Qaeda.' I had said to US officials that Al Qaeda would intensify their work against the resistance." Abdullah dismisses the idea that the assassins knew in advance about the attack on the World Trade Center and were trying to kill Massoud before it occurred. "Osama bin Laden wouldn't have risked that," he said. "What if they had been caught? But maybe they were given a target date" for their part of the work.

Abdullah is skeptical also about Sayyaf's involvement in the plot to kill Massoud. "I, personally, don't believe it," he said. Sayyaf made it possible for the Arabs to get to Massoud, but this could have been justified if they had been legitimate. "They behaved like journalists," Abdullah said, "although when I went to see them they were very rude." This was at the meeting of Northern Alliance leaders in the Panjshir that took place when the assassins were Sayyaf's guests. "I introduced myself and they gave me a look of hatred. I blame myself for not having picked up on that." There had been other attempts on Massoud's life, and in the end this one succeeded because of the kind of man Massoud was. He tried to accommodate people. "Commander Massoud was a careless person," Abdullah said. "He took some security measures, but he liked to be alone in those interviews. And he never could have had one hundred percent security. We should have been able to identify the risk when those guys stayed in our area for three weeks. But we didn't."

YAHYA MASSOUD, THE ELDEST OF AHMAD SHAH MASSOUD'S FULL brothers—he is fifty-two—took me on an overnight trip to the family's hometown of Bazarak, in the Panjshir Valley, three hours northeast of Kabul. Bazarak was Massoud's base during the jihad against the Soviets, and it is where his body is buried. Ahmad Shah Massoud was the second of the four brothers. Wali is the youngest. The other brother, Ahmed Zia, is now Afghanistan's ambassador to Moscow. Their father, an Afghan military officer who was killed in a car accident in 1993, had three wives. There are two more sons from the other marriages, and there are several sisters, although, as is customary in Afghanistan, Yahya didn't mention them. Yahya has been living in Warsaw for the last few years, where he was the first secretary at the Afghan embassy. He has a wife and six children in Switzerland. He doesn't plan to bring them back to Afghanistan, although he is living in Kabul for the time being, helping Wali organize the new Massoudist party.

Abdul Wadoud, a handsome, fair-skinned young man who is the son of one of Massoud's sisters, drove Yahya's luxurious Toyota Land Cruiser. Their other guest was an old family friend, Nur Sultan, an architect who was visiting Kabul after a fourteen-year exile in Reading, England. We traveled north across the Shamali plain. The Taliban methodically destroyed the Shamali after they seized power in Kabul, in order to create a no-man's-land between the capital and Massoud's front line, near the north end of the plain. It is now a vast mud Chernobyl of roofless and crumbling adobe farmhouses, collapsed walls, and barren fields. Many of the fields and roadsides are still planted with land mines, and here and there, uniformed de-miners wearing protective armor and safety helmets with transparent visors kneel or crouch, their faces close to the ground.

When we crossed the old front line, the landscape was suddenly transformed into a green arcadia. The farmhouses were intact, the orchards tended, and the vineyards bursting with new leaves. People walked and bicycled along the roadside, and mountain water burbled in irrigation ditches. The Taliban had once or twice pushed beyond this point, but never held the territory long enough to destroy it.

At the little market town of Charikar, we stopped to have lunch with General Bismillah Khan. Sofas and chairs had been placed in a large circle on the lawn, and Khan sat in the head chair and engaged his guests in conversation. After about a half hour or so of this, a jeep pulled up and men ran across the lawn toward us with large trays and bowls containing towers of white ice cream. We ate the ice cream, and then drove by convoy down a dirt road that led along an irrigation canal built in the sixties by the Chinese, and into a farmstead, where a group of men in turbans waited. Carpets were laid out under the trees around a pond. A birdcage with a white parakeet in it hung from one of the trees. Tea and bowls of *kishmish*—almonds and raisins and sweets—were served, and then we all filed into a long L-shaped room, where we were shown to our places on cushions placed around the walls. The entire floor was covered in tablecloths upon which was arrayed a feast of Afghan dishes: bowls of salad, rice pilaf with raisins and almonds, mutton, yogurt, soup, fruit, chicken and lamb, and basins full of tiny broiled quail, cooked whole. There must have been five hundred of them. The little blackened cadavers rested in piles of scorched wings and feet and skulls and beaks and sunken eye sockets. Taking my cue from the men around me, I popped one in my mouth, and began crunching. I found that after four or five vigorous jaw movements, it was possible to swallow the thing and be done with the experience.

After the feast, Bismillah Khan and his entourage returned to Kabul, and we journeyed on into the Panjshir, which is really more of a canyon than a valley. A single narrow dirt road snakes alongside the Panjshir River, which runs between high mountains of gray and black scree and rock. At the mouth of the river, we drove through the small town of Gulbahar, where the two Arab terrorists had stayed, in one of the Northern Alliance's guesthouses, after they crossed over from Taliban territory and were received by Abdul Rasul Sayyaf. Just outside town, Yahya pointed to a clutch of stone and brick buildings in the can-

Mujahideen fighters at night near Kunduz, November 2001.

THOMAS DWORZAK/MAGNUM PHOTOS

yon wall, and said: "That was where Mr. Sayyaf lived." He said that his brother had accommodated Sayyaf and his several hundred fighters in that spot after Kabul fell to the Taliban.

In a couple of hours, we reached the promontory above Bazarak where Massoud is buried. Abdul Wadoud drove the Land Cruiser up a newly bulldozed road on the knoll and parked. We all got out and trooped over to a kind of dug-out-cave recess in the summit of the hill. It was surrounded by a brick wall with open arched windows and had a plastic-and-tin roof that was supported by stripped saplings and spiked with green flags with Koranic sayings on them. The tomb, a long dirt mound, was covered with a burgundy cloth with gold brocade decorations. Yahya and Abdul stood there, silently cupping their hands in prayer, with their eyes closed. Their friend, Nur Sultan, was overcome by grief. He fell on his knees at the base of the tomb, weeping silently, gasping now and then in a strangled way for breath.

Nur Sultan stayed at the tomb for about half an hour, and then we took refuge from the rain in a nearby building, and Yahya introduced me to a man he described as the engineer in charge of turning Massoud's tomb into a proper mausoleum complex and pilgrimage site. He pulled out some blueprints and pointed to a ditch that ran along the scree all the way from Bazarak, about a mile distant. Soon, he said, it would carry water to this barren hilltop; the idea was that it would become a green parkland, planted with trees and flowers. The present, temporary tomb site would become a proper domed mausoleum, and Massoud's old headquarters, a yellow painted stone building that stood nearby, would be transformed into a Massoud museum. "We've kept everything exactly as it was when he was alive," Yahya said, "we haven't even moved a chair or desk." He said that there would be a library: "He had many books—over three thousand—and the museum will have his uniforms, his guns, and such things. It's a big project," Yahya said, looking around at the dismal hilltop.

A few hundred meters outside Bazarak, the road drops down the mountainside toward the river. The Massoud family compound, a hamlet-sized collection of flat-roofed adobe compounds, is on a steep slope overlooking the water. We drove up to a sentry hut, past a modern, white-painted cement house that Yahya said belonged to one of his sisters, who lives in Holland. The young soldier at the hut saluted and lowered the rope barrier, and we drove up the muddy track and parked alongside Massoud's grandfather's house. A smaller whitewashed building attached to it had belonged to his father and was where Ahmad Shah Massoud was born. For a period during the jihad, Yahya said, Massoud had lived here and used part of the house as his command post.

A big rock wall topped with tin had been built into the steep hillside above their father's house. The wall formed a shining semicircle against the dark scree of the barren hill, enclosing a swath of terraced gardens that led to a modern, white house. Six or seven torrents of water arced gracefully down the hill from the house, bouncing from one terrace to another, and a stone pathway led up through a series of orange-colored latticed arbors. "This was the home Massoud was building for his family," said Yahya. "It was almost finished when he died." His wife and six children live in Iran now.

The house was a simple two-story structure made of concrete, but it had lots of windows and a glorious southern exposure. You could look down to Massoud's grandfather's house and to the curving river and the mountains beyond. The cement veranda surrounding the house had a snow-fed swimming pool, and a half-built sauna was set against the mountainside. Behind the house, a small canal was spanned by small bridges that led into an impressive stone wall with several doorways. Yahya explained that Massoud had built a network of fortified cave rooms for his family in case their home was subjected to an aerial attack. On the next terrace down, there was a lawn and swings and a slide for

Massoud's children, and farther down, a large orchard of almond, mulberry, apricot, and apple trees.

We walked back down along a pathway that led past the orchard and went into Massoud's father's house. It had recently been modernized, and the interior walls were painted a pale peach color. A single portrait hung on the wall. It was a pencil drawing of Massoud, smiling. That night, we slept on velveteen sleeping pads that had been placed for us in the room where Massoud was born.

A FEW DAYS LATER, IN KABUL, I MET YAHYA AT A MASSOUD FAMily house in the Wazir Akbar Khan neighborhood, where he introduced me to Commander Aziz Majrou, one of Ahmad Shah Massoud's oldest and most loyal mujahideen officers. Aziz had been badly wounded in the war against the Soviets. His left hand was scarred and missing a thumb and he limped. "Majrou means 'wounded person,'" he explained to me, shyly.

Aziz had met Massoud in 1978, when the first of Afghanistan's Marxist leaders, Taraki, was in power. Aziz was a twenty-year-old mechanic and Massoud was one of the emerging Islamist leaders who were trying to organize guerrilla insurgencies. He wrote a letter to the people in Aziz's village, Dasht-i-Debat, in the Panjshir Valley. "The elders gathered the men of the village in a secret place and read out the letter," Aziz recalled. "It said that there was a Communist regime in Afghanistan that wanted to change our culture and that we must defend ourselves." The letter was a summons to holy war. Aziz said that he and a hundred or so other men from the village began to organize themselves, although only a few of them had guns or fighting experience. The elders in Safichir, a nearby village, had also received a letter from Massoud, and men there began to organize also, and to wait for Massoud to come to them. "About a month after the letter came," Aziz said, "Massoud arrived, and then a third village, Paian, joined us. These were the first three villages in the Panjshir to organize."

Massoud came with about twenty men, including several relatives and friends. "I thought that he was going to be a big man, with a big beard and a turban," Aziz said. "Someone maybe in his forties or fifties. But he was almost the youngest man in the group." Massoud would have been about twenty-six years old then. "He was an honest man," Aziz recalled. "He didn't seem to be interested in money, and he acted like a leader." Aziz stayed with Massoud until he was assassinated. His duties changed over the years, especially after he was injured, but he remained a mujahideen. At the end, he said, he had worked as a deputy division commander in the Panjshir.

I asked Aziz who he thought had killed Massoud. "There is no doubt it was the terrorists," he said, the Taliban and Pakistan. "But, unfortunately, most of the provincial commanders in the Panjshir did not pay enough attention to the dangers he faced. His security was not very well organized. We had warned him to be careful."

Were the assassins able to kill Massoud because of the negligence of his officers? I asked Aziz. Or was there a betrayal from within the Northern Alliance?

"Sayyaf is, of course, very suspicious," Aziz replied. "Perhaps he knew of the plan. Or perhaps he didn't know what the terrorists were up to and was used by them."

I MET BISMILLAH KHAN AGAIN IN LATE MAY, AT HIS BASE IN Kabul. He shared it with a Swedish contingent of the ISAF. He has an office on the rooftop of a building that has a rose garden and a lawn and a huge, sixties-style swimming pool. The Swedes were giving a Taste of Sweden barbecue when I arrived, and Bismillah Khan and his men were lined up with paper plates and plastic utensils to get their food. They were obviously ill at ease, and not a little offended, since at an Afghan feast a guest sits and is served.

Some of the Afghans didn't know how to eat with forks and knives, and those who did helped them. They whispered about what was on their plates: barbecued beef, chicken, potatoes, and bamboo shoots. They didn't know what bamboo was, and most of them didn't touch it. They had never eaten potatoes with the skins on. A few of the men cracked jokes in Dari about the meat, which they thought might be dog, or pork. Others said that it wasn't *halal*, that is, that a butcher had not uttered "God is great!" when the animal's throat was cut.

At the end of the meal, the Swedish chef announced that he wanted to wish one of the other soldiers happy birthday, and, as was the custom in Sweden, he would present him with a gift. This was all translated to the Afghans, who were puzzled, since they don't celebrate birthdays. The chef unwrapped a bottle of whiskey and handed it to the soldier. "And now," the chef said, "our friend must share his gift, as is the custom in Afghanistan, with everyone here. It will take, I estimate, five minutes." And he laughed at his joke.

Two of Bismillah Khan's aides ran over to the Swede's translator and pointed out that this was a big mistake. Fridoun, my translator, muttered, "Don't they learn anything at all about Afghan culture before they come?" The whiskey bottle was removed, and Bismillah Khan, who had politely eaten everything on his plate during dinner, rose and thanked his hosts and shook the officers' hands.

Later, in Bismillah Khan's office, I asked him about one of the key elements in Sayyaf's explanation of his role in the matter of Massoud's assassination. Sayyaf had told me, and others, that he had warned Bismillah Khan and Massoud that the Arabs might be dangerous and that he didn't trust them. Bismillah Khan said only that Sayyaf had told Massoud that the Arabs seemed "strange." He became testy when pressed and said that I should talk to Sayyaf. He also said that he hadn't sent a car to pick up the Arabs. They had been picked up by Sayyaf's men. "Who brought them from the front line to Kabul?" I asked.

"I don't know," Bismillah Khan said. "Maybe the Taliban."

The Arab assassins had been taken to Sayyaf's house and given tea, and were introduced to a man named Qazi Karamatullah Siddiq, who spoke Arabic and was assigned to accompany them while they were in the Panjshir. Siddiq is a Muslim scholar and a graduate in Sharia law from Dawa'a al-Jihad, Sayyaf's university near Peshawar. He now works in one of the ministries in the interim government, and I talked with him about the Arabs. Although Siddiq is a Sayyaf loyalist, he contradicted several of Sayyaf's recollections, most notably the one about the assassins almost getting into the meeting of Northern Alliance leaders in the Panjshir, supposedly to kill them all. This was a story that I had heard repeatedly as evidence that Sayyaf was not involved in the plot to kill Massoud, since he would have been killed himself. But Siddiq says that the Arabs never got near the meeting, because Sayyaf had refused, in advance, to give them permission. He says that Sayyaf then arranged for the Arabs to interview Massoud in Khoja Bahauddin. Siddiq also said that Sayyaf never mentioned any suspicions about the Arabs until after the assassination, although Siddiq didn't seem to think this implicated Sayyaf. "Professor Sayyaf and Ahmad Shah Massoud were like brothers," Siddiq assured me. "No one was more sad than Professor Sayyaf when Massoud died."

Conspiracy theories are given credence in Afghanistan not least because there have been, historically, a lot of conspiracies. The reigning political ethos is survival of the fittest, and alliances are fluid. Afghans are geographically isolated, xenophobic, and cynical from years of war. Sayyaf helped the assassins, and most of the people I spoke to who were close to Massoud—relatives, intelligence agents, military commanders—believe that he must have had some sense, if not explicit knowledge, of the assassins' plans. But he was only one—perhaps the final—link in a chain of people who made it possible for the two Arabs to get to Khoja Bahauddin with their sophisticated explosives and well-choreographed suicide plan. For instance, among the CDs and notebooks and verses from the Koran found in the Arabs' things after the assassination was a letter of recommendation written by the head of the Afghan Red Crescent Society (shocking documentation of the culture of complicity and appeasement that had developed between NGOs and the Taliban). Massoud's assassins were linked to Osama bin Laden and Al Qaeda and, by inference, to the World Trade Center attacks. "These links are so strong," an Afghan intelligence agent close to the investigation of Massoud's death said to me, "that they leave no doubt to anyone in intelligence, with knowledge of terrorist organizations, and of Afghanistan, that the two events were connected."

One afternoon toward the end of May, I went to lunch at Wali Massoud's house. He had several guests, including a group of Afghan American businessmen. One of them, who lives in Virginia and works for DynCorp, an American defense contractor, told me that he had been away for twenty-five years but was thinking of returning if he could do some business for his company.

Wali and I were able to talk for a few minutes in a corner, and I said to him that an Afghan intelligence officer had told me that, although several European intelligence agencies are investigating his brother's murder, there isn't much of an investigation taking place in Afghanistan.

"That's right," he said. "There is no investigation here at all."

I asked Wali if people were preoccupied by the intense preparations for the Loya Jirga. I had been struck by the fact that Sayyaf seemed to be very involved in the dealmaking that was going on. Why would so many of those who revered Massoud be prepared to cut deals with a man who is suspected of betraying him?

"All of these people," Wali said, "are involved in politics."

# 9

## THE MAN IN THE PALACE

O n May 11, riots broke out in the city of Jalalabad, in eastern Afghanistan. The violence followed a *Newsweek* story—which has since been retracted—on new allegations that American interrogators at Guantánamo Bay had desecrated the Koran. In the next few days, the protests spread to the capital, Kabul, and throughout the country. In some provincial towns, police fired into crowds. But early on there were signs that the violence had less to do with *Newsweek* than with Afghanistan's president, Hamid Karzai.

On the first night of rioting, copies of an anonymous letter circulated in the streets of Kabul. This Night Letter, as it was called, was a vehement exhortation to Afghans to oppose Karzai, whom it accused of being un-Islamic, an ally of the Taliban, and a "U.S.A. servant." The letter said that Karzai had put the interests of his "evil master" ahead of those of Afghans, and it called for leaders who were proven patriots,

This chapter was originally published as "The Man in the Palace," *The New Yorker*, May 29, 2005.

mujahideen—a synonym, in this case, for members of the Northern Alliance, many of whom are now warlords and regional strongmen—to
defy him. The timing was opportune: Karzai was on a trip to Europe,
in search of financial backing. His next destination was Washington,
where he planned to discuss a pact that would guarantee the United
States a long-term military presence in Afghanistan.

Karzai seemed unsure of how to respond. Even as the unrest continued, he stuck to his itinerary and, from Brussels, called the riots a "man-
ifestation of democracy." When he finally arrived home, several days
later, he held a press conference, at which he blamed unspecified "enemies of peace" for the violence. He asked, "Who are they who have such
enmity with Afghanistan, a nation that is begging for money to build
the country and construct buildings, and during the night they come
and destroy it?"

The nineteen thousand American and eight thousand NATO troops
stationed in Afghanistan were placed on high alert, and government
officials met with protesters. By the time the violence abated, at least
seventeen people were dead, and government buildings and aid-agency
offices had been torched. It was the largest display of anti-American
feeling since the fall of the Taliban, in late 2001.

THE NEXT WEEK, *THE NEW YORK TIMES* PUBLISHED, IN RAPID
succession, a State Department memorandum saying that Karzai was
"unwilling to assert strong leadership" to end drug trafficking—
Afghanistan is the source of most of the world's heroin—and a new report on the abuse of prisoners in Afghanistan. The prisoner-abuse story
described how American soldiers had beaten two Afghan men to death
at Bagram air base, north of Kabul. One of them was a twenty-two-year-
old cabdriver who appeared to have no connection to terrorism. Karzai

was in the incongruous position of defending his record as a steadfast ally in the war on drugs while expressing horror at the reports of American abuse.

There are other contradictions. Afghans don't generally question Karzai's good intentions, but they complain about his ineffectiveness and the corruption in his government. Karzai is an odd combination of decency and diffidence, a committed democrat but a regal figure who is comfortable leaving the business of governing to others—including his American advisers. Habiba Sarabi, whom Karzai appointed governor of Bamiyan Province, making her Afghanistan's first woman governor, said of him, "He was quite popular during the transitional period. And he still is, because there are no alternatives to him. His character and his democratic inclinations are higher than those of all the others." Unfortunately, she said, "sometimes he makes promises he can't follow up."

When I spoke to Karzai in Kabul, not long before the riots, he told me repeatedly that Afghans had actively sought close ties to the United States. When the Taliban were in power, "it was Afghan people that kept going to see the US and asking it to come and help Afghanistan— and also asking to help the US," he said. "*We* were the persuaders. *We* brought the US in. It's been a success. And that's why I got the vote." Now he was confronting the limits of that success, and he appeared surprised and aggrieved.

Last week, as he headed to Washington, Karzai said that he would demand "justice" for Afghan prisoners and control over US military operations in Afghanistan. The requests only underscored his lack of authority; the alleged abuse had taken place in his own country, and if American troops weren't there, Karzai almost certainly wouldn't be, either. As it turned out, Karzai signed an agreement at his meeting with President Bush that affirmed the US military's right to operate freely. And when, at a press conference, with Bush at his side, he was asked

about prisoner abuse, he said that it made him "sad," but quickly added
that the actions of a few soldiers should not sully the image of the US
government. After his brief flash of assertiveness, he seemed more a sup-
plicant than ever. His relationship with Washington—which gave him
security, status, and a certain amount of pride—revealed itself in all its
dependency and weakness.

When I arrived in Kabul this spring, after Afghanistan's most severe winter in many years, the snow on the jagged black mountains that
ring the city had begun to melt, and the streets, most of them unpaved,
were either clogged with mud and raw sewage or, on the days the sun
shone, concealed by swirling clouds of dust. But it was easy to see how
profoundly Kabul had changed since the fall of the Taliban. The last
time I was in Afghanistan, in the summer of 2002, the honeycomb of
wattle-and-daub houses on the slopes surrounding the city was mostly
uninhabited. The ghost houses gaped at the city below—their windows,
their tin roofs, their doors had all been ransacked. Now, as refugees have
flooded back to Afghanistan—three million have returned since the
fall of the Taliban brought an end to major fighting—the houses have
mostly been reoccupied. Down on the flatlands, new neighborhoods
have appeared among the ruins of old ones. Several high-rise commercial buildings, with colored mirrored glass, Dubai style, are being built.
The population of Kabul has multiplied, from about a million to an
estimated three million inhabitants, and it is still growing.

In the narrow streets of the city center, thousands of newly imported cars compete with cyclists, water buffalo, and poor Hazara men,
who take the most menial jobs, pulling carts. The armored convoys of
the NATO peacekeeping forces and the Humvees and Land Rovers
of American and British troops speed to and from their bases. Other
Americans, out of uniform and accompanied by gunmen, move around in
large SUVs with smoked-glass windows. Most Afghans assume, probably correctly, that they are Special Forces commandos or CIA operatives;

in any case, they are the most overt reminder that a war against the Taliban and Al Qaeda continues mostly out of sight.

The American operations, which have confined the Taliban mainly to the backcountry and the Pakistani border region, are extremely controversial, especially among Pashtuns, Afghanistan's largest ethnic group. (Most of the Taliban are Pashtuns, as is Karzai.) Ahmad Shah Ahmadzai, a prominent Pashtun politician, told me that, before the recent revelations, when he visited Karzai as part of a delegation to protest the US military's raids and its detention of people from Pashtun communities, Karzai had said, "What can I do? The Americans don't

President Hamid Karzai with US Ambassador Zalmay Khalilzad, other officials, and his retinue of Afghan and American bodyguards, 2005. SAMANTHA APPLETON

listen to me." Ahmadzai threw up his hands in a gesture of incredulity and contempt. "Karzai is president with the will of the Afghan people, but in some aspects he is an American puppet, too," he said.

Karzai was appointed interim president at a UN-sponsored meeting of exiles in Bonn in December 2001, two months into the American bombing campaign. A presidential election was postponed twice because of threats from the Taliban, but it was finally held, last October, and Karzai won, with 55 percent of the vote. (Parliamentary elections have yet to take place.) His main opponent, Yunis Qanouni, a former Northern Alliance official, achieved only 16 percent.

Now Karzai presides over a country of about twenty-nine million citizens, most of whom are poor and illiterate, with an economy that relies almost entirely on international aid and the illicit harvest of poppies, the raw material for opium and heroin. The drug business employs some 2.3 million Afghans, with revenues equal to 60 percent of the legal GDP. Since 2001, the poppy harvest has soared 1,500 percent; by most estimates, Afghanistan is fast becoming a narco-state. The unemployment rate is about 30 percent and the crime rate is spiraling upward.

And yet in 2005 nearly five million children, including nearly two million girls, attended school, compared with under a million total in 2001. Women now have the right to vote, and four million registered for the last election; three of Karzai's thirty-two cabinet ministers are women. International aid organizations have trouble operating outside of Kabul, because of security concerns—dozens of relief workers have been assassinated—but teams led by British and American forces are laying roads and building bridges and schools in much of the country. (While Operation Iraqi Freedom has cost the lives of more than 1,600 American servicemen and women, 144 American soldiers have died in and around Afghanistan.)

How much credit or blame Karzai can take for these developments is unclear. Most of Karzai's government ministers have an American counterpart who is a member of the so-called Afghan Reconstruction Team. One American official in Kabul described the team to me as a sort of shadow government: "Khalilzad's cabinet"—a reference to Zalmay Khalilzad, who has been the American ambassador in Kabul since 2003. The official said that the team members acted as "senior counselors" to the Afghan government. He noted, for example, that they helped write Karzai's inauguration speech.

Virtually every Afghan I spoke to was troubled by Karzai's close relationship with Khalilzad. The ambassador is often referred to, sarcastically, as "the second president," or, sometimes, simply as President Khalilzad. Habiba Sarabi told me, "The problem is that Khalilzad makes policy pronouncements himself, and speaks more strongly than the president does. So people naturally think he is more powerful than President Karzai."

Khalilzad, who was born in Afghanistan, seems to enjoy the image that he has acquired as Afghanistan's American viceroy. He was an official in the Reagan and George H. W. Bush administrations, and has known Karzai for many years because of his work as a foreign-policy analyst and in Afghan exile circles. On the half dozen occasions I saw Karzai and Khalilzad together, they did nothing to conceal the warmth of their friendship. It was obvious that Karzai was closer to him than to many of his own ministers.

The American official in Kabul, referring to Khalilzad by his nickname, said that, until recently, "it was like Zal had to hold Karzai's hand even when he went to the bathroom. He consulted him on everything before he did anything." But this official also told me that, since the election, things had begun to change: "Now it's more like he calls Zal afterward and tells him what he's done and asks him what he thinks." An American adviser to Karzai said, "He and Zal are really close friends, who spend more time together than most husbands and wives; they eat dinner together almost every night. Karzai doesn't just consult him for decisions—he also gets emotional support from him." Earlier this month, President Bush nominated Khalilzad to replace John Negroponte as the US ambassador to Iraq. The official said, "Personally, I think it's a healthy thing that Zal is leaving. It will give Karzai a chance to become his own man. And it won't be healthy just for Karzai; it'll be healthy for Afghanistan, too."

When I arrived for my first interview with Karzai at Kabul's old royal palace, where he lives and works, I found him walking in the garden with Khalilzad. He gave me a friendly wave, as did the ambassador, and said that he would be with me shortly.

The palace is a complex of buildings in an eclectic mixture of architectural styles and periods: There are fortifications with turrets, slate-roofed roundhouses, and a lovely Victorian mansion. Some of the buildings are ruins, with caved-in roofs, struck by missiles in Afghanistan's recent wars. Karzai's residence is a graceless modernist concrete structure built in the sixties, for one of Afghanistan's former princes, with a small garden, a swimming pool, and a tennis court in back. I was shown into his sitting room, which had a homey but unintentionally retro look, with wood-veneer paneling on the walls. The furniture—upholstered in floral velour—was similar to what I had seen in middle-class Afghan homes.

When Karzai entered, he apologized for the delay—he had been asking Khalilzad if American helicopters could be sent to rescue victims of a flood. Karzai is a lithe man of medium height, with pale skin, a prominent nose, and large, expressive brown eyes. He has a salt-and-pepper beard clipped short, and a finely woven white wool *patou*, or man's shawl, was thrown loosely around his shoulders.

Although he is the leader of one of the most destitute countries on earth, Karzai has an uncanny, if dissonant, sense of sartorial panache. Westerners often assume that his elaborate outfits are the traditional dress of his people, the Pashtuns. In fact, Karzai assembles them as homages to Afghanistan's disparate ethnic groups—they are costumes, roughly akin to the baseball caps that an American politician might wear while campaigning in different parts of the country. The striped green silk *chapan* cape that Karzai wore to President Bush's State of the Union address in 2002 is Uzbek; the gray karakul hat he often wears is traditionally Tajik. When he is among other Pashtuns, he often wears a turban, as they do.

A few days before our meeting, I had watched Karzai speak at a ceremony in honor of International Women's Day, at the Intercontinental Hotel in Kabul. The event was the first public appearance by Karzai's wife, Zinat, who is thirty-five years old and was trained as an obstetrician and gynecologist. Like Karzai, Zinat is from the southern city of Kandahar and moved with her family to Quetta, Pakistan, during Afghanistan's civil war, where she worked with Afghan refugee women. Karzai, who is forty-seven, married her only six years ago; the marriage was an arranged one, and there is a great deal of speculation about their relationship. They do not have children. During her husband's address, Zinat, a pleasant-looking woman in a modest black chador, sat in the front row of the audience, along with other VIPs. I asked Karzai whether security concerns had kept her from attending such events before, despite her role as First Lady.

"It was Women's Day," he said, smiling warily. "She wanted to go to the last Women's Day. But somehow it was messed up. Somebody came to me the day before, and said, 'Well, can she come?,' and I said yes and I meant to ask her." But, he said, "I forgot." He finally called to invite her just as he was leaving for the event. "She said, 'Get lost, too late,'" Karzai laughed. "This time, I remembered."

His own presence at the event was unusual; he rarely appears outside the palace, even in Kabul. He had arrived surrounded by two dozen heavily armed American guards. His security detail includes scores of American contractors working for DynCorp International, which has a multimillion-dollar contract with the State Department, and a smaller number of agents from the State Department's Bureau of Diplomatic Security. Karzai told me that early in his presidency Lieutenant General Dan McNeill, the first commander of coalition forces in Afghanistan, said to him, "Look, let's get you a security environment. You don't have any professionals here—anybody can get in and blow up this place." He said that he resisted the offer, but then "I started to consult. Everybody, including the chief justice, you know what they said? They said, 'Ring them as soon as possible, so that you can work independently, so that this place becomes independent.'" The Afghan people "know the means of this country," Karzai said. "They know what we can do, what we can't do."

In truth, most Afghans are far less sanguine. During the election campaign, Karzai was embarrassed when his American security men forced him to return to Kabul after a rocket was fired near his helicopter as it was about to land outside the town of Gardez. There are reasons for such caution; Karzai survived an assassination attempt in 2002, and three ministers in the interim government were murdered. But his opponents have used the fact of his US protection to portray him as subservient, and to question his patriotism. Fahim Dashty, the editor of the *Kabul Weekly*, told me, "I don't understand why it is he cannot find Afghans to defend him. He's had three years in power now. If he had wanted to train Afghans, it's more than enough time. It can mean only that he doesn't trust Afghans."

Despite his American support, Karzai has trouble convincing Afghans that he can confront the warlords or the thousands of Taliban fighters who are still at large. Karzai recently offered amnesty to the Taliban on the condition that they renounce violence. I asked Karzai about the offer, which many Afghans saw as a betrayal.

"Afghanistan had bad days before the Taliban as well," Karzai replied. "From the time of the Soviets and from the time of the mujahideen groups—Afghanistan suffered for so many years. We have practically pardoned all those people who were among the murderers of the Afghan people. . . . Now either we have to bring people in to trial and seek justice or we have to forget about it, and live a life by forgetting the past."

When I asked if there was a middle ground, he replied, "What is in the middle? If I go to the middle ground, I will not be bringing total peace to this country. If I can reduce the bomb blasts in Afghanistan by bringing some of the Taliban back home, and put things in order by making them behave all right, then I should do that. Now, if you ask me as a citizen of Afghanistan, 'Karzai, what is it that you want, justice or peace?,' I would say, of course, both—most human beings would. But, if you ask me as the president of Afghanistan, then I have to say, 'Peace gives you continuation of life. Justice does not, necessarily.'" He added, "When we can afford it, we can have justice."

Karzai's relationship with the warlords is ambiguous: Many of them fought against the Taliban as part of the Northern Alliance and, until recently, Karzai had little choice but to share power with them. (As an exile in Pakistan, he opposed the Taliban, but he was not a member of the Northern Alliance, which was dominated by Tajiks and Uzbeks.) When the United States military invaded Afghanistan, in October 2001, it formed a tactical partnership with the Northern Alliance. The Alliance worked with American Special Forces and the CIA, and helped to direct air strikes. As the Taliban defenses in Kabul weakened, the US asked the Northern Alliance to wait to enter the capital until a coalition government that would better reflect Afghanistan's ethnic mix could be formed. But the Northern Alliance took the capital anyway, and, from that position of strength, was able to demand the most powerful jobs in Karzai's cabinet. Muhammad Fahim, its military chief, became Karzai's defense minister and vice president, despite allegations that he is a major figure in Afghanistan's criminal underground. Last July, just before the presidential campaign officially began, Karzai dropped him as his running mate. According to Americans I spoke to in Afghanistan, it was Ambassador Khalilzad who persuaded Karzai to make this move.

Meanwhile, General Abdul Rashid Dostum, perhaps Afghanistan's most notorious warlord, has been offered the post of chief of staff to the commander in chief of the armed forces—that is, Karzai. Dostum, an Uzbek who dominates a large swath of northern Afghanistan, is viewed by most human rights organizations as among the worst war criminals in the country. One recent charge is that under his orders hundreds of Taliban fighters, who had surrendered to his forces, were locked in airless shipping containers and left to die of asphyxiation and thirst. Dostum is extremely wealthy, has a large and well-armed militia, and is reported to be heavily involved in narcotics trafficking. The American adviser to Karzai argued that the new job was mostly symbolic—"It's basically a broom closet down the hall"—and was the best way to reduce his power. But Dostum has not yet arrived in the capital, and many in Kabul question whether he will ever assume his post.

When I mentioned Dostum, Karzai offered a conflicted reply: "I am quite a sentimental person. I might be hurt a lot, when I see something hurt. And this is the only time where I sat down and said, 'Hamid, here you don't get sentimental—you think of this country's future, and provide an opportunity for all to work.' The countryside understands it very well. Afghans are extremely pragmatic." Before he made the appointment, he added, "I consulted extensively. I called all the former jihadi leaders, I called lots of other people, and then I made the appointment. I never do that without consultation. You know, I'm accused of too much consultation. That's my problem."

Hamid Karzai is the fourth of eight children born to Abdul Ahad Karzai, the former deputy speaker of Afghanistan's royal parliament and paramount chief of the Populzai tribe, and his wife, Durkho. The Karzais are connected by marriage to the former Afghan king Zahir

Shah. (Although the monarchy was abolished in 1973, Karzai has declared Zahir Shah, who is ninety, the "father of the country" and allows him to live at the palace.) The family's ancestral home is in the village of Karz, in the parched flatlands just outside Kandahar.

Only two of Karzai's seven siblings live in Afghanistan. The eldest, Abdul Ahmed, is an engineer in Maryland. The next two, Qayum and Mahmoud, own a chain of Afghan restaurants—called Helmand, after Afghanistan's major river—in San Francisco, the Baltimore area, and Cambridge, Massachusetts. Shawali, who is younger than Hamid, is involved in business ventures in Afghanistan, as is Ahmed Wali, who is also Hamid's personal representative in Kandahar. The seventh son is Abdul Wali, a biochemist at Stony Brook University, on Long Island. Fouzia, the only sister, lives in Maryland.

When I visited Kandahar in late March, Qayum, the second-eldest brother, was visiting from the United States. Qayum, who is a slightly fleshier version of Hamid, recounted how his father, who exemplified the old order—the so-called feudals—was arrested in a wave of Leninist terror after the Communist coup in 1978. He was jailed for two years. Upon his release, he left the country and went to Quetta, where most of the family had already fled. Hamid was studying in India, at Himachal Pradesh University. Once he completed his BA and MA, in political science, he followed the family to Quetta. There he joined the Afghan National Liberation Front, one of the more moderate of the mujahideen factions then fighting the Soviets. Hamid was fluent in six languages—English, French, Hindi, and Urdu, as well as Dari and Pashto, Afghanistan's two official languages—and he became the spokesman for the front. (Hamid told me that he occasionally crossed the border to visit mujahideen on the battlefield, and that he had carried a weapon but had never used it.)

Qayum offered to show me the family's village, Karz. We drove in a Toyota Land Cruiser for twenty minutes or so on a rutted dirt track between fields of grapes, which are harvested for raisins, not wine. Qayum told the driver to stop next to a large family cemetery. The tomb of Abdul Ahad Karzai dominated the cemetery, a raised plinth under a canopied roof.

In 1999, Abdul Ahad Karzai was gunned down outside his home in Quetta, presumably by the Taliban. Hamid Karzai and his siblings, together with hundreds of other relatives and tribespeople, defied the Taliban by bringing his body across the border in a vast convoy. They drove 120 miles to Kandahar, and then to Karz, for the burial ceremony. "It was a show of force—it was very audacious," Qayum said. "People said that it was the greatest number of cars ever assembled in Kandahar—or not since the kings used to come. At one count, there were four hundred cars in the procession." Afterward, Hamid was proclaimed head of the Populzai tribe.

Karz is a poor, featureless place, a sunstruck maze of flat-roofed mud dwellings and walls. Qayum pointed out a building that had been the primary school he attended as a boy. The Karzais had had some vineyards but were not one of the great landowning families of Kandahar, Qayum said. Indicating a tiny mud-walled shop, he said, "I used to think that was a huge supermarket." The family moved to Kabul in 1965, when his father became a member of parliament. He was in ninth grade and Hamid was seven years old.

We walked to the collapsed mud walls of what had been the Karzais' home. A displaced family was living in a tent pitched in the middle of the courtyard. Qayum said that when they were growing up he thought Hamid might pursue some sort of humanitarian work. "He always had an enormously soft heart," Qayum said. "Beggars used to come to our house and ask for Hamid." In 2000, he said, "Hamid was visiting us in the US and watching TV, and there was an appeal from Save the Children or one of those international humanitarian organizations, and there was a picture of an Afghan girl sitting there, surrounded by garbage, and he became highly emotional—unbelievable! Tears came to his eyes. He said, 'Can you please turn this off?' He just couldn't handle it." Qayum added, "I never thought that he would become a politician."

In late 2001, Qayum was in Bonn, at the conference where the post-Taliban leadership was being negotiated. He recalled telephoning Hamid, who was in Afghanistan, to inform him that there was a movement to nominate him for president. Hamid Karzai had qualities that made him an ideal compromise candidate: He was a moderate but safely traditionalist Pashtun from a well-known patrician family. He was also favored by King Zahir Shah. Qayum told him, "This is the toughest moment in Afghan history. Are you sure you want to do this?" Hamid replied, "If not me, then who is going to do it?"

Every other day or so, Karzai holds an audience in Gul Khana, or Flower House, the part of the royal palace where he has his office. One afternoon this spring, he received a delegation from Badakhshan, the northeasternmost province of Afghanistan. I joined the visitors—some wearing loose-fitting *shalwar kameez* and felt *pakul* hats, others in military uniforms or Western suits—as they were shown to a long row of tables. A couple of Afghan cameramen stood behind a tripod with a video camera, and Afghan and American armed guards took up positions around the room.

After a few minutes, Karzai entered, and hailed the visitors enthusiastically. He was wearing an elegant blue overcoat and a karakul hat. Everyone fell silent for an opening prayer, and then one of the Badakhshanis stood up to speak.

He began by praising Karzai, who was, he said, a great man, a good man. He reminded Karzai that Badakhshanis had always been loyal to the kings of Afghanistan. And they were loyal to Karzai. But lawlessness and warlordism defined daily life in Badakhshan. "People are beginning to tell us that we shouldn't have voted for you, because you cannot defend us." He said that those who supported Karzai needed something in return.

Karzai said sympathetically, "It will happen, it will happen."

The next speaker said that he had been Karzai's local chairman during the presidential campaign last fall, then he said, "Lately, people have been coming up to me and saying, 'You haven't fulfilled your promises.'" He told Karzai that the solution was to give his people jobs. At that, Karzai called for the video camera to be turned off—"so that we can talk freely."

Another man, a member of Afghanistan's small Ismaili Shiite sect, took the microphone. "Our province is controlled by smugglers, and we have seven districts where we have no local people at all in the official posts," he said. "Everywhere we go, they say, 'You are not Tajik or Hazara; you're not Uzbek or Pashtun. There is no job for you.'"

Karzai looked displeased. "What are you saying? That if you're not from a certain tribe you don't get a job?"

"Yes," replied the man. "Especially in the National Army."

"This is wrong. Everyone in Afghanistan, each tribe, has the same rights, and this is promised in the constitution. What are these people thinking? I prefer an orphan, a child without a father, or, even better, someone who doesn't know what nationality he is than such people!"

Karzai told an aide to get the interior minister on the telephone. When the aide handed him his cell phone, Karzai told the minister what he had heard: "These are educated people telling me these things, and I want to discuss this with you. When can you see me?" Karzai then had a call placed to his army chief, Bismillah Khan. After a brief exchange, he turned to the men in the room and said, "Bismillah Khan says he has space open for officers and soldiers and you should send him your candidates." Everyone applauded.

The lights in the chandeliers that hung from the domed ceiling of the meeting room flickered on and off—presumably as a result of one of the city's frequent power shortages. Karzai noticed a Mongol-looking elderly man who had stood up, and urged him forward. The man had been sitting quietly with several companions, all of them wearing high tasseled fur hats and long black leather boots with their trousers tucked in, Cossack style.

The old man introduced himself as Abdul Rashid, the khan of the Small Pamir, a region at the far end of the Wakhan Corridor, a slender neck of mountainous land—the most inaccessible corner of Badakhshan. The Wakhan borders Tajikistan on the north and Pakistan on the south, and juts into western China. (The khan's people are ethnic Kyrgyz.) The khan had a wispy beard and thick glasses, and spoke in a reedy, tremulous voice. He said that he and his companions had waited three months to see Karzai, and it had taken them four weeks to reach the capital from their village; they had made much of the journey on foot.

"There are no roads where I live," the khan explained. "I am thinking that the Afghan government has forgotten us." There were no schools or hospitals, or policemen to guard the frontier against smugglers or terrorists. After several years of drought, his people had little food. He was ashamed to say it, but they were also afflicted by opium addiction, and needed clinics.

Karzai interrupted him. "Don't worry. I am going to arrange food— I will send you back with food on helicopters," he said. "You will not go home without a solution to your problems. We will arrange what documentation is needed for the clinics, and we will get you your food."

The other Pamiris rose to their feet and walked toward Karzai. One of them produced an embroidered robe and a high peaked cap of many colors, similar to the caps worn by Tibetan lamas. Karzai put on the robe and the fantastic hat, placed his own karakul on the khan's head, and beamed at the men. The video camera was back on now, and the room had an air of celebration. Suddenly, a man dressed in military fatigues took the microphone and called out, "Our province is controlled by mafias and drug traffickers!," but Karzai cut him off, saying, "We will solve it." Surrounded by his security men, he headed for the door, leaving his visitors behind.

Karzai has not been to Karz, his home village, for years. "The last time I saw it was when it was bombed by the Soviets, in 1988," he said. Six months later, the Soviets pulled out, but the fight against their Afghan proxies continued for three years. Finally, in 1992, Najibullah, the last Afghan Communist ruler, abandoned his office, and the mujahideen returned from their base in Pakistan. "We all came together," Karzai recalled. "We spent the night at the edge of the city, and the next morning we all came to Kabul."

As they drove into the city, Karzai said, his elation gave way to foreboding. "I noticed people looking from behind their drawn curtains. We heard a lot of firing in the air. By the second day, it appeared that the city was in the hands of too many different groups, that our lives were going to become more difficult."

Almost immediately, factional fighting broke out. Karzai eventually became the deputy foreign minister in the transitional mujahideen government of President Burhanuddin Rabbani and Ahmad Shah Massoud, his charismatic military chief, who later commanded the Northern Alliance. In a series of shifting battlefield alliances, Dostum, who had been with the Soviets, joined forces first with Rabbani and Massoud and then with Gulbuddin Hekmatyar, a radical Islamist. Thousands of civilians were killed, and large sections of Kabul, which until then had remained intact, were leveled.

During the fighting, Karzai fled. I had heard many tales about what happened to him. There were reports that he had been imprisoned and mistreated, or even tortured, and then had escaped. Karzai's rivals made disparaging jokes and suggested that he was a coward. I asked him to clarify what had happened.

Karzai coughed, as if uncomfortable, but began talking. "It was at the height of this extremely bad period for Afghanistan," he said. One day, when he was at the foreign ministry, one of Rabbani's men came and told him that the president wanted to see him. Karzai was suspicious, but he went along. The man drove Karzai to the office of the intelligence services and led him into a small, dirty room with a bare radiator. Muhammad Aref, who later served as the head of Karzai's own intelligence services, came in. ("I have never mentioned it to him," Karzai said.) Aref and the other man began to interrogate Karzai, asking about alliances against Rabbani. "I said, 'I know nothing of this.' They were very, very nervous, almost pale with nervousness! Just as they asked me the second question, a big bang was heard, and the room filled with smoke and debris from glass and all that, and everybody ran out, and I also ran out. I saw that the roof was not there. I saw that sunshine was coming in."

A rocket had hit the building. In the confusion that followed, Karzai made his way outside, and back to his office. "That's it. I came to the foreign ministry, and the people there were shocked—I was bleeding, I had some shrapnel."

Karzai hired a taxi and began a circuitous trip, by car and on foot, until he was safely in Pakistan. He said that Rabbani later telephoned him and his father to apologize, saying that he hadn't known about the interrogation beforehand. But Karzai did not go back. The people around the president, he realized, had succumbed to paranoia. The next time Karzai returned to Kabul, it was as Afghanistan's president.

During the next few years of civil war, the United States saw the relatively unknown Taliban as potential peacemakers—and so, for a time, did Karzai, who knew many of the Taliban commanders from his years in the anti-Soviet jihad. Early on, he gave them money and weapons, in the belief that they would be the vehicle for what was then his dream—the restoration of the Pashtun monarchy of King Zahir Shah. In 1996,

the Taliban seized power, and invited Karzai to become their UN ambassador. He considered the idea, but decided against it.

"A lot of the jihad commanders in the field were very pragmatic
people," Karzai said. "Just some were very radical." By radical, he meant
"puritanical—not politicized radical types," he said. "They were very
clean people. Almost all of them became the Taliban." He added, "When
the Taliban movement began, we saw it as an innocent movement. When
I say 'we,' I mean we Afghans, a lot of us, me, my friends, many other
members of this community. We thought they were people who wanted
to help this country. But very soon we recognized that among them
there were people who were not from Afghanistan, and who were hor-
ribly cruel to this place—Al Qaeda."

After his father's assassination, Karzai tried to get US support for a
Pashtun anti-Taliban movement. In 1999, he went to see Michael Sheehan, a counterterrorism official in both the George H. W. Bush and
Clinton administrations. Sheehan told me, "At the time, Karzai was
just a nobody, another Afghan exile—I never imagined he'd become the
president. But I had heard he was prominent with the Pashtuns." When
they met, Sheehan said, "he seemed decent. He seemed like a nice guy,
but I remember sitting there looking at him and wondering, How is *he*
going to go after the Taliban?" Karzai talked about his plans, Sheehan
said, and "we agreed on everything, about how evil the Taliban were,
and the need to remove them. But what could I do for him? In terms of
the Clinton administration's policy at the time, there wasn't a lot of
stomach for it." That indifference continued into the Bush administration, Sheehan said, especially since the Northern Alliance was losing
ground. "There were a few guys in the CIA pushing for the Northern
Alliance, but nobody else wanted to touch it," Sheehan said. "Afghanistan was seen as a loser, a sinkhole. Until 9/11, no one gave a shit."

Karzai testified before the Senate in 2000, and also began to coordinate his efforts with Massoud, the military leader of the Northern Alliance. Then, on September 9, 2001, Massoud was assassinated by Al Qaeda suicide bombers. Two days later, the World Trade Center and the Pentagon were attacked.

When Karzai saw the first news reports, he said, "I knew immediately that the United States was going to come and help us." Within two days, "hundreds of people arrived in Quetta to meet with me," Karzai said. "The house became so crowded!" Among them was Khalilzad, who then worked for Condoleezza Rice, the national security adviser. (During the Clinton administration, Khalilzad worked for the RAND Corporation and was a consultant for Unocal, a company that wanted to build a pipeline through Afghanistan.) Three weeks later, in early October 2001, "I moved into Afghanistan," Karzai said excitedly. "Without any help, at that moment—nothing. I just walked into the country."

Karzai and a few companions made their way to Tirin Kot, the main town in the rugged province of Uruzgan, north of Kandahar, and then on to a small village crisscrossed by running streams. He met with tribal elders, he said, "and that's where I learned the significance of the United States to Afghanistan."

The elders were skeptical of Karzai. "A cleric said, 'Look, we know what you're up to, we know that you want to defeat the Taliban, but do you have the backing of the US? Will it give you planes, will it give you weapons, will it give you money, will it help you?' And I said yes." The cleric asked if Karzai had a satellite phone, and when he said yes, told him, "All right, then, call the US—ask them to come and bomb a place near the Taliban governor's office, or the police headquarters in Tirin Kot. The next day, the people will go and take the town, without too much trouble."

Karzai said he told the cleric that he couldn't ask the US to bomb his own country. The cleric pressed him. "He said, 'Well, I'm sorry, this means that you are not interested in freeing the country—you're only here to kill yourself and us, and our children and women, and we're not going to die in a futile war of yours.'"

Karzai stayed in the village for eleven days. The tribal council met and argued with him, telling him that Al Qaeda fighters were coming, and would attack. Finally, they said that the entire village was fleeing into the mountains for safety. "I was afraid there would be a massacre," Karzai said. He decided to make the call.

"When I called the US Embassy in Islamabad, I said, 'I am Hamid Karzai.' To my surprise, they knew who I was. I thought they had forgotten about me!

"They said, 'Where the hell are you?'

"I said, 'I am here in Uruzgan.'

"They said, 'Do you have communications, how do we locate you? Do you have'—what is it called? GTS, GPS? I didn't even know what GPS was. I said, 'I have no idea. I know I am between Tirin Kot and the mountains.' They said, 'Fine.'"

The Americans told Karzai to have his men light four fires on the hills around their position, at least a hundred meters apart, for the next two nights. They complied, and when Karzai called again the Americans told him, "We've found you." Karzai paused and smiled broadly, and said, "Technology."

The Americans told Karzai to set the fires again, so that they could drop a shipment of weapons. ("Hey, great story," Karzai said to me, "if someone can make a movie out of it.") He and the tribesmen lit the fires and waited. Hours passed, but the planes didn't come. Karzai went to sleep in a shepherd's hut. Then, he said, at about one thirty in the morning, "someone came, saying, 'Do you hear the planes?' Just as I came out, a huge black plane flew over us, and then somebody shouted, 'Oh, look at those white things!'" The white things were parachutes, and they were attached to crates of weapons.

"And, by the way, the people had already taken Tirin Kot," Karzai continued. "Exactly what that man had asked me—while we were in the mountains, the US planes had come and bombed some place in Tirin Kot. The next morning, a group of about fifty tribal chiefs went into the town, kicked the governor out of the place, kicked the police out of the place, and took control of the town."

It was in Tirin Kot, two days later, that Karzai realized the tide had finally gone against the Taliban and in his favor. A defecting Taliban commander arrived there alone, and asked him for a letter of safe conduct. Karzai decided to write the letter, to see what would happen. Two days later, the man returned with pickup trucks and weapons for Karzai. "Then I said, 'Wow, we are much wider and much more than we imagined.'"

After the audience at the palace, I went to see the Pamiris at their lodgings, which they had described uncertainly as a "presidential guesthouse." This turned out to be a decrepit two-story building on a dirt lane off a backstreet. The grounds were strewn with litter. The room where the Pamiris were living was dark and cold; there was no electricity. The khan, a reserved, dignified man, said that he had decided to come to the capital nearly four months earlier, right after Karzai's election victory. "Before, there was always war in our country, so we didn't want to come down," he said. "But now a great power has come to Afghanistan." He meant the United States. "We came to congratulate Mr. Karzai for this and to ask him for his help."

They left their homes before the winter snows blocked the mountain passes, and walked for seventeen days before reaching Wakhan, the nearest town with a dirt road. None of the men had been in touch with their families for months. "Where we live, there is not even a telephone," the khan said. "We keep sheep and yaks and we live from their milk and cheese for seven months of the year, and our people make carpets from the animals' wool. Afterward, we take the carpets on foot to the market at Wakhan."

Their visits to Wakhan had exposed them to the drug trade. "We have opium addicts in every family," the khan said. He estimated that one in four Pamiris was an addict, women as well as men. His own son-in-law, he said, "smokes for three days and then sleeps for three days."

The Pamiris told me that their audience with Karzai had been arranged by General Fazal-Azim Mojadeddi, known as Zalmay Khan, who was born in a less remote part of Badakhshan. After my meeting with the Pamiris, Zalmay Khan invited me to his office, in the palace complex. He is a tall, burly, impeccably dressed man; according to his business card, he is in charge of "V.I.P. security" for the presidency. When I asked him why the Pamiris had come to him, he said, "They don't know anyone else."

Zalmay Khan told me that he had come across the Pamiris when he was in the mountains as a mujahideen in Massoud's army, in the early nineties. He stayed with them for three weeks. "It was August, and even then it was really cold," he said. "The Pamiris live remote from one another—families are two and three kilometers apart. I asked why the population was so small and not increasing, and they told me it was because eighty percent of their babies died before tasting their mother's milk. They have no doctors to guide them, no health care." As for their opium use, "They were a sad people, and this was a way for them to escape their problems."

The Pamiris remembered Zalmay Khan, and when they heard on the radio that he had joined Karzai's government, they decided to seek him out. Zalmay Khan told me that, under the Afghan monarchy, his father had been the member of parliament for the region, and the Pamiris seemed to have tapped some dormant sense of feudal responsibility in him. ("They look to me," he said.)

During the interim administration, President Karzai had given orders regarding the Pamiris to several of his ministers, "but they didn't take him seriously," Zalmay Khan said. This time, he believed, the insecurity of the region's border, which was used as a crossing point by Al Qaeda and Uzbek terrorists, meant that the government could not afford its traditional neglect.

The next time I saw Karzai, we talked about the Pamiris. When I mentioned that they had waited three months to see him, he looked shocked. "Nobody told me," he said defensively. "Now I must find out if all the arrangements for the things they were asking for were made or not." Karzai looked over at his aides, and said something briskly in Pashto. One of them began scribbling on a notepad. Karzai looked back at me, and made it clear that he was ready to move on. When the conversation turned to the extremes of Afghanistan's topography, he looked relieved.

The town of Charikar, north of Kabul, where the Shamali plain meets the foothills of the Hindu Kush, is the gateway to the Panjshir Valley. The area was the home base of Ahmad Shah Massoud and other Tajiks in the Northern Alliance. In the election, Karzai's share of the vote in the Panjshir was around 1 percent. Afterward, Tajiks angrily accused him of having "Pashtunized" his administration by removing Northern Alliance men from their government jobs. These days, the Panjshir is something like enemy territory for Karzai. I went along on a visit he made to Charikar in March, for a road opening, and we were flown in on two American Chinook helicopters, escorted by two Apaches, two Black Hawks, and two fighter jets, which circled overhead once we landed. In the hour we were on the ground—just long enough for Karzai to dump a ceremonial load of dirt—dozens of American and Afghan guards stood by.

A few days earlier, I had been invited to dinner in Charikar at the house of Atta, a local strongman who was a former mujahideen commander. The entertainment was provided by a *maskhara*, or traditional

Afghan jester, named Samad Pashean. Long before the recent decades of warfare, *maskhara* performed for the country's monarchs; as in medieval Europe, they had license to lampoon the powerful. Pashean was one of the last remaining *maskhara*. He had survived the Soviet occupation, the civil war, and the Taliban years by wandering from one warlord's base to another, plying his services. According to my host, he was also a hit man, a blackmailer, and a thief.

Pashean regaled us with skits, dances, and gossipy monologues. In one, he described how after a man insulted him, he went to his house, killed him, and stole his shoes—for some reason, everyone laughed uproariously at that detail. Pointing to me, Pashean offered to kill anyone I wanted for the equivalent of $2,000. When I told him that his price was absurdly high, he good-naturedly indicated that he was ready to bargain.

Much of the humor was directed at Karzai, and it was not kind. Karzai was compared to a mountain dog who went hunting by himself, only to lose his way home in the snow. One of my dinner companions interpreted, "Karzai has been away, and with the Americans for so long, he has forgotten what Afghanistan is like." (Not everything was political. There was also a pair of skits about brides on their wedding nights which the *maskhara* performed in partial burkha drag. It was tame, by Western standards, but the mujahideen fighters practically wept with laughter.) Another riff involved militiamen taking part in a demobilization program but turning in only defective weapons. "We Afghans have to learn how to eat for ourselves, like cows, who, with their cuds, know how to find the good stuff to eat, and how to spit out the bad," the *maskhara* concluded. "One day, we Afghans will be able to spit out Karzai."

Ismail Khan was a test case in Karzai's effort to reduce the power of the warlords. It was Khan who, in 1978, sparked the jihad against Afghanistan's Soviet-backed regime by leading an army revolt in his native

city, Herat. He was a legendary battlefield commander against the Soviets and, later, the Taliban. After the overthrow of the Taliban, in 2001,
Khan became the undisputed warlord of the city and the surrounding
province of Herat, which borders Iran. He imposed strict Islamist dis-
cipline and kept the customs duties that were collected at the border
crossings, instead of sending them to Kabul. He used much of the
money to develop his city, and, before long, he was being referred to as
the Emir of Herat. Khan is not as gratuitously brutal as Dostum, or as
personally corrupt as some of the other warlords. But his defiance of
central authority and his close relationship with Iran were a source of
growing anxiety and embarrassment to Karzai and to the Americans.

Last year, during extended fighting in Herat involving several different militias—some were believed to have been acting on Karzai's
behalf—Ismail Khan's son was killed, and his men went on a retaliatory
rampage. At a critical moment, Karzai left Afghanistan to accept an
award in Europe, and Ambassador Khalilzad flew to Herat. Shortly
afterward, Khalilzad went on television to announce that Khan had
agreed to leave Herat and join Karzai's government. In December, Khan
became the minister of energy. It was a stunning turn of events, one that
increased Karzai's authority, even if it had less to do with his strength
than with that of the Americans who stood behind him.

An American diplomat in Kabul told me, "The institutions of the
country are still very weak, and so the fact that the US enjoys a lot of
credibility here was a factor." He added, "The shadow use of force can
have a powerful effect on crushing the actual use of force. We had to
make sure we signaled to Ismail Khan and others that the US supported
the president and his decisions but that we also saw a way forward for
Khan. Finding roles that are dignified—and also more suited to the
new circumstances—is always an important part of these solutions."

Ismail Khan is a stocky, powerfully built man, with hard eyes and
a long, flowing snow-white beard. Upon greeting him, his aides and

followers kiss his hand. I visited Khan at his ministry, in a district of western Kabul that was heavily damaged in the civil war. "You know us as heroes of the jihad, but now we are known by the new title—'warlords,'" he said, smiling bitterly. "During the Soviet times, we were there in the fighting, feeling the fire and smoke of the war, and everyone was awaiting the outcome, wanting us to beat them. Those who call us warlords now were sitting in their air-conditioned homes. I wish they'd spent a night with us at the front line in the war. But I know that these things are being said and done for politics or for the benefit of someone." Khan gave me a significant look, and, as he went on, it became clear that he was referring to the United States.

Relaxing a little, Khan said, "If you go to Herat, you will see the good job I did there." He had built new roads, provided water and electricity, and opened schools—"for both boys and girls. There are fifty-four thousand girl students in Herat." Khan boasted that, in the short time he had been in his new job, "I've raised the electricity in Kabul from fifty-five to a hundred megawatts"—in contrast, he suggested, to the rest of the government, which after three years had been unable to restore basic services.

We talked for a while about the obstacles facing the government. He paused, and then blurted out, "The thing is power. Power is necessary to build, to do what I did in Herat."

I asked whether Karzai had power, and Khan answered by speaking again about Herat. "The projects that I started are still unfinished, and now there is insecurity, too. When I was there, women could walk in the city with their children at night. Now you don't see people out on the streets at night. In all this time, the government there has been at the service of President Karzai."

Khan went on, "I am very depressed. I was injured three times. There are fourteen bullets in my body, and eleven members of my family have been killed. I saw forty-nine thousand people killed in Herat.

In one day alone, during the fight with the Communists, twenty thousand people were killed"—Khan was referring to a vicious aerial bombardment of Herat, in March 1979, carried out in reprisal for the slaughter of Soviet advisers and their families by his forces. "It is only random luck that I am still here. So when it was all over I wanted to rebuild my city. I managed to do some. But since I left it's all becoming undone."

Yunis Qanouni, the Tajik politician who came in a distant second in the presidential election, told me, "The removal of warlordism is fine; it should be done. But people also want democracy, stability, confidence, balanced reconstruction, and economic expansion. The government does not have a proper national strategy. If you ask what is the national strategy, no one can tell you. One day, Ismail Khan is a warlord, and the next he isn't. It is the same with General Dostum."

We were sitting in Qanouni's living room. He lives in an imposing, well-guarded house in Kabul's northern suburbs decorated in an expensive, faux-Georgian style. Wearing a superbly tailored pin-striped suit, Qanouni seemed to have done very well since the fall of the Taliban.

"The problem as I see it is that the leadership is weak," he said. "No government in Afghanistan's history has had the international support this government has had. Karzai has been unable to take advantage of these opportunities. But maybe another person could." Qanouni added, "These next five years will just be a transitional period."

The drug trade, which has strengthened the warlords and corrupted Afghan officials, is in the background of any discussion of Karzai's administration. The sheer number of people who make their living from opium and heroin has made it politically difficult for Karzai to act. On this issue, he has not had the full backing of the United States. Until recently, the Pentagon kept American troops from taking part directly in counter-narcotics efforts, which were left mostly to the British and the Europeans. Nearly $800 million has been budgeted for counter-narcotics,

President Hamid Karzai in his palace, 2005.   SAMANTHA APPLETON

but an American official in Kabul admitted that the US was at a loss about how to solve the problem. Karzai has vehemently objected to one approach, the aerial spraying of poppy fields, because of its effect on farmers—a stand that seems to have irritated Washington. Last year, Karzai declared a "jihad" on the drug trade, and he has issued moral, religious, and nationalist appeals to his countrymen to stop growing poppies. He speaks wistfully of farmers returning to traditional crops, like pomegranates and honeydew melons. In the absence of a robust plan for combating the traffickers, it's the sort of sentiment that makes him look like a well-intentioned man but a powerless leader.

A top Afghan intelligence official told me, "What I worry about is Afghanistan becoming like Russia in the mid-nineties." He was referring to the proliferation of gangster capitalism following the collapse of the Soviet Union. There are some signs that it is already happening. Even in the capital, warlords, strongmen, and corrupt officials are carrying out land grabs with a kind of Wild West impunity. The same tactics used for so many years in Afghanistan's wars seem to have been redeployed to accumulate wealth.

In late 2003, the residents of a shantytown at the edge of Kabul's most affluent district were forcibly removed, and their homes were bulldozed by police officers under the command of Kabul's police chief. An inquiry by a UN official revealed that the land had been divided into lots for mansions and allocated to more than three hundred government officials, including twenty-eight of Karzai's cabinet ministers. Fahim and Qanouni were among the beneficiaries. Karzai fired the police chief, but perhaps it was one battle that he decided not to fight, or perhaps he simply forgot about it, because the police chief was given a new senior security job, and the building of the mansions commenced.

Because Karzai is distracted by a host of issues, it is hard for him to keep smaller promises, too. The day before I left Afghanistan, I went to see the Pamiris again. Their mood was ebullient. On their first visit to the health ministry, they had practically been laughed out of the building, but now they had once more been promised their clinics. And the rural-development minister had told them that, while there wasn't much chance of a helicopter, he was organizing trucks with food and blankets for three hundred families, and some shoes. When I called for an update last week, however, not much more had happened. Zalmay Khan was out of the country, and his assistant reported that, as far as he knew, the Pamiris had returned to the Wakhan Corridor empty-handed.

Hamid Karzai is not a warlord, as most Afghan politicians of the past three decades have been, and this is both the source of his credibility as a democrat and his great vulnerability—he needs the American military in order to have bargaining power. To a very real degree, Karzai is less a conventional president than something akin to a constitutional monarch. His lack of power has rendered him the public face of an administration that, despite the tension in recent weeks, effectively remains an extension of the US government.

Zalmay Khalilzad's departure for Iraq will present a test for Karzai: whether the president can function as a leader without the ambassador at his side. (Last week, the administration named Ronald Neumann, a diplomat based in Iraq, to replace Khalilzad.) Karzai still must find a way to balance his conciliatory instincts—the qualities that make him genuinely likable—with the need to be tough enough to confront warlords and drug traffickers and to make Afghanistan truly independent of the US.

As long as the balance of power remains in American hands, Karzai will appear weak to his enemies, many of whom feel that they earned on the battlefield their right to power, and who would not hesitate to use force to unseat him. In this light, President Bush's unwillingness to cede to Karzai's request for a face-saving role in the US military operations seems shortsighted. Barnett Rubin, a scholar of Afghan affairs at New York University, told me, "Karzai is the most pro-American leader you can ask for in the Muslim world—that is, he's trying to be a leader. But the Bush administration certainly isn't helping him."

In my last interview with Karzai, he told me that he had been in Tirin Kot on December 5, 2001, when he learned that he would become Afghanistan's president. "I was headed up to the top of the hill, because I was feeling very, very cold, and I said I will go up there and get warm. Just as I moved up, a bomb landed; the windows and the doors and everything collapsed on us, and it hit in exactly the same spot as where I was intending to go." Karzai laughed, and said, shaking his head, "God is great."

The bomb, an errant American missile, wounded Karzai and killed eight other people. "Nurses were cleaning my face of the debris, the blood," Karzai said. "A call came, and when I answered it was Lyse Doucet, of the BBC, with news from Bonn. She said, 'You have been selected to lead the government.' So—that is the day the Taliban also came to surrender. Nine, nine twenty, the call about Bonn. Ten o'clock, ten fifteen, the Taliban came to surrender. One hour."

But then I asked Karzai when he had really felt the power of the presidency, and he replied, "I don't know, I don't know. I still don't feel the difference, I still feel the same as if I were moving along, organizing meetings against the Taliban, or as if I were still in Tirin Kot. There's no change. I don't feel like the president or anything else—I don't care about the presidency or being president—I dislike power, I really dislike it. I mean, it doesn't exist for me, I don't feel it, you know? It's a cup."

He held a teacup in his hand and motioned with it. "If there's tea in it, I enjoy the tea."

"But not the cup?"

"I feel the cup—I don't see power. I don't get it. I don't know what it is."

# 10

## THE AMERICANS'
## OPIUM WAR

In the main square in Tirin Kot, the capital of Uruzgan Province, in central Afghanistan, a large billboard shows a human skeleton being hanged. The rope is not a normal gallows rope but the stem of an opium poppy. Aside from this jarring image, Tirin Kot is a bucolic-seeming place, a market town of flat-topped adobe houses and little shops on a low bluff on the eastern shore of the Tirinrud River, in a long valley bounded by open desert and jagged, treeless mountains. About ten thousand people live in the town. The men are bearded and wear traditional robes and tunics and cover their heads with turbans or sequined skullcaps. There are virtually no women in sight, and when they do appear they wear all-concealing burkhas. A few paved streets join at a traffic circle in the center of town, but within a few blocks they peter out to dirt tracks.

This chapter was originally published as "The Taliban's Opium War," *The New Yorker*, July 9 & 16, 2007.

Almost everything around Tirin Kot is some shade of brown. The river is a khaki-colored wash of silt and snowmelt that flows out of the mountain range to the north, past mud-walled family compounds. On either side of the river, however, running down the valley, there is a narrow strip of wheat fields and poppy fields, and for several weeks in the spring the poppies bloom: lovely, open-petaled white, pink, red, and magenta blossoms, the darker colors indicating the ones with the most opium.

One afternoon this spring, at the height of the harvest, I drove through the area with Douglas Wankel, a former Drug Enforcement Administration official who was hired by the United States government in 2003 to organize its counter-narcotics effort here. Wankel, who is sixty-one and has piercing blue eyes, was stationed in Kabul as a young DEA official in 1978 and 1979, during the bloody unrest that led up to the Soviet invasion. "I left on a flight to New Delhi a couple of hours before the Soviets rolled in," he said. "People thought it was because I knew it was coming. I didn't; I just happened to be leaving on a trip. But the Soviets branded me a CIA agent, and so I couldn't come back—until now, that is."

Working first with the DEA and then with the State Department, Wankel helped create the Afghan Eradication Force, with troops of the Afghan National Police drawn from the Ministry of the Interior. Last year, an estimated four hundred thousand acres of opium poppies were planted in Afghanistan, a 59 percent increase over the previous year.

AFGHANISTAN NOW SUPPLIES MORE THAN 92 PERCENT OF THE world's opium, the raw ingredient of heroin. More than half the country's annual GDP, some $3.1 billion, is believed to come from the drug trade, and narcotics officials believe that part of the money is funding the Taliban insurgency.

Wankel was in Uruzgan to oversee a poppy-eradication campaign—

the first major effort to disrupt the harvest in the province. He had brought with him a 250-man AEF contingent, including forty-odd contractors supplied by DynCorp, a Virginia-based private military company, which has a number of large US government contracts in Iraq, Afghanistan, and other parts of the world. In Colombia, DynCorp helps implement the multibillion-dollar Plan Colombia, to eradicate coca. The AEF's armed convoy had taken three days to drive from Kabul, and had set up a base on a plateau above a deep wadi. With open land all around, it was a good spot to ward off attacks.

Much of Uruzgan is classified by the United Nations as "Extreme Risk / Hostile Environment." The Taliban effectively controls four-fifths of the province, which, like the movement, is primarily Pashtun. Mullah Omar, the fugitive Taliban leader, was born and raised here, as were three other founders of the movement. The Taliban's seizure of Tirin Kot, in the mid-nineties, was a key stepping stone in their march to Kabul, and their loss of the town in 2001 was a decisive moment in their fall. The Taliban have made a concerted comeback in the past two years; they are the de facto authority in much of the Pashtun south and east, and have recently spread their violence to parts of the north as well. The debilitating and corrupting effect of the opium trade on the government of President Hamid Karzai is a significant factor in the Taliban's revival.

The Taliban instituted a strict Islamist policy against the opium trade during the final years of their regime, and by the time of their overthrow they had virtually eliminated it. But now, Lieutenant General Mohammad Daud Daud, Afghanistan's deputy minister of the interior for counter-narcotics, told me, "There has been a coalition between the Taliban and the opium smugglers. This year [2005], they have set up a commission to tax the harvest." In return, he said, the Taliban had offered opium farmers protection from the government's eradication efforts. The switch in strategy has an obvious logic: It provides opium

money for the Taliban to sustain itself and helps it to win over the farming communities.

Wankel had flown in from Kabul five days earlier to meet with the
governor of Uruzgan, Abdul Hakim Munib, about the eradication operation, only to discover that Munib had left for Kabul the day before.
Wankel was told that a sister of the governor had died or fallen ill—
there were several versions—but nobody believed this was the real reason
for his absence. Munib, a former Taliban deputy minister, was suspected
of retaining ties to the movement. And, Wankel noted, there were poppy
fields within sight of Munib's palace.

"We're not able to destroy all the poppy—that's not the point. What
we're trying to do is lend an element of threat and risk to the farmers'
calculations, so they won't plant next year," Wankel said later. "It's like
robbing a bank. If people see there's more to be had by robbing a bank
than by working in one, they're going to rob it, until they learn there's a
price to pay."

We came to a wide bend in the river, a stretch of good, flat growing
land with broad poppy fields. The fields were neat and well tended, and
the swollen bulbs beneath the blossoms on their long green stalks were
dripping with dark brown opium. A heady, acrid odor like stale urine
hung in the air. Small groups of men and boys were in the fields, scor-
ing the bulbs to bleed the opium. They stopped and stared at us when
we drove past, and then continued their work.

Before Doug Wankel could do anything in Uruzgan, he had to talk
to the Dutch. In a bewilderingly complicated arrangement, NATO
member states have been put in charge of military operations in different Afghan provinces—the British in Helmand, for instance, and the
Canadians in Kandahar. Since August 2006, the Dutch have been in
Uruzgan. A 1,700-member Dutch force occupies a sprawling walled
base southwest of Tirin Kot. Smaller bases within the walls house con-

tingents of Australians, US Special Forces, and the Afghan Army. Military aircraft land at and take off from an airstrip there at all hours. There are small firebases elsewhere in the province, but troops at the main base rarely venture far from Tirin Kot.

Suicide bombings and IED attacks, major features of the Iraq insurgency, were rare in Afghanistan until 2005, but they have become common, and not just in Uruzgan. On June 17, a suicide bomber blew up a bus in Kabul, killing dozens of people. Although a threatened Tet-style spring offensive by the Taliban never quite materialized, the level of violence has risen significantly. Some five thousand people were killed in the war last year, including 191 foreign troops and at least a thousand civilians. By contrast, half that number of people were killed in 2005. As the war gets worse, incidents involving the killing of Afghan civilians by American troops, unintentional or not, have increased, causing widespread discontent. In May, the upper house of the Afghan parliament called for an end to offensive military operations by foreign troops and for dialogue with the Taliban. Karzai has complained publicly about the civilian deaths, but he is dependent on the foreign forces to prop him up. (Thirty-five thousand troops from thirty-seven nations are now in Afghanistan under the NATO umbrella; seventeen thousand are American. Another eight thousand American troops operate under US military command.) Karzai seems isolated and weak, and his authority barely extends beyond the capital.

The effects of the war and the drug boom are evident in Kabul. There are more security barriers and anti-suicide-blast walls in the city, and United Nations personnel and relief workers must adhere to constantly updated safety guidelines and curfews. The rules are even stricter for American diplomats and officials, who live and work within their own new embassy compound. Meanwhile, in nearby Sherpur, a downtown neighborhood, dozens of gaudy "poppy palaces" have gone up—mansions owned by former warlords and by senior officials in Karzai's government, built on public land that had housed war-displaced families until they were forcibly removed by police.

The official corruption and judicial impunity that have taken root under Karzai are seen as his greatest failings, and feature heavily in Taliban propaganda. Two years ago, his government announced a plan for fighting the opium trade, based on "eight pillars," including building the justice system, eradicating the poppy crop, and funding alternative development programs that would provide seeds for other crops and credits for fertilizer. The plan is backed by a commitment of billions of dollars from the US, but so far there has been little to show for it.

A Western official in Kabul told me, "The narcotics issue is an example of the problems this government faces—corruption, tribal politics, and lack of central institutions. Here it's not *re*construction—you're starting from zero on a lot of issues. We're trying to impose all of it at once, and it's hugely frustrating." The official went on, "Right now you've got to work with what you've got, and here you've got people who've figured out how to survive through thirty pretty horrific years. There's a lot of dealmaking. We have to be realistic about whom we're dealing with. And we have to show we're going to be dogged on this."

In Uruzgan, the Dutch have advocated a policy of nonconfrontation and the pursuit of development projects. (The Dutch commander, Hans van Griensven, was quoted in *The New York Times* in April as telling his officers, "We're not here to fight the Taliban. We're here to make the Taliban irrelevant.") A European official told me that the Dutch had doubts about Wankel's mission; they feared that it might be counterproductive, because it was only about destroying poppies and did not include any of the other seven pillars of the national plan. "There was concern that it might crosscut other activities focused on security and development," he said.

Wankel was frustrated by the wariness of the Dutch. "Most or all

Europeans are opposed to eradication—they're into winning hearts and minds," he said. "But it's our view that it isn't going to work. There has to be a measured, balanced use of force along with hearts and minds." He conceded, however, that the Uruzgan operation fell squarely on the use-of-force side of the scale. Later, he told me, aid, seed, and fertilizer would be offered to the farmers around Tirin Kot, but not yet. Other Americans were frankly contemptuous of the Dutch policy, which they regarded as softheaded.

The Western official told me, "We don't have a lot of time here. If we don't get a handle on this soon, we'll have a situation where you can't get rid of it, like we had in Colombia for a while, where the narcos owned part of the government and controlled significant parts of the economy. And we have a lot of evidence of direct links with the Taliban. These problems, and organized crime, too, are being embedded here while they're talking about 'alternative development.'"

Soona Niloofar, a member of parliament from Uruzgan, found the debate over development versus forceful eradication somewhat abstract; she didn't think much had been accomplished on either front. "Before the Dutch arrived, I told them, 'You must do reconstruction and help the farmers.' And the Ministry of Agriculture also spoke about helping them with alternative livelihoods. But nothing happened," she said. "They have done little reconstruction. There is a big gap between them and the people." The Dutch presence was felt only around Tirin Kot, she said, and, as far as she knew, the only significant things they had done were to repair a damaged bridge and set up a women's sewing cooperative. (A spokesman for the Dutch government said that there had been other projects, including one called Cleaning Up Tirin Kot, which involved painting storefronts and helping with garbage disposal.) At the same time, security had deteriorated. "The Dutch policy is a very weak one, and it makes the enemy stronger," she said.

Niloofar, who is twenty-seven, is a striking woman with a strong face and high cheekbones, and on the day I met her, at the Parliament, she wore, instead of a burkha, a brilliant turquoise *shalwar kameez* and headscarf—all the more noticeable in the assemblage of drably suited and robed male MPs. The Taliban have targeted women in public life, including teachers at girls' schools, and a number have been killed. Niloofar said that she could no longer safely travel to her home in Uruzgan or stay there overnight.

"People are getting very angry with Karzai," Niloofar said. "At the beginning of the year, he promised to sack the governors where opium is grown." She smiled sarcastically. "Nothing has been done."

"There is a fairly strong consensus view here that eradication alone, in the absence of the other seven lines, will not curb poppy cultivation or opium production," Chris Alexander, a Canadian who is one of the top-ranking United Nations officials in Afghanistan, said. "But in Helmand and Uruzgan all of these steps depend on improved security, which must remain the overriding priority. The Taliban have partnered in intimate ways with the drug networks over the past two years. Their alliance deserves to be exposed for the opportunism and criminality it represents." He added, "This Taliban is no fresh-faced Islamist movement. It is a violent, drug-fueled rabble with a narrow and highly unappealing ideological base. Their defeat—or at least reduced influence—can open the door to a much more effective counter-narcotics policy."

After a meeting with the Dutch, Wankel returned to the AEF's camp, looking tired and exasperated. He had a map approved by the Dutch, showing a tight quadrant of land within which his team was to confine its work. It was miles away from the Dutch base. "They're as nervous as whores in a church," Wankel said.

THE ERADICATION TEAM SET OFF EARLY THE NEXT MORNING for their first day's work. There were nineteen Americans and a hundred

Afghans in a convoy made up of twenty-four all-terrain vehicles—similar to small dune buggies—eighteen Ranger pickup trucks carrying Afghan policemen, and four of DynCorp's white Ford F-250 pickups. I rode in a truck driven by David Lockyear, an amiable six-foot-seven-inch Tennessean in his thirties, known as Doc Dave. Lockyear, who had a goatee and was covered with tattoos, was a paramedic from Nashville who joined the Marine Corps after September 11. ("I was just pissed off, like a lot of people, and wanted to do something," he said.) He fought in the first siege of Fallujah, and in 2007 he went to work for DynCorp. He smoked a Marlboro and held a cup of coffee in one hand as he drove.

A great dust cloud formed as the ATVs hyperkinetically whizzed past us and the trucks kicked up plumes of swirling yellow powder. Picking up speed, Lockyear exclaimed, "This is redneck heaven. You get to run around the desert on ATVs and pickups, shoot guns, and get paid for it. Man, it's the perfect job!"

When we reached the target area, men on ATVs cut through the fields, dragging metal bars on chains, which knocked down the poppies. Other members of the team whacked at the poppies with shovel handles. Around the edges of the fields and on small hills above them, armed Afghan Interior Ministry policemen stood guard. Wankel had attended a *shura*, or council of local elders, a few days before to explain the mission, and a small group of local Pashtun policemen were on hand, but the AEF team consisted mostly of men from other areas of the country. Major Khalil, the deputy commander, was an ethnic Tajik, and didn't trust the Pashtuns. (Like many Afghans, Khalil uses only one name.) He came from the same village in the northern province of Panjshir as the mujahideen hero Ahmad Shah Massoud, who was assassinated by Al Qaeda two days before the September 11 attacks. Khalil described the area where we were as "the heart of enemy territory."

Doug Wankel walked up to an angry-looking farmer who was watching his field being destroyed and asked him, through an interpreter named Nazeem, how much he got for his opium. Twenty-one thousand Pakistani rupees for a four-kilo package, the farmer said, and he harvested three to four kilos per *jerib* (a local land measurement equivalent to about half an acre). He added, "I get only a thousand rupees per *jerib* of wheat, so I'm obliged to grow poppies." That comes to about $33 from an acre of wheat, and between $500 and $700 from an acre of poppies. In Uruzgan, the opium was sold to middlemen who then smuggled it out of Afghanistan to Pakistan or Iran.

"How long have you been growing poppies?" Wankel asked him.

The farmer looked surprised. "When I was born, I saw the poppies," he said.

When we were ready to move on, the farmer said, as if to be polite, "Thank you—but I can't really thank you, because you haven't destroyed just my poppies but my wheat, too." He pointed to where ATVs had driven through a wheat patch. Wankel apologized, then commented that it was only one small section. "But you have also damaged my watermelons," the farmer insisted, pointing to another part of the field. "Now I will have nothing left."

Wankel turned away. As we walked on, the farmer called out, "Are you destroying all the poppies or just my field?"

About a dozen men and boys gathered on a low dirt wall next to another field and watched the proceedings impassively. A young girl wiped away tears with her scarf and yelled angrily at a policeman. Nearby, several Americans were resting in the shade of some mulberry trees, talking to each other. One of the local men, who wore a black turban, said to them, "We're poor—we're not with the Taliban or anything. You've made a big mistake. Now we'll grow more against you." He added, "I have to feed my children."

Nazeem, the translator, spoke to the men in Pashto, and recited passages from the Koran proscribing opium. One of the men retorted, "The

Koran also says to fight against *kafirs*"—that is, infidels. His companions stirred and nodded.

A farmer approached Glen Vaughn, one of the DynCorp medics, and told him that he had pains in his back which made it hard to move his legs. He had gone to the Dutch base to be treated at the hospital there, but had been turned away. Vaughn, a stocky former fireman from Denton, Texas, began to examine him. As he did so, another man made a lunge for Vaughn's holstered sidearm. Vaughn jerked backward and the man dodged away, grinning. "I'll shoot you in the head if you try that again," Vaughn said in English.

Nazeem and a couple of Afghan policemen formed a protective circle around Vaughn. The other farmers, seeing Vaughn's alarm as a display of fear, laughed at him. Nazeem spoke to them sharply, saying, "I'm Pashtun, too, like you, and I'm not afraid of you." Staring coldly at him, the oldest farmer, a gray-bearded man, said, "You will be afraid when the time comes."

Back at the base camp, Wankel changed into shorts and a T-shirt decorated with the Stars and Stripes and an eagle, and lay down on the cot in his tent to read Bob Woodward's most recent book, *State of Denial*. On balance, he was pleased with how the first day had gone; it had been a good start. "It's not fair to judge the eradication program against the figures for drug cultivation, because it's really just getting off the ground," Wankel said. "Corruption is a huge problem, though, and no doubt some of the guys we're involved with are up to some stuff. But you just have to try and steer them."

ON THE SECOND DAY OF THE OPERATION, THE LOCAL POLICE, who were supposed to show up at seven, were forty minutes late and, when they finally arrived, there were only a few of them. This was worrisome, because after the previous day's foray there was more potential for trouble; the presence of the police was seen as a guarantee of local cooperation, and therefore of security for the eradication force. Mick Hogan, a tall, muscular man of fifty with a silver beard, who was Wankel's manager in the field, stood silently, watching the convoy get ready. Hogan was a veteran of Special Forces anti-guerrilla operations in Central America during the 1980s, and of the Bureau of International Narcotics and Law Enforcement Affairs' counter-narcotics programs in Colombia, Guatemala, and Bolivia. He remarked evenly that the late arrival of the policemen was "not a good sign."

The convoy moved out anyway. We traveled slowly in a long line of vehicles. I was in a Ford truck with Eric Sherepita, one of two DynCorp commanders of the operation in Uruzgan. Sherepita was a burly man in his thirties with a shaved head and tattoos, a goatee and a Fu Manchu mustache. The other DynCorp commander, Kelly, a former policeman from Arizona, also goateed, was driving another. The remaining DynCorp trucks were packed with guns and men, including two specialists in land-mine and explosives removal: a husky, soft-spoken Samoan named Suani, who often wore a sarong and draped a kaffiyeh over his head, like an Arab sheikh, and Anton, a Croatian from Mostar, who rarely spoke.

As we entered the nearest village, children gathered along the track waving and holding their hands out, and some of the DynCorp men tossed them gray plastic packages. "*Halal* MREs," Sherepita explained. "The kids love them." He threw a few, and the children scrambled to retrieve them. Some opened them immediately and began eating the contents, while others threw them under the tires of the trucks to watch them get squashed.

The area chosen for the day's mission had been relayed to Wankel and the DynCorp team by the Dutch only the evening before. The drive, on the opposite bank of the river from the camp, took nearly two hours. We bivouacked on some sloping open ground above a village on a bluff. Below were poppy fields and the river; behind us was a row of bare hills and, a half mile or so farther away, the steep flanks of the mountains.

Two helicopters, called Diablo One and Diablo Two, flew in and landed on the ground near us, disgorging a small group of television journalists, including Dutchmen and a couple of Australians, who were to film that morning's eradication work. They stumbled toward us, clutching plastic water bottles and their gear, and were introduced to Doug Wankel, who led the way down the hill.

Wankel climbed on the back of an ATV driven by Mick Hogan to get across a stream at the base of the bluff, and, at the last minute, one of the Dutch newsmen got on, despite Hogan's warnings that his weight would throw off the balance. The ATV cleared the stream but toppled off the steep embankment on the other side. The Dutchman leaped clear; Wankel and Hogan were pitched into the field as the ATV flipped over.

Wankel was on his back, and both his legs were pinned under the vehicle. Several of us lifted the ATV and saw that his legs had deep, ugly gashes; on one, the white bone of his shin was exposed. Hogan, unhurt, began cursing the Dutchman, who had vanished. Someone brought a stretcher, and Wankel, managing a pained smile, was carefully loaded onto it and carried to one of the choppers, which would fly him to the Tirin Kot base.

Policemen were already busy whacking and crushing poppies, using sticks and ATVs. They were spread out over several hundred meters. Unlike the day before, there were no children or any other civilians in sight.

AS I WALKED ALONG A TRAIL BETWEEN THE POPPY FIELDS, GUN-shots rang out. Men began running, taking cover, and looking up toward the village on the bluff; the firing seemed to be coming from the

American military contractors and Afghan soldiers on an anti-opium operation, on alert after coming under fire from Taliban gunmen in Uruzgan, 2007.   AARON HUEY

mud-walled compounds there. Kelly, the ex-cop from Arizona, yelled at me to take cover. I headed toward a stand of trees with Aaron Huey, the photographer who was traveling with me; from there we could no longer see any other Americans. A group of six or seven Interior Ministry policemen—almost all of the local police had disappeared as soon as the shooting started—ran past with their guns drawn, and we followed.

Moments later, we were in an open section of the village, and under fire. There were now twenty or so policemen, in small groups bunched up against mud walls, shooting in various directions. One of them had been shot in the shoulder and was bleeding. I tried, with Huey, to make a run for where I thought the American convoy was, but we were turned back by gunfire.

Some of the policemen began pointing at a distant farm compound. "*Dushman!*"—enemy—one yelled. They fired an RPG at the compound. The grenade exploded, sending up a large black burst of smoke and dust.

Major Khalil appeared, leading a few of the policemen and a prisoner in a brown robe; they had tied his hands behind his back with his own shawl. Huey and I joined them as they made their way down an alley and toward the fields. When we were in the middle of the poppy field, Khalil screamed, "Taliban! Get down!" Then he and his men, firing their guns, advanced, with us among them.

We could see the helicopters flying over the village and the river, seeming to leave the area. Several of the policemen asked me why they weren't firing at our attackers. I didn't know what to tell them. (Later, I learned that they were evacuating the television journalists.)

As we approached a steep hill, from which the Afghan policemen were firing rockets and Kalashnikovs into the village, Khalil told everyone in our group to lift our hands and weapons in the air, and he began calling out loudly, identifying us to the policemen above us, telling them to hold their fire. As they covered us, we climbed the hill to join them.

It had been about ninety minutes since the shooting began. As we looked for cover on the hill, Khalil directed his men to fire into the village. Bullets came cracking at us. The prisoner, his arms still bound, crouched next to me. There was a plume of black smoke; the men said that it was one of our vehicles burning. Khalil, seemingly panicked, ordered everyone to run. (He later told me that he had seen movement below and feared that the Taliban were about to surround us.) We headed for another hill, from which I was finally able to see the convoy, about a half mile away, across a wadi.

A group of men had gathered in a large foxhole at the summit of our hill, and I spotted Mick Hogan, who was looking through his gun's scope at the village below. I crawled up to him. Below us, I saw a man dressed in black move quickly through the village and dodge out of sight behind a wall. The men in the foxhole pounded bullets in his direction.

Hogan told us to get to the convoy; the Americans wanted to pull out right away. As Huey and I headed down, one of the Afghans came running past us, pointing to a hole in his trousers where a bullet had just missed his leg. I congratulated him on his good luck. Then I spotted Kelly driving one of the white pickups and we got in with him.

We had to get back across the river, but the route we had used that morning was too dangerous; some Afghan policemen had just been ambushed in an attempt to head that way. Our way to the river cut between two walled orchards, and the convoy, a long line of slow-moving trucks, was taking fire from both sides. Kelly called the helicopters on his radio, and soon we heard the grinding sound of the helicopters' miniguns—.30-calibre machine guns that fire up to four thousand rounds per minute.

When we reached the river's edge, we saw that one of the white pickups was stranded in the water and some of the ATVs were submerged. Men were clambering about—trying to hold on to vehicles, calling for towropes—and returning fire. Kelly stopped midstream to help them. Two of the ATVs were towed out, but the others, and the pickup, were abandoned. The DynCorp men ripped the radio out of the pickup so that the Taliban wouldn't take it. Kelly managed to get his truck to the other side, where the shooting continued.

Nearby, a DynCorp crew had opened full automatic fire on a group of gunmen who had moved from deeper in the orchard to the tree line on the opposite bank and were shooting at us. Aaron Huey and I took cover behind a truck as Kelly joined the fight. Rockets exploded near the Diablos, and then the choppers disappeared. (They had both been hit several times, but made it back to the base in Tirin Kot, one with a fire on board.) After a few more minutes, the decision was made to retreat.

The road was almost obscured by the dust kicked up by the trucks in front of us. We passed another orchard, and, again, there were gunshots from both sides of the road. In the back of our truck, Bulmaro Vasconcelos, a machine-gunner from Hemet, California, fired into the orchard with a heavy machine gun. I saw a military cap in the road in front of us, and then a man lying face down. We couldn't tell if he was alive or dead, and swerved to avoid running over him. It was one of the Afghan policemen. Kelly yelled for the truck behind us to pick him up.

A few seconds later, the window on Kelly's side exploded and he yelled, "Shit! I've been hit!" He grabbed his leg, but kept driving, feeling the leg with one hand. He looked at the hand: There was no blood. The bullet, evidently slowed by the metal door, had not pierced his skin. "I'm all right," he said. A bullet hit my side of the truck, and another struck the back. A minute or two later, we were out of the orchards and into more open territory, headed toward the camp. For the first time in four hours, there was no shooting.

About ten minutes after we got back to camp, we heard loud explosions coming from the river. The Dutch had dispatched an Apache helicopter to destroy the abandoned pickup with a Hellfire missile.

In addition to the man we had found in the road, who had been shot in the head and was barely alive, four Afghan policemen had been shot, of whom two were critically wounded. One was spouting blood from the femoral artery in his right leg. Another had been shot in the lung and the liver. Sylvester Pocius, known as Sly, another goateed Dyn-Corp contractor, had been grazed on the neck by a bullet that ricocheted off the bolt of his gun. The wounded were rushed into camp for emergency treatment and driven to the Special Forces hospital. (A month later, the policeman who had been shot in the liver died of his wounds.)

Later, Major Khalil said that he had been informed that eleven other Afghans were wounded and eight killed during the attack. There was conflicting information about the identities of the dead, and uncertainty about whether the reports were accurate, but the victims were said to have included an old woman, or possibly an old man, and a twelve-year-old girl.

THE ERADICATION TEAM REMAINED IN CAMP UNDER A TIGHT security lockdown for ten days. The camp was set up like a kraal, with thirty-odd trucks parked in tight groups to form a large, fanlike defensive circle. Within this perimeter, the team members pitched their tents, with the DynCorp men in one area and, in another area, the Afghan police, some of whom slept on cots in the backs of trucks. Each group had its own cookhouse tent and its own toilet truck. The Americans also had a shower truck and a laundry truck. Beyond the camp, at each point of the compass, Nepalese Gurkhas hired by DynCorp maintained sentry positions in foxholes and in sandbagged machine-gun nests on the roofs of trucks.

The DynCorp men spent their time swapping stories, watching DVDs, surfing the web, and catching up on email; the camp, which had its own satellite gear, was wireless. Camp life soon acquired a *Groundhog Day* routine. Every afternoon, Pocius and Vasconcelos lifted weights, and then Pocius sunbathed. Tyrone, a fifty-seven-year-old logistics man, called his wife in North Carolina every evening, using Skype, and talked to her for hours. Kevin, a personable Ohioan, brewed Starbucks coffee that had been sent from home.

Most of the DynCorp men were Southerners or Midwesterners, and all but a couple were ex-military men. Almost all had children, and told me they had become contractors because they were able to earn a great deal more money than in civilian jobs back home. Their contracts obliged them to stay in Afghanistan for six-month periods, after which they received a month of paid vacation. Money was not their only motivation, however. Many spoke about wanting to recapture the camaraderie and adventure of military life. Being in Afghanistan also gave them a sense of purpose: They were patriotic, and saw themselves as participating in the war on terror.

Hook, a former army man and prison guard, had been hired by DynCorp just the month before. One morning, he said, "The real problem in this war on terror is you guys, the press. Ties our hands. The only way to fight this is to give them back the same medicine, like Operation Phoenix, in Vietnam. My Lai—what Calley did there was probably just on orders."

Tyrone, who was a Vietnam veteran, said he thought that the war could not be won the way it was being waged. "We're really not fighting it," he said. "The Taliban are just right over the ridge there. The Dutch are tolerating it."

By this time, news had circulated that Khalil's prisoner, who had been tied up and kept in a tent for four or five days and interrogated at the US Special Forces base, had talked. Allegedly, the day before the attack, men from another village had brought in weapons and a group of fifteen to twenty Taliban fighters, and had told the village men to evacuate women and children. (The AEF men estimated that there were forty to fifty attackers in all.)

Mick Hogan had debriefed each of the men who had been in the field on the day of the attack, and he was angry at the Dutch. They hadn't sent an ambulance for the critically wounded Afghan policemen, he said, or treated them at their hospital. From the beginning, Hogan said, the Dutch had issued petty rules that had made it harder to accomplish the mission. "They gave us a grid less than nine clicks by two to operate in, and something my time in the SF taught me was that unpredictability is the key to survival," Hogan said. "The more people know what you're doing, the more likely something bad can happen to you. They said, 'Oh, you can't go here, you can't cross the river there.' Makes you think that our so-called international allies are not our friends."

One of the senior members of the AEF told me that it appeared that the fields in the target area belonged primarily to the Alokozai tribe, leaving those of the Populzai—Karzai's tribe—relatively untouched. "So the Dutch, wittingly or unwittingly, appear to be favoring the Populzai," he said. "By targeting the Alokozai, it was almost mandated that they would retaliate."

After hearing so many recriminations, I tried to arrange an interview with the Dutch military. They declined to speak to me while I was in Uruzgan. But when I returned to Kabul I spoke to a European official based in Afghanistan, who dismissed the reports that the Dutch had been unwilling to treat the wounded; the problem was that their hospital had been full at the time, and the Special Forces hospital had had space available. (Later, a Dutch government spokesman said that they had never received a formal request for an ambulance. The spokesman also said that the target area was selected in conjunction with the Afghan government and others in the international community, and was meant to be "tribal neutral," although there were other factors at work, including security and the richness of the fields.)

The ambush, the European official said, should not have surprised anyone, especially that late in the season. "You can put the eradication team wherever you want, but it's not really a fighting force," he said. "If you get attacked, you can only retreat."


ONE PROBLEM WITH ERADICATION OPERATIONS SUCH AS THE one in Uruzgan is that they tend to set up confrontations between armed men and poor farmers: The only American a farmer ever meets might be the one who is destroying his harvest, rather than someone who is building a school or a clinic. Another problem is that knocking down or plowing under the flowers is time-consuming. "The per-acre cost of forced eradication is also excruciatingly high," Chris Alexander said.

A way around this would be to spray the poppies with chemicals from the air, as coca is eradicated in Colombia. This is a highly controversial approach, however, because of its indiscriminate destruction of crops and the uncertainty about its health effects. As a compromise, the Americans have strongly advocated ground spraying from tractors. The Western official said, "You have to get past manual eradication and discuss chemical spraying. The Europeans are adamantly opposed—just look at the whole genetically-modified-crop debate in Europe. If they decided to spray over the next few months, we would need to have an information campaign on spraying, telling the Afghans they're not going to have two-headed babies but also telling them so in Europe, in The Hague and in Rome."

The official said that last year Karzai had authorized ground spraying, but, under pressure from the Europeans, decided to wait. "Karzai is balancing a lot on this. If the international community goes to him in a united front, he can make the hard decision. But on this issue we weren't united, and he couldn't make the decision."

The narcotics issue, like almost every other piece in the Afghan jigsaw puzzle, poses a conundrum to the Americans. While attempting to pacify Afghanistan, they must stabilize it politically and rebuild it, too;

as the eradication issue shows, the actions required for one can under-
mine the other. Added to this is the absence of a unified international
strategy, and the resultant infighting between the US and its allies.
There is disunity not only on the opium problem but on how to fight
the war. Doug Wankel said, "Americans have this image of being
cowboyish and pushy, and we've suffered in this from what's happened
in Iraq."

Distracted by Iraq, the US only belatedly began serious counter-
narcotics and reconstruction efforts in Afghanistan. In the vacuum, the
Taliban returned, and most of the foreign experts and Afghan officials
I met with acknowledged that they, not NATO or the Karzai government, held the initiative. No one speaks with any assurance about
"winning"—only about the long road ahead. In Chris Alexander's carefully phrased appraisal, "The trend is not monolithically positive."

Karzai, in his efforts to mollify his restive fellow Pashtuns, has
made conciliatory gestures to the Taliban, which have alienated Tajiks
and Uzbeks who helped him come to power. There is the danger of a
broader divide between north and south. A coalition of former warlords
and politicians predominantly from the north recently formed an opposition front to challenge Karzai, who is up for reelection in 2009. A
group of retired generals—again, mostly Northerners—have called for
a more hard-line approach in the war against the Taliban. While in Afghanistan, I traveled several hours north of Kabul to the Panjshir Valley, and met with Ahmed Kushah, a nephew of the assassinated Ahmad
Shah Massoud. Kushah was living with a band of armed followers high
up in the mountains, to prepare for the new guerrilla war he believes is
coming. He told me he felt certain that Karzai's policies, backed by the
West, would lead to a Taliban takeover, and he was preparing to defend
the north, just as his uncle had once done. He told me that although he
had no immediate plans to attack Americans, he would do so if they
moved against him. Islam, he told me, was his inspiration.

Among ordinary Afghans, conspiracy theories are rife. Major Khalil asked me one day, "If the Americans can put a man on the moon, why can't they defeat the Taliban?" His implication was that, if the Americans didn't win, it was because they didn't want to badly enough.

I ARRANGED TO BE ESCORTED TO THE POPPY FIELDS BY A LOCAL police unit, so that I could speak to farmers freely, without members of the eradication team present. The policemen, who arrived in a pickup, did not inspire confidence. There were six or seven young men, most of them wearing *shalwar kameez* instead of uniforms, under the command of a tiny hunchbacked man who walked with difficulty, using crutches. He wore a rakish turban and a dirty robe, and he spat constantly. Suppressing my misgivings, I went with them.

At the edge of a wadi, we found several men and a boy at work, harvesting opium. The policemen stood at the edges of the field as I waded into the poppies with a translator, a local young man named Saibullah, who had learned English as a refugee in Pakistan. Once he had explained that I merely wanted to see how they collected the drug, they were friendly enough. The boy showed me how he ran his thumb over the oozing bulbs and then scraped the gooey brown opium into a glass he held in his other hand. When the glass was full, he emptied the contents into a large bowl. It was eight twenty a.m. and the harvesters had been working since five a.m. It looked as though they had already collected about two kilos. Nazir Ahmad, a bearded man in a long, opium-stained smock, said that he had twenty people to support and four *jeribs* of land, from which he expected to harvest twenty-five kilos of opium.

The development projects meant to offset the loss of the poppies didn't benefit people like him, Ahmad said. "The Karzai government doesn't give the money to poor farmers growing poppy. It gives it only to its friends who grow it"—corrupt officials and landowners with political influence. (Many of the farmers were sharecroppers.) "We would be happy to stop growing opium if they would give us some help, and stop giving the money meant for us to thieves." Instead of receiving aid from government officials, Ahmad said, "if they tell us to break the poppies, we must pay them not to."

Ahmad's younger brother said that he had just returned from the harvest in Helmand Province—the source of 40 percent of Afghanistan's opium. The opium farmers there often had to pay bribes, he said. This echoed what the DynCorp men had told me about their experience in Helmand the previous month. There, after *shuras* with elders, the local policemen had guided them to certain fields while leaving others intact. Presumably, the farmers whose poppies were spared were well connected or had paid bribes. Chris Alexander told me, "In Helmand and Uruzgan, eradication has been subject to political manipulation and corruption. It has also proven virtually impossible to conduct in districts where the Taliban are relatively strong, thereby inevitably penalizing farmers in pro-government districts."

Before I left the field, Ahmad looked at me directly and said, "I know the opium is turned into drugs that destroy young people, and I am sorry, but we are twenty people and we have no help. We must grow it to survive. If we get help, we won't grow it next year."

Driving up out of the wadi, we had to wait for a convoy of three armored personnel carriers, with Australian flags, to pass. In Tirin Kot, we parked in the traffic circle at the center of town, where a large group of turbaned and bearded young men had gathered, waiting for opium farmers to come along and hire them as day laborers. The men looked at us with suspicion. Several covered their faces. One of the men was the farmer who had tried to grab Glen Vaughn's pistol on the first day of the mission. Saibullah, the translator, said, "We should go now—there may be suiciders." As we drove on, he said that there were Taliban among the men in the crowd: "They were the ones who covered their faces."

When we returned to the camp, I heard that a suicide bomber on a motorbike had blown himself up next to an Australian convoy, wounding a number of soldiers and civilians. Most likely, this was the convoy that had passed us.

THERE WERE DOUBTS ABOUT WHETHER THE ERADICATION would resume; the embassy in Kabul was not sure that it was worth the risk. The Americans had always been cagey about the number of acres of poppies they hoped to eradicate in Uruzgan, claiming that it "wasn't about numbers" but about making their presence felt. They had intended to spend at least ten days in the fields, and thus far had managed only one—in which, by their rough calculations, they had destroyed less than two hundred acres. (By contrast, earlier in 2007, in a monthlong operation in Helmand, they had destroyed an estimated 7,500 acres—out of an estimated 175,000 planted with poppies.)

"We've been and shown we can mess things up," Hogan said. "Sure, we've taken our losses, too, and maybe we lost the battle, but we haven't lost the war."

After a week, the DynCorp men were told that the Uruzgan mission was complete. The Nepalese Gurkhas slaughtered a goat in celebration. That night, however, Hogan reported that the US ambassador and the Afghan minister of the interior had decided that the team should not leave Uruzgan without a final show of force.

Major Khalil came to see Kelly. The local Afghan Army commander, he said, was worried about accompanying the eradication team into the fields—one of his patrols had recently been ambushed.

"So what are you saying?" Kelly asked warily.

Khalil suggested another *shura*, to get the cooperation of the village elders. He also urged that they move quickly, because the harvest was almost over—the fields were already "trash." Kelly said, "It's true, the fields are shit now, but that's not the point. The point is to go back in there and kick some ass."

Kelly told Khalil to set up the *shura*. Rolling his eyes, he said, "This is just the way it was in Helmand, with the *shuras* repeating themselves over and over again, all the same fucking shit. It's a stalling tactic."

Limping, but managing without crutches, Doug Wankel reappeared the next morning. He had flown from Kabul with Gene Trammell, the head of the DynCorp counter-narcotics program. Colonel Marouf, Major Khalil's superior on the AEF, met us at the governor's palace with the local police chief, Qassem. The errant governor of Uruzgan, Abdul Hakim Munib, who had finally returned from Kabul, arrived a few moments later.

Munib began talking about his commitment to eradication. "We've tried to do as much as we could, but we're hampered by lack of tools and equipment," he said. "I was happy when I heard you were coming." The Americans listened quietly, their faces neutral. Then Munib announced that he had met with the elders, and they had agreed to eradicate half their poppy fields by themselves—there was no need for the AEF to do it.

Qassem stood up. He said that there were two areas where eradication could still be conducted. Before he could continue, Wankel cut him off, and announced that President Karzai and the Afghan minister of defense had been informed about the attack on the team. "Kabul says it's very important for the government to come back and eradicate for one, two days in the area where it happened, to show that the government has the ability to exercise the rule of law in Tirin Kot," Wankel said.

Qassem said, "We can come and show you where to go."

"You will have to come early. We leave at seven sharp," Wankel said, standing up. "Thank you, that's it."

QASSEM ARRIVED ON TIME, ALONG WITH SEVERAL JEEPLOADS
of his policemen. I rode with David Lockyear, the Tennessean. Overhead, we could hear the whine of a Special Forces drone. We passed a
man on a motorbike; Lockyear exclaimed that he had a Kalashnikov,
and radioed to the Afghan police truck behind us to pick him up. The
poppy fields were on both sides of the road where we had come under
fire during our retreat, running toward the river on one side and toward
the desert on the other. Several fields were already brown, drying in the
sun, but others were still green. The eradication team entered the fields
on the desert side and began whacking the stalks with sticks.

Several farmers ran up to Colonel Marouf, yelling furiously, "We
are all Muslims! Why are you doing this to us?" Marouf told the policemen to keep them at the edge of the fields. Allen Barnes, one of the Dyn-
Corp medics, was standing guard nearby. He was wearing a khaki kilt,
claiming relief from the heat and some Celtic ancestry. One of the other
contractors called him a "gear queer." Barnes laughed.

Marouf called off the men once they had destroyed two-thirds of
the poppies—to leave the farmers with something, he said. The farmers
were released. As they left, one of them said to Marouf, "If we had
known you were coming to do this, we would have fought you." Calling
after them, Marouf retorted, "When you fight, you use your women and
children as shields!"

Governor Munib and the intelligence chief arrived with a clutch of
elders. They made their way to a shady spot under a mulberry tree at the
edge of a field and sat down. I saw the hunchbacked police commander
approach Munib and kiss his hand. Wankel went over and told Munib
that the plan for the next day was to destroy poppies on the other side
of the road, down by the river, where the fields were bigger and richer,
in order to be "fair." Munib just nodded.

Afterward, I asked Munib about the links between the Taliban and the opium trade; he had, after all, been a deputy minister in the Taliban regime.

"In the areas where the poppies are cultivated and there are Taliban, it is under their influence. But elsewhere it is not fully so," Munib said. "We know that the Taliban are telling the people to oppose the government's eradication strategy, but, as you also know, the Taliban, when they were in government, eradicated all the poppies."

He added, "When the Taliban imposed their decree, there was follow-up. They were capturing and punishing people, so the people stopped growing opium. Also, there was no opposition—the Taliban had all the power."

MUNIB AND THE ELDERS DID NOT SHOW UP THE NEXT DAY. QAS-sem and his local policemen appeared, however, with a village councilor. They led the eradication force to the same side of the road where we had been the day before. Doug Wankel was furious. After the policemen had spent half an hour whacking one small field with their sticks, he told them to stop. He said again that he wished to eradicate poppies in the fields toward the river. The councilor told Wankel that he would not accompany the men if they went on that side of the road, nor could he guarantee their safety.

Wankel insisted. He ordered Major Khalil and the DynCorp men to set up a good security perimeter. Qassem and his men stayed behind. Wankel and Trammell and a group of men, guns drawn, walked down into the fields below, a checkerboard of green wheat and luxuriant poppies. After a few minutes, Marouf received a call from Qassem on his field radio saying that he and his men were pulling out. Alarm spread among the Americans and the Afghan policemen who were with us.

"Someone powerful obviously controls this area," Wankel told

Trammell. "The local authorities' leaving has sent out the message that we're unsafe and can be attacked. We should go."

We climbed back up the bluff. Qassem was standing there with several of his men. Doug Wankel didn't approach him. Marouf went to talk to Qassem, and then came back and told Wankel, "The police say you can eradicate *there*"—he pointed up to the other side of the road.

"Fuck the police," Wankel snarled, and he turned and walked away. He told his men that it was over.

I walked past one of the jeeps where some of Qassem's policemen, dressed in robes and sparkly skullcaps, were laughing and talking with the opium growers. I caught a whiff of something burning as I passed. They were smoking hashish.

Back at camp, everyone was in a bad mood. Hook, the former prison guard, remarked, "We ought to take all those guys and hang them in public, beginning with the governor." He laughed, and added, "Good thing I'm not an idealist—I'm just here for the money."

# 11

## DAY OF THE SUPERWADI

As the Taliban have refined their war-making skills and escalated their attacks, US military bases in Afghanistan have come to resemble sci-fi movie sets, a surreal blend of the primitive with the futuristic. Combat Outpost Terminator, in the district of Maiwand, a little under forty miles west of the city of Kandahar, is such a place. An almost imperceptible intrusion on a dun-colored desert plain, the base, inhabited by some four hundred men, has fifteen-foot-high walls made out of stacked-up Hesco barriers—large canvas and wire mesh boxes filled with rocks and dirt—abutted here and there by primitive-looking watchtowers, and a skyline broken by radar and digital telecommunications masts. Inside, three hundred American soldiers live in large tents laid out in rows, alongside a hundred or so Afghan soldiers.

Everything at Terminator is both high-tech and utilitarian. Instead

This chapter was previously unpublished but written and prepared for publication in *The New Yorker* as "Letter from Maiwand," November 2010.

of the powder-fine gray moondust that blankets the desert floor outside the base, a blanket of industrial-grade gravel covers the ground. Staff offices are tents or constructed out of banged-together plywood, inside which officers view satellite surveillance video on plasma screens, and plot out operations on laptop computers. There is a chow tent, a gymnasium tent with barbells and cross-trainers, and an internet shack. Here and there are men driving around khaki-painted armored earthmoving equipment filling Hescos in camp-expansion activities, and on forklifts, shifting crates of bottled water, prefab building materials, and boxes of military food supplies. Air-conditioning ducts and electrical cables stretch from large metal relay boxes into each tent. Green and gray plastic latrines stand in huddled ranks around the edges of the base. Once a day, a stinkwagon operated by a pair of local Pashtun men rattles into camp and, using special hoses, sucks up their contents, and makes its way noisily and pestilentially along the graveled lanes of the camp. They are roving-eyed chancers and do not inspire feelings of trust; a detail of armed soldiers watch over them as they go about their smelly business.

In a mustering yard sit a couple dozen huge Stryker and newer MRAP (mine-resistant ambush-protected) military vehicles, painted desert yellow and built with angled V-shaped hulls to better withstand the explosions set off by the Taliban's IEDs.

A constant humming sound comes from all the generators, the idling engines, and the buzz of men who live day in and day out in constant preparation for war. Occasionally there are explosions, too, not always explained, and the frequent sound of high-flying aircraft. Jets give off distant full-sounding roars and whooshes that fade quickly while drones emit an irritating high-pitched whine that persists for long periods. At least several times a day, military choppers come in and land amid great storms of dust and then, like lethal metallic insects, clatter out and away again.

The Americans are in their late teens and early twenties, and many have the doughy muscularity of young men who spend their days lifting weights and eating protein powder and living off carbs and red meat. The shorter, smaller-bodied Afghans look undernourished and scrawny by comparison. The Americans walk around in wide-elbowed alpha male struts; very conscious of their carriage, they seek to project an image of physical strength. The Afghans, by contrast, are more discreet in their movements, and seem instead to want to deflect, not attract, attention. While many of the Afghans wear beards and have shaggy hair, the Americans have the short back and sides and oddly tufted top-of-head haircuts that are US Army style.

Every afternoon, a couple of young Americans take out a laptop and a drone—it is the size of a model aircraft—and they send it up, flying, to soar high above and to wheel about, sending back real-time video of the surrounding desert and the nearby wadi, a dry riverbed, which cuts through a sprawling farming community of mud-walled compounds, irrigation ditches, and fields of marijuana, grapevines, and opium, and peters out in the bushy flood scree of the Arghandab river valley. The wadi is dry in October, but when it runs with water, the river it feeds, the Arghandab, is Kandahar's main lifeline, and the labyrinth of farming villages that are clustered along its banks are the heartland of today's Taliban insurgency.

Just beyond the wadi's end, the great Registan desert begins, climbing hundreds of feet up into the air from the riverbed to meet the unrelentingly blue horizon in an undulating rise of rose-colored sand. The Americans call it "the Reg."


ON THE MORNING OF OCTOBER 7, A FUNERAL WAS HELD AT COP Terminator for Joseph T. Prentler, a young man from Fenwick, Michigan, killed three days earlier when he drove over an IED just outside the base. He was a driver for his company commander, what the army calls

a specialist, one rank below sergeant for an enlisted man. Prentler's photograph, blown up and mounted and set on a stand, showed a young
man with a pleasant full-cheeked face and wearing glasses, posed in his
uniform in front of an American flag, and next to it, the yellow flag of
his regiment.

Prentler was born on February 11, 1990, and he died on October 4,
2010; he was still four months short of his twenty-first birthday. He had
joined up right out of high school. As Prentler's friends, young soldiers
like himself, stepped up to a podium that had been set up, and spoke
about him, quite a few soldiers cried. One of the three speakers was especially distraught; he had been Prentler's closest friend, and he spoke
of him with his voice breaking, how Prentler had been the funny one,
how he'd always been ready to party, and, when they had had their
nights off, back in Germany where they had been based before being deployed to Afghanistan, back in June, he had invariably gotten dressed
in a pink shirt that was too small for him. The other soldiers hugged the
soldier who told this story as they stepped up to pay their respects.

Three Afghan Army officers came and stood for a time next to
Lieutenant Colonel Bryan Denny, the tall and lanky commander of
the Third "Wolfpack" Squadron of the Second Cavalry Regiment that
Prentler had belonged to. The Afghans looked skinny and a little lost
in their uniforms, which were greener and more old-fashioned-looking
than the Americans' digital desert camouflage. They looked as if they
felt awkward, too, as if they were not certain they were welcome. No one
spoke to them, and, after a time, as the ceremony went on, and scores of
soldiers came up in pairs, stepping forward to kneel and pray briefly before the small altar made for Prentler, they vanished.

A recording of Scottish bagpipes playing "Amazing Grace" over the
camp's PA system, over and over, in a continuous loop, elevated the occasion and made it more poignant too. Soldiers stood stiffly with overly
taut faces that were on the verge of crumpling; some had teary eyes, and

swallowed repeatedly. A few wiped their eyes. From Lieutenant Colonel Denny's bowed face, the tears streamed openly.

Afterward, a young officer, who looked not much older than Prentler had been, stood fussing around the altar; he asked what I thought of the picture—it was one he'd taken himself. One of the men had criticized it, he said; they had said the portrait was too bleached out, or something. I reassured him, telling him that it was fine; it showed Prentler's smile and his convivial spirit, which his friends had spoken about, and that meant everything at such times. He nodded, smiling, seeming to eat up my words. I asked him about the medals and insignias that some of the men had stripped off their uniforms and laid on the little altar. The items would be sent to Prentler's mother, he explained, along with his uniform and personal effects. Not the *actual* uniform, he added, explaining that it was terrible what an IED could do to a man's body, and in Prentler's case, there was not any uniform left to send. They would send her a new uniform. He had also gone through all of Prentler's personal belongings, he said, to make sure there was nothing that might offend or hurt the feelings of his survivors. It was a routine they always did with all the dead soldiers, out of a sense of compassion, and also tact, for their relatives. Along with the remains, the items were then sent to a special place in Delaware, where other army personnel went through everything again, just in case. They went through his laptop, if he had one, his letters. They always did that.

Lieutenant Colonel Denny was standing on his own, and some of the soldiers were going up to him to give their respects. It was as if he had assumed the role of Prentler's absent father and mother. Denny was wearing his regimental hat, a wide-brimmed black Stetson adorned with gold braid and a brass insignia of crossed sabers. The sabers are supposed to evoke the regiment's warrior tradition on the Union side in the American Civil War, in the Indian wars that followed it, in the Mexican-American War, and in the war against Spain. (Formed out of the Second

Dragoons in 1836 by Andrew Jackson, the regiment's first operation was against the Seminole Indians.) Denny's face was tight and pink. His clear blue eyes met mine. I said I was sorry about his loss. He thanked me quickly and looked away, blinking and swallowing, and said no more.

PRENTLER WAS THE FIRST FATALITY IN DENNY'S SQUADRON since it had arrived in Maiwand from Germany a little over three months earlier. They had suffered a few injuries, almost all from IEDs, and especially in the past two weeks, ever since Denny had ordered his men out of Terminator and into the wadi to erect a mile-long Hesco wall down along one of its banks, all the way to where the Arghandab begins. The idea was to cut off the Taliban's so-called ratlines between Helmand and Kandahar; it seemed that they used the river, and the network of villages strung along it, to move back and forth, which meant that Maiwand was strategically located. With NATO's long-awaited "Dragon Strike" offensive against the Taliban in and around Kandahar finally having begun in mid-September—with the brunt of the action focused on Zhari and Panjwai, a network of villages west of the city of Kandahar, and in the Arghandab Valley to the north—it was Denny's task to cut off the Taliban's escape to the west. Terminator had been built for that purpose, and since the wall had gone up in the wadi—with a few Afghan and American troops sharing a bivouac or two along its length (and a tiny outpost, "Golden," set up a few hundred yards beyond, in the Reg, to do overwatch)—Denny's men had been hitting IEDs every day, virtually every time they drove out of camp. Denny himself had run over an IED the day after Prentler had died; it had blown his Stryker onto its side; Denny had bruised his legs, but he and the men with him had been lucky; no one was seriously injured. Denny, an athletic forty-two-year-old, said ruefully that the fact that his legs were still hurting was a reminder that he was "not twenty anymore."

Denny is from a farming family of German Irish extraction—"They still make their own sausages," he told me with a flash of self-deprecating pride—and he was born and raised in Oxford, North Carolina, where his parents and siblings still live. He is the only soldier in the family, and pursued a military career against their wishes, he says, because "I always wanted to be a soldier and nothing else." After joining the ROTC in college, he graduated from Appalachian State University in 1990 and immediately joined the army, just in time to take part in the first Gulf War. Later, he served in Bosnia. After a stint teaching and writing military doctrine, Denny attended the US Army Command and General Staff College, and in 2003, he earned an MA in military history. Denny has also done several tours in Iraq. Since 2006, he has lived in Germany, where the Second Stryker Cavalry Regiment is now stationed. Denny is married and has an eleven-year-old son. In his spare time, he likes to ride his Harley-Davidson motorcycle, and whenever he can, he travels to commemorative military reenactments on some of Europe's World War II battlefields. He is, basically, a redneck military geek, and proud of it. "I love it, man, just love it," he said more than once.

TERMINATOR IS THE MOST FRONTLINE OF THREE BASES CALLED COPs (combat outposts) in Kandahar's westernmost district of Maiwand, with one FOB, or forward operating base, Ramrod—a kind of rearguard headquarters—under Denny's command. Ramrod is a large base, with about a thousand men and comfortable facilities that include prefab container housing rather than tents, decent shower facilities, a properly equipped gym, and a PX that sells Red Bull and Snickers bars and Odor-Eaters, but Denny has spent little of his time there since building Terminator. His Wolfpack squadron was deployed under the US Army's Second Brigade Combat Team, 101st Airborne Division, in charge of the Combined Task Force "Strike" for NATO's Regional

Command South, which is responsible for all of southern Afghanistan. NATO and US counterinsurgency efforts are directed at undermining and isolating the Taliban from the civilian population, shoring up the Afghan government, and training, operating with, and ultimately handing control over to the Afghan military as quickly as possible, so that the NATO troops can leave. When I asked Denny, bluntly, if he thought his mission was possible, he wiggled his eyebrows and cracked a wry smile. "It's a tall order," he said. "But I'm sure going to try."

DESPITE ITS STRATEGIC IMPORTANCE, DENNY'S DISTRICT IS barely inhabited, with a mere eighty thousand inhabitants, and only one town, Hutal, the district capital, a scrubby little pit stop next to Highway One, the main road leading west from Kandahar to Helmand. (Terminator is situated about ten miles south of Hutal in the desert; Ramrod is about fifteen miles to the west along the highway.) Some forty thousand people live in and around Hutal, and Denny maintains a base there, too, called COP Rath, alongside a contingent of the Afghan National Army (ANA) and the Afghan National Police (ANP). Just outside Hutal, the police have their base in a very large, oddly shaped dirt mound that rises inexplicably up from the flatland next to the highway. It is what remains of a fortress built by Alexander the Great on his conquering sweep through this area twenty-three hundred years ago. In Hutal itself, there is another fort as well, of more modern vintage. Built in the mid-nineteenth century and called simply "the British fort," it is a crumbling compound with crenellated parapets and a series of domed and pillared rooms below. This is where the British expeditionary forces based themselves in 1880 during the Second Anglo-Afghan War.

It was from here, on July 27, 1880, that Brigadier General George Burrows set out with 2,476 British and Indian troops to intercept what he believed would be a rabble of Afghan warriors under the warlord Ayub Khan. When the two forces met in the desert hills about four miles north of Hutal, Burrows discovered that Khan's force had already taken the strategical advantage by seizing the hilltops, and had encircled his own force with some twenty-five thousand men. It was a bloody encounter, and in the end, after hours of close-quarters fighting, much of it in hand-to-hand combat, the British were routed. A tattered remnant of the British force managed to escape, having lost 969 men, and retreated all the way to Kandahar. It was one of the greatest defeats of the Second Anglo-Afghan War. A few years later, Rudyard Kipling memorialized the terror felt by a fictional British survivor of the battle in "That Day," one of his Barrack-Room Ballads. In one stanza, he wrote:

> I 'eard the knives be'ind me, but I dursn't face my man,
> Nor I don't know where I went to, 'cause I didn't 'alt to see,
> Till I 'eard a beggar squealin' out for quarter as 'e ran,
> An' I thought I knew the voice an'—it was me!

One afternoon during my visit, a group of American soldiers unlocked the padlock on the large metal gate at the main entrance to the British fort and proceeded to fire their weapons at paper targets that they pinned to some Hescos. As they fired, some young Afghan boys found a hole in the outer wall and, despite admonishments, repeatedly peeked their heads through to call out excited, unintelligible greetings. Waving their hands, the Americans yelled out *"Daanga,"* which means "Go away" in Pashto.

A COUPLE OF DAYS BEFORE PRENTLER'S FUNERAL SERVICE, I'D met Denny at a "security *shura*," a biweekly meeting he holds in Hutal

together with the district governor, the local police chief, and the intelligence chief, with elders from Maiwand's outlying communities.
Such *shuras*, which amount to air-clearing sessions about security and
other issues, are a key element in NATO's counterinsurgency program in Afghanistan, providing a venue for what it calls "Key Leader
Engagements"—a way to build relationships with local religious, tribal,
and village leaders in Afghanistan's complex society.

The Americans believed that some of the Maiwand community
leaders who attended the *shuras* came at the behest of the Taliban, to be
their eyes and ears. One of Denny's officers, Major Matthew Brown,
said of the arrangement: "We don't mind. As long as they're coming to
the table and we can discuss a way forward on issues, that's OK with us."
The Taliban, Brown suggested, were an ineludible fact of life in Maiwand. He reminded me that the district had been the birthplace of the
Taliban movement, emerging out of madrasahs established in the early
1990s in the villages around Zhari, where its leader, Mullah Muhammad Omar, was born and raised. According to Brown, the Taliban administration ran a shadow government in Maiwand, complete with its
own "high crimes Sharia judge," who served as the district's maxi-
mum judicial authority. It was a fact of life that NATO's International Security Assistance Force (ISAF) was still unable to compete
with, because the local Afghan government authorities had no judicial structures in place whatsoever. Eventually, it hoped to help get
some kind of a judiciary up and running, but meanwhile, he acknowledged, the US military was still on a steep learning curve when it came
to knowing Maiwand and its personalities. "We're still in the process
of trying to find out if the local leaders are corrupt," Brown said can-
didly. For the time being, for property disputes and other common
crimes and misdemeanors, he said, the locals took their problems to
the Taliban judge.

IT SOUNDED AS IF IN KANDAHAR, THE MORE THINGS CHANGED the more they had stayed the same. Hutal was just a few miles down the road from the hamlet of Pashmul, where, twenty-one years earlier, I had had an audience with a pair of Islamic judges who were implementing Sharia law on behalf of the Afghan mujahideen. At the time, the city of Kandahar was held by troops loyal to the Afghan government of President Najibullah and his departing Soviet military allies, but the various mujahideen factions, backed by Pakistan, the United States, and Saudi Arabia, had the city surrounded. The roads around the city were heavily pocked from aerial bombardments and littered with the charred hulks of Soviet military vehicles that had been destroyed in mujahideen ambushes. The war was a reckless, almost casual affair at that point; there was little frontal combat, but the mujahideen spent their days firing rockets into the city from their bivouacs in the desert, meanwhile running the affairs of the rest of the province according to their own laws—much as the Taliban do today.

There was a lot of aerial bombing taking place from overflying Soviet MiGs, however, which were constantly overhead. In order to reach the Sharia court in Pashmul, my mujahideen hosts had to drive across dangerously exposed open land, and zigzag at high speed down a section of the highway leading west from Kandahar. We turned off the highway into some farmland a few hundred yards from a besieged government fort that closely resembled the Alexander the Great fortress that was being used by the police in Hutal. It happened to be under attack at that moment; we could see bursts of smoke rising from around the fort.

The Sharia court was located two hundred feet from the highway amid a pleasant maze of grape vineyards and farmers' mud-walled homes. There, protected by a heavily armed honor guard of mujahideen fighters, two elderly *maulavi*—holy men—from the Kandahar mosque were sitting on a large black cloth that had been laid out for them under a tree. They had with them the tools of their trade: a pair of Korans and a pile of hadiths—interpretative works of the Koran.

It was January 1989, long before the astringent Taliban made their subsequent appearance in the area, but the *maulavi* had been exercising Sharia law for several years. My host, Mullah Naquib, an influential mujahideen commander in the Arghandab Valley north of the city of Kandahar, where I was living with his fighters, had taken me with him to see the judges in order to find out whether it was true, as rumors had it, that they had banned music in the province. It turned out that they had. The *maulavi* explained that they had decided that the playing of music should be prohibited among the mujahideen because they felt it might distract them from their Islamic duties in the jihad. Mullah Naquib absorbed their words with a look of solemn obedience, but he said nothing.

I sensed that the edict was not to Naquib's liking. The Pashtuns of Kandahar are great lovers of music, and in Naquib's camp, which was under regular aerial bombardment, his mujahideen, mostly adolescent boys, regularly listened to music. It was their only entertainment in a life that was otherwise dominated by fervent prayer and making war. The music they seemed to enjoy most was traditional Pashtun music, wild and rhythmic melodies played with drums and sarindas and songs sung by boys their own age crooning about unrequited love and the beauty of flowers. I asked the judges what other cases they had tried. They consulted their ledgers and informed me that they had sentenced eighteen murderers to death by shooting, usually by their victims' relatives; one thief to have a hand amputated; and two pairs of adulterers to be stoned to death. They recalled, after some discussion between themselves, that in one of the two cases, the man had only been flogged, because he was unmarried, while his lover, a married woman, had been stoned to death.

Later, back in his camp, Mullah Naquib informed his men about the music ban, and suggested that they adopt a "don't ask, don't tell" policy, in which they could carry on playing their music, but no longer play it in his presence.

THE *SHURA* WAS HELD IN THE DISTRICT GOVERNOR'S OFFICE, A newly built villa in a walled compound on the edge of Hutal's road junction with Highway One. With a smattering of American and Afghan soldiers tensely fanning out in front of and around our group for protection, Denny led the way on foot, striding out of COP Rath's secure confines and down the small main road, past a few gawking Afghan men and boys. Denny waved and smiled breezily, and walked on. Inside the compound, Denny warmly greeted the police chief, Colonel Naimatullah, who wore a gray uniform and wide-brimmed cap. Together they entered the villa, where the "DG," Haji Obeidullah Bawari, a stocky man in civilian clothes, was waiting. Another man with a black goatee and a furtively watchful expression, I learned, was Abdul Ghafar, the NDS (National Directorate of Security)—or intelligence—chief of Maiwand. I knew from remarks made by some of Denny's officers that they liked and trusted Naimatullah, but were still unsure how they felt about Obeidullah, the district governor. They still knew nothing about Abdul Ghafar or his background. Curiously, Denny's predecessors in Maiwand had not learned anything about him, either.

As the officials moved into positions at the head of a conference table set in a long, narrow meeting room, there was light banter between Denny—through an Afghan American interpreter who stayed constantly at his side—and Obeidullah and Naimatullah. Denny deferentially insisted that Obeidullah sit at the end of the table in the most powerful position, while he sat to one side, and Abdul Ghafar, the intelligence man, sat on the other. Then, amid a great scraping of chairs and friendly

back-patting, Denny made Naimatullah sit between him and Obeidullah. As the elders began filing into the room, the sly-faced intelligence
chief asked Denny how he had spent his night. Denny replied: "Well, I
don't have a new wife, so I slept well!" He grinned; it was intended as a
good-natured quip—Ghafar was recently married—and once Denny's
remark was translated, he laughed, and so did all the other men in the
room. With a pious expression but with eyes twinkling, Ghafar said:
"When your wife is not with you, God is on your side." Everyone laughed.

Next to Denny sat a State Department adviser, a couple of Canadian military men, and two lanky US Special Forces men who wore
shovel beards and outdoor clothes and made little eye contact with anyone else. If it weren't for the fact that they were in Afghanistan, and
therefore in context, they might have been mistaken for Appalachian
good ole boys.

The Afghan elders filled the chairs that faced Denny on the opposite side of the table all the way down the room. They ranged in age from
their early thirties, at a guess, to white-bearded wizened men in their
seventies. One had dyed his beard a shocking orange color. They wore
waistcoats over traditional *shalwar kameez* tunics and pantaloons, and,
on their heads, turbans, or else the little sequined and embroidered skullcaps favored by Pashtun men. They bore themselves with gravitas and
wore blank looks, but listened attentively to everything that was said.

After asking each of the elders to introduce themselves, Obeidullah
spoke to them: "As you know, the coalition forces are here to deal with
an emergency, to fight a war, but also to provide security to the population. Please help us on the security. If you help us once, we will help you
twice." He then asked them to tell anyone they knew who was "educated," but had left Maiwand, to return. His administration was short-
handed, and needed qualified people.

The meeting began. An old man stood up. He said that his three
sons had run away from home because they were "frightened of the co-

alition forces," and now he didn't know where they were. He said this in a chastising way. The intelligence man, Abdul Ghafar, said: "If they want to come back home, let them, and if they have no problem, they can go back to work. If they have joined the Taliban, that's another issue, and not our problem."

Another man complained that the coalition forces had built a road through his farmland without his permission. This provoked an acrid exchange between Naimatullah and the farmer. Colonel Denny's interpreter explained that he was accusing the farmer of being deceitful in order to make money off the Americans; there had always been a road there, he said. The farmer denied this. After listening for a while, Denny said that Abdul Ghafar, the intel man, should investigate whether or not the claim was true. If it turned out not to be a "preexisting road," then the US Army could write up a "land-use agreement" as it had done with other properties it was using, and the farmer would be paid for his trouble.

An elder from an outlying community stood up and complained that the coalition forces had shot dead a deranged man a few days earlier in his neighborhood. The man had been running around a field and was armed, but was harmless, he said. They had shot him from a helicopter. He went on to complain about other recent alleged shooting incidents. Irritated, Abdul Ghafar rounded on the speaker. If what he was saying was true, Ghafar growled, why was it that only he had come to the *shura*? "Why haven't they come?" he asked. "Do you know any of the victims' names?" The man shook his head slightly. He did not say anything, and sat down.

Two men were summoned by their names and came forward. They stood silently and expectantly as Denny ceremoniously produced, and then handed to Obeidullah, a large stack of Afghan paper currency, some 290,000 afghanis—the equivalent of about $5,000—which was then handed to them. It was explained that they were being compensated for the destruction of their shops in Hutal by some Afghan policemen who had run amok in an unexplained incident some months before. The shopkeepers received their money and retreated again with grateful expressions.

A gaunt-looking man in his thirties stood up next. He said his name was Sardar Mohammed, and that two days earlier, helicopter gunships had fired machine-gun bursts into his compound, killing his three-year-old son and wounding his twelve-year-old daughter. Denny listened closely and expressionlessly to the man, and then to one of his own intelligence officers, who came up to where he sat and explained his version of the incident. It seemed that there was a surveillance video, which he had seen. The American intelligence officer spoke to Sardar Mohammed, and said that he regretted the death of his child, but that the video he had seen clearly showed a Taliban suspect fleeing on a motorbike, driving right past his compound. Sardar Mohammed said that it was not his concern what happened outside the walls of his home. His children had been at home; bullets from coalition helicopters had been fired into his family compound. In addition to the bullets that had killed his son and wounded his daughter, he had found many shell casings around the yard.

Tersely, Colonel Denny told Sardar Mohammed that he would investigate the incident. Then he said, speaking loudly, in such a way as to send a message to everyone in the room: "This doesn't lessen the loss, but I have stopped counting how many civilian deaths have been caused by IEDs since I've been in Maiwand. The fact is, those who place IEDs seek refuge in the civilian population, and I suspect those helicopters engaged IED emplacers who were hiding in the population."

Sardar Mohammed said: "Yes, I was out in my field and I heard the noise of a motorcycle. So why didn't the helicopter shoot him? Why did it shoot into my compound?"

Denny replied a little defensively. He said that he wanted to clarify to Sardar Mohammed that his squadron did not possess its own helicopters, so those involved in the incident would have belonged to another unit. Then, looking directly at the father, he added: "But as the battle space owner of Maiwand, it is my responsibility to investigate, and if helicopters have done this, we will make amends."

Obeidullah spoke to the elders in the room. "Don't run from coalition aircraft. They don't know whether you are guilty or not if you are running." One of the men retorted: "The people run because they're afraid of being taken to Bagram."

Winding up the meeting, Obeidullah ceremoniously thanked Denny for his presence, and he intoned: "There is no sweetener to war, just blood. I'd like the insurgents to come to the table and negotiate. War will not get us anything. Peace is everything."

The police chief, Colonel Naimatullah, stood up. He bitterly criticized the local men who had demanded compensation money in exchange for the use of their land. "The coalition is having to do these things because the Taliban is using your land to attack them," he said. "What are all of you doing about it? Do you pay any taxes? Are you putting any men into the Afghan National Police or the Afghan National Army? No! You just come and complain and ask for money! Looking at you, just talking and growing marijuana and poppy and doing nothing to help us, I am embarrassed."

Some of the elders wore offended looks, but most of them remained as impassive as they had throughout the meeting, which had lasted over three hours. Everyone filed out of the room. The *shura* was over.


THE SITUATION THAT THE US MILITARY FINDS ITSELF IN IN AFghanistan is an odd one. Formally speaking, it has been deployed in Afghanistan since the autumn of 2001, and yet, in areas like Maiwand, it is essentially a newcomer. The Americans arrived there in mid-2008,

replacing a small Canadian contingent. With the troop surges authorized by President Obama, there are now five thousand soldiers where
there had previously been only fifteen hundred. The fact is that, until a
couple of years ago, there were very few Americans in the field in southern Afghanistan; the war, such as it was, was being fought by a fractious
and largely inadequate grab bag of its NATO allies: British, Canadians,
Dutch (now withdrawn), and Australians. The Americans, so to speak,
are still doing catch-up, and in Maiwand so far, their performance has
been questionable.

In a pre-trial case still under investigation by US Army prosecutors,
soldiers in Denny's predecessor unit, the Fifth Stryker Combat Brigade
of the Second Infantry Division, which was deployed in Maiwand in
July 2009, have been charged with involvement in several so-called sport-
killings of Afghan civilians between January and May 2010. Although
twelve soldiers have reportedly been implicated in the crimes, four have
been formally charged pending a trial at the Stryker Brigade's home
base at Joint Base Lewis-McChord near Seattle. Most of the alleged
crimes are said to have occurred at the instigation of Calvin Gibbs, a
twenty-five-year-old staff sergeant from Billings, Montana. In a front-
page story on October 1, the US Army newspaper *Stars and Stripes* reported that Gibbs had been charged with "conspiring with other soldiers
from the 5th Stryker Combat Brigade of the 2nd Infantry Division to
murder three unarmed Afghan civilians, allegedly for sport, and dis-
membering and photographing the corpses." Gibbs, who previously
served a tour in Afghanistan and two in Iraq, is also suspected of having carried out similar previous killings in Iraq. He is reported to have
a tattoo on the calf of his right leg showing a crossed pair of pistols surrounded by six skulls, each representing a different "kill": three colored
red, supposedly representing his Iraq murders, and three in blue, representing those he carried out in Afghanistan.

After comparing the potential consequences of the unfolding scandal to those caused by Abu Ghraib, the *Stars and Stripes* disclosed that army investigators were "scrambling to locate dozens of digital photographs that soldiers allegedly took of one another posing alongside the corpses of their victims. Military officials worry disclosure of the images could inflame public opinion against the war, both at home and abroad."

Although Maiwand's sport-killings had been prominently covered by the US and international news media, I was intrigued by the fact that, during the two weeks I spent with US troops in Maiwand, no one mentioned the case. I asked Lieutenant Colonel Denny whether the revelations had affected his relationships with the local Afghans when he had taken command, or whether he'd felt he'd had to make amends in any way. "No," he said. "This may come as a surprise, but no one has mentioned it to me, ever."

Given all of the challenges faced by field commanders like himself, a don't-look-back-or-too-deeply philosophy was probably the only way forward for Denny. Another time, after the security *shura*, he asked me for my impressions of Abdul Ghafar, the intelligence man. When I asked why he wanted to know, Denny said, "Well, it was just that that's the first time he's ever spoken up in one of those *shuras*." I asked Denny what he knew about Ghafar's background. He shook his head. "I don't know anything about him," he said. "Nothing?" I asked. He smiled and kept shaking. "Nothing at all." Surely his predecessor had debriefed him about his Afghan counterparts when he had assumed command three months before? Denny nodded. "They didn't know anything about him either," he said, shrugging. He added, as if his remark explained all the mystery: "Hey, it's Afghanistan!"

When I arrived at Terminator, all the talk among Denny's men was about the impending "superwadi" operation. It had been two weeks since they had erected their Hesco wall in the wadi; the results had been quick in coming. In a special *shura* meeting that had been held at the request of some of the elders from the adjacent communities, the locals

An Afghan officer working with the US military in Maiwand waves money at Afghan elders seeking compensation in exchange for relatives killed and property damaged by US military actions. October 2010.    JOÃO PINA

had complained that the wall cut them off from one another, separated farmers from their lands, and prevented shepherds from grazing their flocks of fat-tailed sheep. As a solution, Denny had agreed to construct two secure openings in the wall to allow for the free passage of "legitimate" civilians, farmers, and their livestock. In return, he planned to build fortified sentry posts in order to screen people. The work would begin on the day of the "superwadi" operation, which would also involve mine clearance, because in the days since the wall had gone up,

Denny's men had run across IEDs almost every day—including the one he'd hit.

Denny had used the occasion to suggest that the farmers contribute some young men to a "sons of the *shura*" initiative—or a local police force. (The growth of grassroots militias—aka "local police auxiliaries"— is a central part of the counterinsurgency strategy being promoted by General David Petraeus.) His overture had elicited no reaction whatsoever, Denny said, but he regarded it as a beginning. Before he'd built the wall, they'd had no interaction at all. Now they had something to talk about.

Denny had to go and brief General Petraeus, and left Terminator for a couple of days; in his absence, he ordered his operations chief, Major Ivan Salgado, to take a "reconnaissance" patrol to the wall. A short, wiry, easygoing man, originally from Hermosillo, Mexico, Salgado took me with him in one of the new four-seater MRAP ATVs, high above the ground, with a robotic turret gun. We wore earphones to be able to speak over the engine noise; Salgado sat next to the driver and I sat behind, next to the gunner, who looked continuously into an infrared computer screen that also functioned as his turret gun's targeting system. He moved a toggle stick, as in PlayStation, to move his gun-mounted camera around. (After nightfall, the driver flipped down a similar screen and looked at it—instead of out at the road—to drive.)

The purpose of the day's mission, Salgado explained, was to go over the wadi with a unit of Marine Corps engineers, who had arrived in Terminator with special armored minesweepers. They would determine where to clear, and also choose where to put the gauntlets in the wall. He quipped: "First there was the Great Wall of China, Hadrian's Wall, and the Berlin Wall, and now there's the Wolfpack Wall."

As we set out of the base in the big monster truck and were immediately enveloped in a fog of dust, Salgado spoke about the prevalence of IEDs, and said: "One of the issues we have is that women and children are putting in the IEDs." The gunner volunteered laconically: "We got white phosphorus for that, sir." Salgado replied: "Well the problem then is the counterinsurgency [formula] kicks in and you just have thirty, forty more insurgents to deal with."

Salgado said he'd been in Maiwand before, back in the "good old days" of 2004, when the Taliban had mostly gone to ground after being chased into the hills, and had not reemerged. With two platoons, "eighty-something men," he had been in charge of Maiwand, Zhari, and Panjwai—he named another district or two—out of Kandahar. "We just used to drive around in an open-top Humvee with our feet on a sandbag," he said nostalgically. "Different days."

WE TRUNDLED HEAVILY ACROSS THE MOONSCAPE, AND DOWN into the wadi; after half an hour, we stopped, and Salgado and I climbed out. The drivers and gunners of our small convoy stayed inside their vehicles, engines running, vigilantly surveying the terrain, while we walked along the wall. The Hesco wall had been set on top of one of the banks of the wadi, making, in effect, a twelve-to-fifteen-foot-high barrier. A gaggle of Afghan soldiers were camped along the edge. They did not look so much vigilant as concerned with mundanities like shade and food and water. Most of them sat listlessly in the shade of a sandbagged shelter, staring at us as we walked by. One man was boiling water in a big metal pot, using empty plastic water bottles to burn in lieu of firewood.

There were no civilians in sight; the village was a mosaic of low-level compounds and a small mosque with a megaphone—that was it. After a few minutes, a small boy emerged down a footpath. He motioned to the soldiers; behind him came an elderly man. Salgado recognized him, and seemed wary. He told his interpreter (they are called "terps" by the US military) to tell the old man to stay where he was, and sent him to go find out what he wanted. Salgado pointed to a small house and attached general store next to the wadi. It was a few feet from where Lieutenant Colonel Denny's vehicle had been blown up a few days earlier. The old man's house had been searched and found to have IED-making paraphernalia, said Salgado, and it had been sealed off. The old man, of course, had denied all knowledge of the IED materials. The terp returned and told Salgado that the old man said there were some things he needed from the house. Salgado thought for a minute and decided to let him come, but told the terp he wanted him watched.

After a few hours spent in the wadi with the engineers looking over suitable spots for the sentry points and gauntlets, we headed back. It was just before nightfall. Five or six minutes after our convoy had left the wadi, there was a dull boom and an explosion a couple hundred feet off to our left. The convoy stopped. The gunner swiveled his gun-mounted camera to take in the scene; I could see some figures standing next to a pickup truck. After some initial confusion, we learned what was happening. One of the Afghan commanders we had met down in the wadi had taken a secondary track and had hit an IED. It was a dud, apparently, or at least had not unleashed its full explosive charge; he was unhurt and so was his driver; their pickup, however, was heavily damaged and could not be moved. It would need to be towed. For the next hour, as the afternoon ended and night fell, our convoy stayed in place, as assistance was ordered from Terminator and a truck dispatched to retrieve the damaged truck. At one point, there was a muted crackle of small-arms fire up ahead; a voice in one of the vehicles ahead reported that they had received some harassment fire. We returned to base with lights off, moving slowly forward via the driver's infrared computer screen. Looking through my thick, bulletproof side window, there was nothing to be seen; it was pitch-black outside.

———

RELATIONS BETWEEN THE AFGHANS AND THE AMERICANS AT
Terminator were very poor. Denny's men grumbled openly about the
Afghans, whom they accused of being lazy, dirty, and of defecating
in the shower stalls. Denny conceded that the cultural differences between the two groups had not made their partnering easy. He also knew
that the "shower-shitting" incident was a sore point with his men, and
said he had requested separate shower facilities, which he hoped to get
up and running soon. When Americans and Afghans passed one another
on the camp's pathways, I noticed, they did not say hello, and they did
not sit together in the chow tent. One day, in the chow line, an American soldier came charging over from the nearby weight-training tent
and began yelling angrily at some Afghans who were in line for lunch.
He demanded to know, in English, if one of them had taken his sunglasses. The American soldiers wear special protective sunglasses called
Eye Pros. "Who's got my Eye Pros?" he demanded repeatedly. Smirking,
one of the Afghans produced the sunglasses from one of his pockets,
and said he had taken them as a joke. The weight lifter was furious and
screamed at the Afghan, calling him a thief. A hullabaloo ensued until
Denny's informal diplomat-in-arms, Sergeant Major James Bodecker, a
rangy man in his forties, mediated and warned the Afghan not to play
such "jokes" again. Barely mollified, the weight lifter stormed off.

I SLEPT ON A COT IN A TENT WITH EIGHT OF DENNY'S NCOS, ALL
in their early twenties. When they were not on duty, they spent their
time sleeping or playing war games. The tent boomed with the noise
of their on-screen avatars repetitively running, panting for breath, or
shooting and dying, all amplified hugely on a laptop's speakers. Their

shooting was punctuated by a cyber scorekeeper's voice that advised them curtly, "You're dead" or "Good kill," in an approving purr. They also watched DVDs, endlessly, and seemingly indiscriminately—everything from the vroom-vroom fast-car movie *Fast & Furious* to the animated feel-good *Kung Fu Panda*. Several of them slept a lot—overmuch, to my eye, even during the daytime. There was almost never any conversation between them. None of them cleaned up around themselves in the tent. Plastic water bottles lay where they dropped them; it was the same with food wrappers and used clothes. They behaved, in fact, as if they were clinically depressed.

After I had been in Terminator a week or so, I made this observation to Denny, and he did not dispute it, but pleaded mitigating circumstances. "First and foremost they had a good guy killed"—Prentler—"and that hurts; it doesn't go away for a while. Secondly, it's the enormity of the task they are confronted with. It's a Herculean task to do what I've asked them to do. It's tough to hold this wall and do it intelligently and to partner with the Afghans, and then not to see the fruits of their labor—and they have not yet seen the Afghan Army be successful—and that's tough on them. This is a tough place to be."

Denny conceded that the Afghan troops he was supposed to "transition" with exhibited some huge deficiencies, but he had detected one or two company commanders with leadership qualities he thought he could help develop; with luck and perseverance, he was hopeful, he said, that he could turn the situation around before it was time for him to leave next summer. It was important to him, he said: "I want to make our casualties count. I don't want to stay here twelve months taking hits and not have our casualties count for something."

"What's victory going to look like for you?" I asked him.

"What will make me feel good is turning Maiwand over to an Afghan force. At least in that little ribbon of it along Highway One and this little section down to the Arghandab. I want to be able to hand it off to an Afghan battalion and know they will be able to hold on to it. That's victory in my mind."

THE DAY OF THE SUPERWADI FINALLY CAME. DURING THE NIGHT, magnesium flares called "ilumes" were fired repeatedly into the sky from Terminator to light up the land below, just in case, as some intel had reported, the Taliban tried to bring fighters into the area or plant new IEDs during the night. Everything was set for dawn, when a dedicated Predator drone would be sent from Kandahar into the sky above; there was to be air support on standby if needed, as well. Just before daybreak, the whine of the drone could be heard overhead. A company of Americans went out on foot first, teamed with a couple of companies of Afghans, to take up advance positions in the wadi. I followed with Denny and a convoy of his men in Strykers and MRAPs, along with the two "mick-licks," special mine-clearers operated by a small crew of US Marines. By early morning we were in the wadi, watching as every few minutes the mick-licks went ahead and, like mechanical dragons, shot out their explosive devices on leash-like tongues before them, detonating mines in front of them. As the bombs set off, secondary explosions could be heard, and the sky filled with columns of dark smoke. A vehicle drove back and forth in front of the village, with megaphones belting out a message in Pashto on a recorded loop: "IEDs kill innocent women and children and other Muslims, so don't plant them. Thank you for your attention." In the doorway of a house in the near distance, a few children and women huddled, looking out. There were no men in sight.

After an hour or so of this, Denny led a task force on foot into the village for the first time. There was no one about. A hundred meters down the path, with his men setting up ambushes along the way, a combined group of Americans and Afghans went into the first compound.

One of the Americans had an explosives-sniffing dog with him, a specially trained Belgian hound. Almost immediately, yelling could be heard. I went into the compound. A couple of young girls and children were standing on one side of the compound, and a pair of teenage boys were talking with some Afghan soldiers; their squad leader was arguing with Denny's terp and Sergeant Major Bodecker. A handful of American soldiers, including the dog handler, were standing aside, looking nonplussed. As I came within earshot, Bodecker was angrily demanding a reason why the Afghans were not proceeding with a search of the house.

"They are saying they are not going to go on patrol with you guys," the terp said. He was upset. The Afghan squad leader was still talking loudly and truculently. Bodecker angrily raised his voice: "Yes you *are* going to do a patrol with us, we are going to assist you doing this patrol, and our dog, a military working dog—" But the squad leader interrupted, drowning him out; Bodecker said, "Let me fucking finish—" only to be cut off again, then he stepped back. The terp and the Afghans resumed their argument. At one point, in a very low and even tone of voice, Bodecker said to the terp: "You tell him to search the compound."

After some more shouting, it was agreed. The terp said: "Yeah, OK, they're going to take care of it." Bodecker said, "No problem." He asked the terp to tell him what they had agreed to. The terp explained they had agreed to let the dog in to sniff the compound, but without the Americans present, and the women's part of the compound would not be searched. I asked Bodecker if this was acceptable. He shrugged. It wasn't, but they needed to get on with the rest of the search; there were over one hundred compounds to go.

The "clearance" of the community continued for several more hours. In most of the compounds, there was no one home. Where the gates to compounds or homes were locked shut, the soldiers kicked the doors in. The families would be paid for the damage later, I was told; it was US

Army policy. It was very hot. The Afghan soldiers who accompanied the squad I was with seemed very unmotivated, and I watched as one man, supposed to be guarding the approaches as a search went on, dozed off.

Denny approached a man and his young son who were watering some newly furrowed sod in a field. Denny asked him what he was planting—corn—and for a few minutes, they discussed fertilizer and irrigating. Denny told him he was the son of a farmer. As we took our leave, the man said to Denny to take care, and to go with God.

Back in the wadi in the midafternoon, it was blisteringly hot. Denny took stock. All the squads had reported back; most of the community's compounds had been searched. There had been no resistance. Five mines or IEDs had been uncovered and blown up by the mick-licks, as well as one stepped on by a hapless dog at the entrance to a compound. Some homemade explosives ingredients were found in one house. Shots were fired at a group of searchers in a far corner of the community, but no one was injured. No one was killed or arrested, for that matter, in the entire operation. If there had been any Taliban around, they had mostly cleared out.

Just before dusk, Denny and a small group of men walked gingerly on a footpath that cut between ripe marijuana fields where the plants stood a good eight feet high. A young man they had arrested two weeks before as a Taliban suspect was returned to his father, who lived at the edge of the village to the east. His son had been arrested after "intel" had determined that several senior Taliban had met at his home. The Taliban had gone, but the son of the house had been taken in for questioning. Other than the information about the suspects who had come and gone, there had been no other compelling evidence to keep holding him, however, and the young man as well as his father had firmly denied all Taliban links. There had been pressure from the community in one of Denny's last *shuras* to free the youth, and so he had.

As the family poured out of the compound to greet the young man and take him back into their compound, his father, a bearded man with wary eyes, made expansive gestures of gratitude to Denny. Denny gracefully accepted the father's blandishments to drink some tea. Denny's soldiers set up a vigilant watch while he and some of his officers and NCOs sat down on a cloth spread at the edge of the nearest field. The father and another man dragged a fat-tailed sheep out between them to a spot about twenty feet away and slit its throat with a knife and then stood there, hands bloodied, praying, momentarily, as it shook and bled to death.

The sun began to set. One of Denny's men, looking through his telescopic sights, spotted a man standing a hundred or so yards away, in the next field, boldly staring in their direction. He guessed aloud that it was a Taliban officer, making his presence known. Denny mentioned discreetly that he had arranged for a show of force by an F-16 fighter jet, which appeared after a few minutes, roaring out of the sky; it swooped down low and blasted across the nearby landscape, shockingly close and loud.

The Afghans watched the jet unblinkingly. The freed suspect's father served Denny and his men more tea. As Denny rose to leave a few minutes later, he begged him to stay for dinner; they would eat the sheep they had just killed, he said. Denny politely excused himself, and the suspect's father, just as politely, accepted his excuses, with polite regrets.

AT ABOUT TEN FORTY A.M. THE NEXT MORNING, AN EXPLOSION resounded from somewhere outside Terminator. The word soon came back to base that a truck that was hauling lumber down to the wadi to build the checkpoints there had run over a mine. The driver, a young American soldier, had been injured. He was from another unit, part of a small logistics team that had been sent to Denny as backup for his superwadi operation. Denny radioed for a medevac chopper from the Kandahar Airfield hospital, but by the time it reached him, the soldier was too far gone. Instead of coming back to Terminator, the chopper headed straight for Kandahar, but the soldier didn't make it.

# 12

## FORCE AND FUTILITY

The first time the United States tried to kill Osama bin Laden was in the summer of 1998, in Khost, Afghanistan. A dusty, mountainous region in the southeast of the country, Khost was a hospitable place for radicals; the Taliban controlled the area, and Pakistan, which frequently supported Islamists, was just across the border. Bin Laden had recently built a training camp there, and invited terrorists from around the Muslim world—Pakistan, Kashmir, Chechnya, Saudi Arabia—to learn how to conduct jihad. The camp, which he called the Lion's Den, was situated in a place of some personal significance. During the anti-Soviet jihad, in the 1980s, bin Laden had participated in a legendary battle there between the mujahideen and the Soviets. The experience, he felt, had transformed him from the politically inclined heir to a construction fortune into a warrior.

This chapter was originally published as "Letter from Khost Province: Force and Futility," *The New Yorker*, May 9, 2011.

In May 1998, bin Laden summoned journalists to a press conference near his base, at which he discussed "bringing the war home to America" and expressed the hope that "by God's grace, the men . . . are going to have a successful result in killing Americans and getting rid of them." On August 7, suicide bombers trained at his camps attacked the US embassies in Dar es Salaam and Nairobi, killing 224 people, including twelve Americans.

Two weeks later, the Clinton administration struck back, attacking a factory in Sudan that was thought to be an Al Qaeda chemical-weapons plant. The same day, it fired seventy-five Tomahawk missiles from warships in the Arabian Sea at the base in Khost. According to the CIA, bin Laden was scheduled to be at the base that day, presiding over a summit meeting. Some twenty terrorists were killed, but bin Laden escaped; he had reportedly left hours earlier, alerted by a former chief of Pakistan's intelligence service, the ISI.

George Tenet, the director of the CIA, put a $5 million bounty on bin Laden's head, and, three years later, after the attacks of September 11, 2001, the United States invaded Afghanistan, in pursuit of bin Laden and his deputies. Whether or not the ensuing war has been intended principally, as President Obama says, to "disrupt, dismantle, and defeat" Al Qaeda, it has certainly been intended to prevent places like Khost from harboring terrorists.

In ten years, some things have changed in the region. As the American military has adopted the counterinsurgency principles advocated by General David Petraeus, the soon-to-be-replaced commander of US forces in Afghanistan, it has come to believe that it is essential to enlist Afghans as our allies. Accordingly, the army's main fighting unit in the area—War Squadron, four hundred men spread out over four bases— works side by side with Afghan soldiers and strives to engage local leaders. But, after more than fourteen hundred American lives lost and countless billions of dollars spent in Afghanistan, the southeast remains in many ways unchanged from the place that housed the Lion's Den: an area of tribal intrigue, anti-American sentiment, and quickly shifting loyalties.

A FEW MONTHS AGO, A GROUP OF VISITORS FROM WAR SQUAD-ron held a meeting with Pacha Khan Zadran, a leader of the influential Zadran tribe, to ask for his help in fighting the Taliban. Zadran, who is in his late sixties, is an extraordinary-looking man, with a face like something devised by a Claymation animator. At the meeting, he wore a black turban topped with a flamboyant cloth fan and trailing a yard-long train. He has a horizontal stripe of eyebrows dyed jet-black, a great proboscis, a handlebar mustache, and basset-like jowls. His ears are massive, resembling dried apricots loosely attached to the sides of his head.

A young American soldier assessed the warlord's appearance with raised eyebrows. As he shook his hand, he grinned and said, "Wassup, pimpin'?" Zadran looked quizzical and didn't seem to understand. The commanding officer, Lieutenant Colonel Stephen Lutsky, cuffed the soldier's shoulder and pushed forward to introduce himself and his entourage. Zadran waved his guests to sit down on sofas, which ringed a meeting room in his local headquarters, in a mountain pass between the strategic cities of Khost and Gardez. Outside, a large billboard displayed Zadran's picture.

The meeting was conducted through an interpreter, a muscular young Afghan whom the Americans called Arnold, after Arnold Schwarzenegger. Lutsky, a small, wiry man of forty with a boyish face and a New Jersey accent, leaned toward Pacha Khan and told him that he had been looking forward to their meeting. Lutsky arrived in Khost Province in January 2010, taking command of a volatile wedge of territory

along the Afghanistan-Pakistan frontier that included Zadran's traditional turf. He was meeting Zadran to try to persuade him to assemble
a paramilitary security force.

The force would be part of the Afghan Local Police Initiative, a US
and NATO program that supplies weapons and rudimentary training
to as many as twenty thousand Afghan villagers, in the hope that young
men employed by the government won't be tempted to work for the Taliban. The program is a key element in the counterinsurgency doctrine,
and, for the Obama administration, these local units are crucial. The
United States has announced that it will begin withdrawing troops
from Afghanistan in July and will complete the process by 2014; President Hamid Karzai said recently that the Afghans will assume control
of seven of the country's thirty-four provinces this summer. But the Afghan National Army and the police are widely seen as ineffective and
corrupt. If there is to be an orderly "transition" to Afghan control of the
battlefield, the US needs better allies in the area.

The problem is that Khost borders the Pakistani province of North
Waziristan, a lawless place that serves as a sanctuary for jihadis. After
the fall of bin Laden's base at Tora Bora, his fighters retreated to hiding
places inside Pakistan. To all intents and purposes, North Waziristan
remains their headquarters. It is also the home base for Jalaluddin
Haqqani, an Afghan jihadi leader whose group of Pashtun fighters is a
linchpin in the alliance among Afghanistan's Islamists, Al Qaeda, and,
despite its denials, Pakistan's intelligence service. It was Haqqani who,
after Tora Bora, hosted bin Laden in his Pakistani refuge.

Although the US has thousands of troops in the area, the Haqqanis operate across the border with impunity, taking advantage of their
tribal connections and knowledge of the local smuggling routes to carry
out audacious strikes. In recent years, with the aid of the ISI, the Haqqanis have become increasingly active, fostering spectacular suicide com-
mando attacks in Kabul, Khost, and elsewhere. The most recent of these,

a suicide car bomb that exploded in a Khost marketplace in February, killed eleven Afghans.

Lutsky was interested in Zadran partly because his tribe had long been rivals of the Haqqanis. During the 2001 invasion of Afghanistan, the Haqqanis allied themselves with Al Qaeda, while Zadran's men fought alongside the Americans. "We need a leader of the Zadran tribe to unite the subtribes and defeat the insurgency," he told Zadran. "And when I think of the person who can do this I think of you."

Zadran smiled and made an offer: "If you pressure Karzai to name me as the head of these three provinces"—the contiguous, tribally linked provinces of Khost, Paktika, and Paktia—"I promise you no more problems in them." Zadran, in a long career in Afghan politics, has not made a virtue of constancy. He fought against the Soviets in the eighties, before joining the US-backed campaign against the Taliban, in 2001. After the ouster of the Taliban, he was named governor of Paktia Province, but locals protested his appointment. Karzai removed him from the post, and, soon afterward, Zadran shelled the cities of Gardez and Khost. For a time, Zadran resorted to banditry, with his fighters extorting money from motorists on the road that passes his headquarters. Nonetheless, he was allowed to participate in the 2005 parliamentary elections, and he won a seat. In the most recent elections, he was voted out, a result that he claimed was due to fraud.

Lutsky alluded tactfully to Zadran's electoral problems. "Even if it were to turn out that, for whatever reason, you were no longer a member of parliament, we know that you would still be the leader of the important Zadran tribe," he said. "And we look to you in that role."

Zadran said that he was ready to help Lutsky, but complained that the Americans had not always acted upon the information he had given them, allowing enemy suspects to escape. (The opposite was also true. In 2002, more than sixty Afghan tribal elders were killed by US warplanes after being misidentified as members of Al Qaeda. The US military

apologized for the incident, calling it a tragic case of "mistaken identity," but there were reports that Zadran had relayed false information
in order to eliminate rivals.) Lutsky countered politely that he had been
acting decisively since he arrived in Khost. "I know the government's
weak," he said. "I want to work more through the tribes, because they
are strong."

Zadran offered to organize a tribal militia, an *arbakai*. Or, he said,
he could pick twenty men to work with the Americans as a special liaison force. Such a group would need arms, vehicles, and communications
equipment, as well as American financing. Which would he prefer?
Lutsky hedged, saying that if Zadran could organize a local police
force, under his own leadership, it would be "very helpful." In the meantime, if Zadran's men could lead the Americans to Taliban weapons
caches, he was authorized to pay out reward money.

Ignoring this, Zadran said, "When my men have intelligence, you
will pick them up in Black Hawks, and they will lead you to where the
enemies are, and you will drop bombs on them."

"We should work on both initiatives," Lutsky said, and then changed
the subject. He had heard that Zadran was building a house in the city
of Khost, and he asked when it would be finished. Zadran said, "When
you guys give me enough money to finish it," and they both laughed.

The two men exchanged cell phone numbers, and Lutsky and his
men climbed into their armored vehicles and drove off. He was pleased.
The meeting had allowed him to check off a couple of important boxes
on the score sheet of counterinsurgency doctrine: a "key leader engagement" that offered an opportunity to secure greater control of a "key
terrain area." As an American counterinsurgency adviser explained it,
"What we're doing here is a very big hand wave. The idea is to work as
best we can to create little bubbles of civilization and see where it gets
us, see if we can't connect them up." The adviser stressed that, in and

around Khost, "partnering with Afghans is a key element of what we're doing."

In 2009, there were only about five hundred "partnered" operations; in 2010, there were more than ten thousand. Still, tense relationships are common among the coalition partners. In 2010, the US ambassador to Afghanistan, Karl Eikenberry, reportedly characterized Hamid Karzai as erratic and clinically bipolar. Worse, in April 2011, an Afghan military pilot killed eight American soldiers and a civilian contractor at Kabul's airport; it was the eighth such attack in 2011. Situations like these underscore the quandary that confronts the United States and its partners in Afghanistan. The Taliban are canny and ruthless, and they share cultural and religious links with the civilians living on the battlefield. How can the US find reliable local proxies to train and arm and share intelligence with? Who, ultimately, can take over Afghanistan's security?

LUTSKY'S AREA OF OPERATIONS—HIS "AO," IN MILITARY PARLANCE— feels like a place at the edge of the known world. His base, Forward Operating Base Clark, sits on a flatland about twelve miles from Khost. On the far side of the city is Camp Salerno, NATO's regional military headquarters, and FOB Chapman, an adjacent CIA base. Set behind dreary defensive fortifications punctuated by high-tech communications masts, the bases seem like mirages on the Afghan plain. In daytime, the skies flash with metallic light as helicopters come and go, and F-15 jets roar past. At night, the only noise is the barking of dogs.

The small city of Khost is situated in a mountain valley crisscrossed by dry riverbeds and bullock-tilled fields. The mountains rising eastward to the Pakistan border glisten with minerals. To the west, a road leads up a deep canyon and over the mountains to Gardez, passing through a

Afghan civilians walking past a US military patrol in Khost Province, 2009.

smattering of hamlets carved out of mud and stone. Except for the occasional shepherd, few people are visible. The road is periodically clogged
by convoys of gaudily painted "jingle trucks," cargo wagons festooned
with dangling metal ornaments that clank tinnily as they move. The
rest of the traffic is nearly all military.

The center of Khost is a welter of traders' streets, arrayed around the
governor's mansion and the police headquarters. The town is crowded
with people, motorbikes, and brightly decorated shops, but it retains a
conservative provincial air. Unlike Kabul, where there has been a construction boom in recent years, only the outskirts show evidence of new
wealth: a handful of colorfully painted villas with ornate wrought-iron
balconies.

Khost has a long tradition of resistance to political and social change.
In 1924, the local Pashtuns rose up against King Amanullah, a modern-
izer who sought to emancipate Afghan women. During the Soviet war,
the mujahideen besieged the Russians and, for a time, surrounded their
airfield on the edge of town—today's Camp Salerno. In the spring of
1991, after the Russians had withdrawn, Jalaluddin Haqqani seized the
city; it was among the first to fall to the mujahideen.

In part because of the Haqqanis' persistent influence, Khost Province remains one of the most dangerous places in Afghanistan. A recent
study showed that, of the 497 US casualties suffered in Afghanistan last
year, 408 occurred in the provinces that border Pakistan. Mike Boettcher,
a veteran network news correspondent, who is also a terrorism expert at
the University of Oklahoma, told me, "In the context of what's going
on in Afghanistan and Pakistan, Khost is the centerpiece. It's right up
against North Waziristan, which is the one place the Pakistani Army
won't go."

On December 30, 2009, a Jordanian suicide bomber posing as a defector blew himself up at FOB Chapman, killing seven American CIA

agents, in one of the most lethal attacks ever carried out against the agency. Nonetheless, the CIA station continues to provide much of the raw intelligence for the US Army's field operations in the area. When American military officers allude to their CIA colleagues, they refer to them as "OGA," meaning "other government agencies," and it is clear that their work in the area is of primary importance. While the US Army often points to its efforts to engage with civilians and train the Afghan Army, the CIA and the Special Forces have been carrying out violent covert operations, like the spectacular killing of Osama bin Laden. Boettcher said that North Waziristan, just next to Khost, is where "the secret war is going on at its fiercest—over eighty percent of the drone attacks are there." CIA drones with laser-guided missiles regularly target Al Qaeda, Taliban, and Haqqani suspects. In September 2008, a strike against the Haqqanis killed at least twenty-three people, reportedly including one of Jalaluddin Haqqani's wives and ten other relatives. The CIA also operates an Afghan paramilitary force of three thousand fighters out of secret bases along the border with Pakistan, several of which are in Khost. All of this has created an atmosphere of suspicion that makes collaboration, of the sort that Lutsky is supposed to encourage, very difficult to achieve.

STEPHEN LUTSKY WAS BORN IN CLINTON, NEW JERSEY, WHERE his father worked as a municipal engineer and his mother as a secretary. Clinton, in the central part of the state, has remained rural, because, Lutsky says, "it doesn't have an off-ramp." He enlisted in 1987, straight out of high school, and then "went green to gold," meaning that he went to college in order to receive an officer's commission. He attended Valley Forge and Lock Haven, both in Pennsylvania, and earned a biochemistry degree in 1992. Lutsky was assigned to Fort Hood, Texas, and then served in Bosnia, Albania, and Kosovo. He and his wife, Denise, whom he married in 1995, have a ten-year-old son and an eight-year-old daughter at home, in Fort Campbell, Kentucky.

Since 2003, Lutsky has had three deployments in Iraq; Khost was his first in Afghanistan. In all of them, he has developed a reputation for seeking out combat. In Iraq, he said, a rocket-propelled grenade hit his Humvee, and he was peppered with shrapnel, some of which is still inside his body. He'd had a dental X-ray recently and what looked like a cavity in one of his molars was revealed to be a metal fragment in his jaw. In Afghanistan, he has the distinction of being one of the few American officers to survive a suicide bombing—two of them, in fact. The right side of his face is scarred with red welts, from his cheek to his eyebrow.

The first bombing was on March 8, 2010, three weeks after Lutsky took charge of FOB Clark. That morning, he told me, he was reviewing operations and intelligence at his tactical operations center, or TOC, a large room in a prefab warehouse on the base. Lutsky shared command of the area with his Afghan National Army counterpart, General Mohammed Asrar Adqas, but their respective groups of soldiers didn't mingle much. At Clark, the Americans live alongside about a thousand Afghan soldiers, in separate but adjoining compounds; the Afghans are trained by a special team of US military instructors. At the TOC, the two groups of officers meet each morning for a briefing and planning session. The meetings are conducted through interpreters like Arnold, because few of the Afghans speak English and almost none of the Americans speak either of Afghanistan's two main languages, Pashto and Dari. While the Americans peer at laptop computers connected to their field units, the Afghans communicate orders through bulky field radios that they lug with them.

Lutsky and Asrar were at a morning briefing when the news came that a group of suicide bombers had entered Khost and were being pursued by the police. One bomber had detonated himself; the ANA had killed another; and the police had two more trapped inside a building. "General Asrar said he needed to be there to see what was going on," Lutsky told me. "I said, 'I'm going, too—I'm your partner.'"

When they arrived, one of the bombers had climbed to the roof, and the situation had become a standoff. "To end the thing, me and four or five of my guys had to kill the guy on the roof with grenades," Lutsky said. They fired into the building three times, using a grenade launcher, and when they entered they found the remaining bomber wounded but still alive, sitting propped up against a wall. "He had a detonation cord on him, and I saw his hands move," Lutsky said. He shot the bomber in the head, and one of his NCOs shot him in the chest. "That's when he exploded."

Lutsky was about fifteen feet away. "My right arm was numb, but I thought I was fine, that I had just been hit by debris," he said. Later, doctors at the base found six ball bearings in his neck, his right arm, and his right leg; others had been deflected by his sunglasses and flak vest. The doctors dug out four of the ball bearings but left one in his arm and another in his leg, because they were too deeply embedded. Lutsky rolled up his sleeve and pointed to a spot on his forearm. "You can feel it," he said. I pinched the flesh and felt a hard round shape. Lutsky smiled. "I can get it to come to the surface with a magnet."

THE SUICIDE BOMBERS HAD BEEN SENT FROM PAKISTAN BY THE Haqqanis, apparently to attack the Afghan government's administrative complex in Khost. Lutsky was wounded only because he had put himself in the action. But, a few months later, on October 10, he was the object of what seemed to be a more targeted attack: A suicide bomber blew up a vehicle as his convoy drove past.

Lutsky thinks that General Asrar may have known about the

bombing. In the preceding weeks, relations between the two men had grown tense. "Initially, we thought Asrar was a really good commander. We'd been working together for nine months." Then, at election time, in September, "something happened," he said. "There was a rumor that Asrar was going to be replaced. He wouldn't interact with us anymore, and wouldn't leave his office."

A few days before the bombing, Asrar confiscated a truck loaded with acid. "We thought it was going to be used for making HME"—homemade explosives—Lutsky said. "We found out later it was for cutting opium. He had plans to sell it. He also had some detainees he was planning to release—he was planning on getting paid to release them."

Without revealing his suspicions, Lutsky seized the truck, and, working with Asrar's deputy, with whom he had built an alliance, he devised a way to keep the detainees in custody. "In the morning update at the TOC, Asrar said, 'We have got to release these detainees—we can't hold them this long.'" His deputy suggested that they be handed over to the provincial police chief. Lutsky, on cue, offered to transport them to the office. "I said, 'I can take them there, because I've got to take the acid there, too. We can do that in the afternoon at fourteen hundred.'"

Asrar was obligated to come along, Lutsky told me: "We are partners, and we're supposed to do everything together." But that afternoon Asrar was nowhere to be found. A little after two, Lutsky's convoy left the base and turned onto the road the soldiers called Virginia, leading to Camp Salerno. After a few kilometers, a car pulled over to let the convoy by, "like every car does," Lutsky said. "Our ANA escort passed, the acid truck passed, my vehicle passed. And then that's when it blew up." The bomber triggered a six-hundred-pound bomb, creating a thunderous explosion. "Fortunately, he pulled the button either too late or too early. So we had damaged vehicles, but it didn't hurt any of us."

Lutsky jumped out of his vehicle and heard a woman screaming, "My son is dead." Three boys were injured, one of them ten years old, one fourteen, and one a six-month-old infant. Lutsky says he ran to the ten-year-old. "We grabbed him, and that's when the blood started spraying. Femoral artery. Chunk of the vehicle took a huge piece right out of his thigh." While Lutsky was tending to the boy, he said, he looked up and saw Asrar standing over him. No one else from the base had yet arrived. "It was just very strange that General Asrar was the first guy on the scene. He was there *quick*." Shaking his head, Lutsky said, "I suspect that he knew something was going to happen."

Asrar denies any wrongdoing. "If the Americans prove that I had any relationship with the opposition forces, then I am ready to be court-martialed," he said. "I served in Khost for four years and nobody ever filed a single complaint against me." A spokesman for the Ministry of Defense later said there was no evidence that Asrar had collaborated with the enemy. But Lutsky maintains that Afghan soldiers and local officials privately accused Asrar of corruption. "There will always be some level of corruption in this country, but we refuse to accept corruption that affects the morale, training, and effectiveness of the ANA soldier, and any corruption that will affect the coalition," Lutsky said. "If he wants to have illegal checkpoints and extort money, OK. If he wants to sell off some gas, OK. If he wants to give his soldiers second-rate food and sell what he's getting for them from us, well, we can work with that. But if he wants to tell the enemy when we are going to conduct an operation, then we just won't tell him."

ASRAR VANISHED THE DAY BEFORE I ARRIVED AT LUTSKY'S BASE, and the rumor among the Afghan soldiers was that he had left for Kabul. Lutsky told me that Asrar's deputy had written to the defense minister and asked for the general to be removed. There had been no official response, so Lutsky didn't know what Asrar's absence meant, but, he said, "I sure hope it means he's gone."

Lutsky drove into Khost to see the police chief, General Abdul Hakim Ishaqzai, with whom he was friendly, to ask about his missing partner. We traveled, as Lutsky did whenever he left the base, in a convoy of three MRAPs—mine-resistant ambush-protected vehicles. Oncoming cars pulled off the road as we approached, and when they didn't our gunners cursed and aimed their machine guns at them. As we drove into Khost, the Pashtun men on the streets either ignored our convoy or noted it with neutral or hostile expressions.

Hakim was a thin, bearded man wearing a dark blue uniform covered with medals. He received Lutsky graciously in his office, a large room with heavy drapes and an old-fashioned wood bureau set with surveillance monitors. After the two men exchanged formal pleasantries, Lutsky said that he had a problem and would be grateful for Hakim's advice. A day or two earlier, his troops had come upon a group of men, wearing civilian clothes and armed with AK-47s, who were detaining other men, presumably to extort money. The robbers had turned out to be ANA soldiers, one of them an active-duty major. Lutsky explained that he had turned them over to the ANA, but he wondered what he should do to follow up. Hakim said, "Unfortunately, such abuses are occurring throughout the security forces. This won't change overnight, but it is up to the commanders to make sure their forces are clean."

Lutsky asked if he ought to raise the matter with Asrar when he returned to Khost. Hakim gave an irritated look and said, "I've known General Asrar ever since I was a child. We went to school together. But here in Khost it has hurt my heart to see that he doesn't have the whole province in mind, only his own interests."

It wasn't just Asrar that Lutsky was concerned about. He had recently urged that two police officers whom he suspected of working with the Taliban be fired; he later learned that they were back at their jobs. Studying Hakim's face, he said, "I was surprised to see they had letters from you authorizing them to have their arms returned to them."

Hakim nodded and said, "I was pressured by the Ministry of the Interior to do this. Believe me, if there was no pressure I would disarm these people. They will not help build this country."

ONE MORNING, LUTSKY MUSTERED A TEAM OF HIS MEN FOR AN operation in Shembowat, a village a few miles from Clark. Intelligence had come in that insurgents had stayed in the village overnight and cached explosives in a latrine there. Lutsky asked an ANA unit to accompany him, but the unit, led by a moonfaced young captain, arrived forty minutes late. Lutsky's men spoke contemptuously of the Afghan soldiers, calling them lazy and unreliable.

Outside the village, we made our way through stubbly fields to a group of walled farmhouses. The Afghan soldiers fanned out to provide security; some of them were local men, who wore black face masks to protect their identity. A few farmers eyed us blankly; a man working the ground with a wooden hoe carried on as if we weren't there. A man and a woman were making fuel patties out of dung and straw, slapping them onto a dirt wall to dry in the sun.

With Arnold translating, Lutsky told the ANA captain to explain to the villagers that he and his men needed to search their houses. The officer looked distinctly uncomfortable, and he hung back, scowling, as Lutsky led his team in the searches. For the next four hours, they went from compound to compound, and the Afghan soldiers trailed along. Women appeared in doorways to shout at the Americans. To show respect for the villagers, Lutsky told the Afghans to conduct the house searches while the Americans went through the compounds' walled yards, picking their way amid tethered cows and rudimentary outdoor kitchens.

In one compound, Lutsky found a suspicious recess in the base of a haystack, and he wondered aloud if that was where the explosives were.

There was nothing there, but Lutsky was still suspicious, and he asked one of his men, a lanky red-haired sergeant named Rhyss Heeter, to climb down into the family's sewage pit to investigate. Heeter sighed and began descending, inching his way down the rounded sides of the pit until he vanished. As Lutsky waited, the ANA captain chatted amiably with the owner of the house, a bearded man in his thirties who smiled throughout the search. Heeter eventually climbed back out, his pants and boots smeared with excrement; he had found nothing.

A few minutes later, on a pathway outside the compound, one of Lutsky's men found a small adobe structure and opened its wooden door. He gave a shout. The explosives were inside, attached by wires to a cell phone. Lutsky barked at everyone to step back as the bomb-disposal team was summoned. After a few minutes, a small, wheeled robot was sent in to disengage the phone from the explosives. As everyone took cover, the explosives were blown up in a sudden blast of noise and dust. We left the village as we had come, followed by the blank stares of the locals.

Back at the base, I asked Lutsky, "Who is your real enemy here?"

"You mean what is keeping us from being successful?" he responded. "I'd say it's somewhere between apathy and misunderstanding. To us, the solution seems very simple: All the villages and the people and the subtribes have to do is join together and agree, 'We're just going to say no to the Taliban.' If they did that, the Taliban wouldn't be able to survive. But, unfortunately, because this war has gone on so long, people are tired. They just want to be able to have an honest job, have food on the table, let their kids go to school, and be able to go to sleep at night without their house blowing up. . . . They're in survival mode. My guess is that if the Taliban come to their door and ask, 'Will you let me sleep here tonight?,' they're probably going to say, 'OK,' and not say anything to us about it, because, if they do, they're afraid the Taliban will kill them." When I asked about the moonfaced Afghan Army captain, he shrugged unhappily but said nothing.

TWENTY-FIVE OF LUTSKY'S SOLDIERS LIVED AT AN ISOLATED base called Combat Outpost Spera, situated high in the mountains, just a few hundred yards from the border with North Waziristan. Spera was subject to constant Taliban mortar fire, and though the men were rotated out every three months, Lutsky was often concerned for their safety. One of the men at FOB Clark described Spera as "a bullet sponge," maintained purely as a marker of the American presence on the front line.

The American counterinsurgency adviser told me that Spera would likely be shut down, because it didn't conform to the new US counterinsurgency strategy for Afghanistan. For a start, he pointed out, Spera wasn't anywhere near a "district development center," the army's label for a populated hub. "We're looking at our presence in places where there aren't many people and asking, 'What are we doing there?' Spera is one of those. It's on an insurgent ratline, yes, but the truth is that the insurgents can go around it."

Lutsky took me on a three-day visit to Spera, which was accessible only by helicopter. The camp, surrounded by pine-covered granite ridges, was a mess of jury-rigged wooden bunkers and sandbag-lined dugouts for mortars. There were machine-gun towers and observation platforms, a hut that served as a gym, and a deck where the men lounged and smoked cigarettes. Camouflage netting hung overhead. The soldiers' life revolved around the TOC, where they gathered to watch TV and check their email. It operated out of one room of a rustic structure that resembled a hunting cabin, with plank floors and a rough brick fireplace. Three times a day, American-style meals were served by a big man called Cookie. In the evenings, some of the men played Risk or cards. Others fed ammo boxes into the fire to keep warm.

The soldiers pointed toward the ridgeline northeast of Spera, saying that just over the border there was a Pakistani military outpost. Every evening, the young officer in charge of Spera, First Lieutenant Paul Corcoran, spoke for a few minutes with his Pakistani counterpart over a field radio. There was a stilted quality to their exchanges; the Americans suspected the Pakistanis of being complicit with the insurgents who regularly attacked them.

Near the entrance to the base was a room occupied by ten Afghans, including the commander of the ANA contingent. Other Afghan soldiers lived below the base, in an old *qalat*, or family compound, next to the airstrip and the crumpled remains of a white Russian helicopter. The Afghans were rarely seen outside their *qalat*, and the ten who shared Spera with the Americans were apparently there only because regulations required it. They had their own cook fire outdoors, and seldom mixed with the other soldiers.

On the outside wall of the gym shack, someone had scrawled a scoreboard: "ANA 1, Hendrix 2, Cats 9." Staff Sergeant Shawn Buzzell explained that it had to do with "some problems" between the Afghans and an American soldier named Hendrix. When the Afghans arrived on the base, they brought a pet cat with them. "The cat took a shit on Hendrix's sleeping bag, sir, and ever since, he's tried to kill it a lot," Buzzell said. "But the Afghans are pissed off at him, because they say cats are sacred." He joked, "I guess you could say Hendrix doesn't have a great deal of respect for the Afghan people, sir."

One morning, Lieutenant Corcoran, a blond twenty-four-year-old from North Attleborough, Massachusetts, set up a patrol into the surrounding hills. Before first light, fifteen Americans and as many Afghans left the base on foot and climbed to the summit of a large hill to the west. To provide air cover, a surveillance drone was sent overhead. The area looked down on a dry riverbed that extended toward Miran

Shah, a Haqqani stronghold in North Waziristan. Insurgents periodically made their way into Khost by circumventing the Pakistani military base across the border.

Not long into the patrol, Corcoran ordered a group of ANA soldiers
ahead to a hilltop called Texas, which had a good view of an insurgent access route. For an hour, the American soldiers huddled in silence against
the side of a rocky escarpment. Corcoran, speaking over a radio through
his interpreter, asked for a report, but there was none. Finally, the interpreter admitted that the ANA soldiers had decided not to go. An
argument ensued, and at last some Afghan scouts set out toward the hill.
Within minutes, word came back that they had spotted five "Taliban"—
men in civilian clothing carrying weapons—on an adjacent hill. The
Americans checked their weapons and gear excitedly, whispering to
avoid giving away their location. Corcoran issued new orders of position,
and the drone circled closer. After another half hour, we heard the
crack of gunshots from across the hill. Over the radio, an interpreter
told Corcoran that the advance party had fired on the "Taliban"; sadly,
they had all escaped. Corcoran waited for the drone to spot the intrud-
ers, but it found no one. At midmorning, he called off the mission. By
then, some ANA soldiers, tired of the mission, had already left for
the base.

That evening, Corcoran stopped by the cook fire, where Spera's
ANA corps commander, a pleasant-faced young man named Mohammed Hamid Agar, sat warming his hands. Hamid had not gone on the
morning patrol, but had sent one of his junior officers. Corcoran, despite his frustration, had accepted it as the Afghan way of doing things.
But why, he asked, had Hamid's men, against his orders, fired at the
"Taliban"? Hamid replied calmly that he had talked with his junior officer about it; the soldiers had fired at the men "because they saw them
leaving, rather than heading toward the Americans, where they could

be ambushed." Corcoran pointed out that the drone could have spotted them and, if the ANA men had waited, the Americans could have set an ambush. Hamid was silent, and eventually Corcoran gave up.

After Corcoran left, I asked Hamid if the story about Hendrix and the cat was true. He nodded, frowning. He said that, after Hendrix's first attempt to kill the cat, some of the Afghan men had wanted to murder Hendrix, but he had prevented them. He had served in the Afghan Army for five years, he said, and in that time had discovered that Americans fit into two main categories: "There are those who respect our culture, and those who don't."

The Americans refer to the sixty-three miles of road that wind over the mountains between Khost and Gardez, linking the frontier lands along the Pakistani border with the road from Kabul to Kandahar, as the K-G Highway. Its highest point, the nine-thousand-foot K-G Pass, is vitally strategic, and it has become legendary as one of the bloodiest stretches of road in Afghanistan. In 1987, when the Soviet campaign against the mujahideen was in its eighth year, Mikhail Gorbachev ordered his generals to seize the pass. After a protracted standoff, in which hundreds of soldiers died, the Soviets took it. Within a month, they lost it again, to Haqqani's fighters. Three months later, they began withdrawing from Afghanistan.

For the past four years, the United States and its partners have been trying to rebuild the road. In May 2007, two American construction firms, the Louis Berger Group and Black & Veatch, began a $120 million repair project. But last summer, as laborers were subjected to near-daily attacks, the work at the pass had to be abandoned. The attacks were widely believed to have come from a Zadran tribesman named Gul Bad Shah, and, in October, LBG's subcontractors devised an ingenious, if cynical, solution to the problem: They hired Shah to provide security along the vulnerable section of the road. The attacks at the pass abruptly stopped.

Recently, though, work had faltered again, because of contract disputes with Shah. Lutsky, as the ranking US military officer in the area, had an interest in seeing the road completed, and he made an appointment to meet Shah—another "key leader engagement"—but Shah did not show up. During my visit, Lutsky happened to encounter Shah outside Zadran's headquarters. Shah presented excuses for the missed appointment, but Lutsky made light of it, and asked him to come that evening to FOB Wilderness, a base a few miles up the road.

Shah arrived at the outer gate just after nightfall. A big-faced, slow-eyed man with a salt-and-pepper beard, Shah wore a *shalwar kameez* and a *pakul*, the felt porkpie hat favored by the former anti-Soviet mujahideen. Lutsky and a young woman named Melissa Skorka—a social scientist who was studying the Haqqanis for the Department of Defense—met him in the camp's "*shura* room," where Afghans were invited in for discussions with the Americans and their interpreters. It was a large, carpeted room with a few cushions on the floor, and it smelled strongly of feet. Though the room was meant to be a neutral space, Shah was at a distinct disadvantage. He was barefoot, having removed his sandals at the door. His cell phone and other belongings had been taken by soldiers outside. (This was a routine procedure at all bases, but I overheard a discreet discussion about Gul Bad Shah's "things," and was given the impression that during the meeting there would be a minute inspection of his phone. Lutsky suspected Shah of conspiring with senior Haqqani lieutenants, and he wanted to keep closer tabs on him.) An American soldier stood in front of him with a flesh-colored plastic device that looked like a Polaroid camera—a biometric scanner, which the Americans used to take the vital statistics of visitors, to be saved in a digital-identity bank.

As the talk with Shah proceeded, the soldier stepped forward with the scanner and held it over the Afghan's eyes, and then each of his fingers, obliging him to stand still, while Lutsky and Skorka asked him questions. After a minute or two at each position, the soldier would remove the apparatus and step back and register its results. Lutsky and Skorka, despite their repeated apologies about the inconvenience of the procedure, seemed quietly pleased with the situation. It allowed them to assess Shah while he was distracted.

"I've wanted to meet you ever since you won the contract," Lutsky told Shah. "The Louis Berger Group has kept me informed of the security situation, and of its changes, along the road." He mentioned that LBG had raised some "discrepancies" in the number of security guards Shah had promised to provide. Shah glared. "They're lying to you," he said. The problem, he insisted, was that LBG had given some Mangal—members of a rival tribe—a security contract along a portion of the road. Shah said that he had signed a contract for 800 men and had 150 of them ready to go to work. "The Mangal have to be removed so that I can put my own men there," he said. "I told LBG this, but they haven't done it yet."

Shah talked carelessly, as if trying to fill the silence, as the soldier fit his fingers into the machine. He said that Gulbuddin Hekmatyar—a former Afghan mujahideen leader who had allied himself with the Taliban—was trying to "disrupt" the roadwork, as were the Haqqanis.

Lutsky nodded, and said, "Yes, we're tracking everything. What we need to do is have a meeting—you, me, and the Louis Berger Group—to get this security contract resolved."

Shah replied, "Once it's paved, there will be no more problems, no more IEDs." He added, "If the Louis Berger Group can't do the work, I can. I can bring diggers and excavators and five hundred men, and they will do the work! LBG has spent years on this road, and they haven't paved it!"

Lutsky said, "That's why we're excited you're on it. With the Zadran tribe, we'll get it done."

Shah said, "The next time you come to the K-G Pass, I want to throw a party for you." He described his house, in a village next to a washed-out bridge, and said, "We'll have tea and corn bread." When the soldier finished the last finger, Lutsky stepped forward and thanked Shah. Looking a little uncertain, Shah put on his sandals and left the room.

NOT LONG AFTER MY VISIT, GENERAL ASRAR WAS TRANSFERRED to Kabul; he left Khost, he said, because he wanted to be with his family. Lutsky finished his tour and returned to Kentucky. Before he departed, he oversaw the closing down of Spera. In a carefully orchestrated operation, the American soldiers were evacuated by helicopter, along with their Afghan partners. Before leaving, the Americans burned everything they could not take with them, so that nothing would be left for the insurgents, who would again have full control of the area.

Mike Boettcher, the terrorism expert, was skeptical about the pullback. He said, "Khost is the one place where we're going head-to-head with the new Al Qaeda"—the insurgents in North Waziristan. The greatest threat, he told me, came from Jalaluddin Haqqani's son and heir apparent, Siraj. In 2009, the US offered a $5 million reward for information leading to Siraj Haqqani's capture or execution, like the one offered for bin Laden in 1998. "Siraj is the poster boy for the new generation of Al Qaeda," Boettcher said. "The old generation—that's Jalaluddin—was basically about the regional war, but Siraj is a believer in the global jihad, which was bin Laden's contribution."

Despite the threat from Pakistan, the American soldiers' presence at Spera was principally symbolic. The outpost's small number of men couldn't do much to stop insurgents from moving across the border. Their attempts at forming allegiances had been frustrated; they had only token cooperation from their Pakistani counterparts on the other side of the mountain, and precious little from the Afghan soldiers they lived alongside.

In any case, it is not ground troops or ANA soldiers who are proving most effective in fighting insurgents. As the killing of bin Laden showed, some of the most successful work in Afghanistan, in Pakistan, and against Al Qaeda is being done covertly, by the CIA, the Special Forces, and the Navy SEALs. Pacha Khan and others often told Lutsky that, to win the war, he should forget about everything else and go hit the enemy in Pakistan. Lutsky always answered, "That's way above my pay grade." He said this in a joking way, but he was right: There is a larger concern in Afghanistan that only political leaders can solve.

US counterinsurgency doctrine places great emphasis on what used to be called "winning hearts and minds." But, after nearly ten years, it is unrealistic to expect that the army can still win people over in Afghanistan. The coalition has huge numbers of troops there, armed and housed at vast expense. Many have acquitted themselves honorably, and in some areas they have succeeded in pushing back the Taliban. But the task of building a nation out of warring interests has for the most part proved overwhelming. It seems, regrettably, that whatever we can accomplish in Afghanistan will be achieved by force, not by making friends. Lutsky told me, "The cultural complexity of the environment is just so huge that it's hard for us to understand it. For Americans, it's black or white— it's either good guys or bad guys. For Afghans, it's not. There are good Taliban and bad Taliban, and some of them are willing to do deals with each other. It's just beyond us."

# 13

## ANNALS OF ASSASSINATION

### I.

### Ahmed Wali Karzai (July 13, 2011)

Hamid Karzai is a middle child, one of seven sons and a daughter born to the late Abdul Ahad Karzai, the former deputy speaker of Afghanistan's royal parliament and paramount chief of the ethnic Pashtun Populzai tribe. (After the Taliban assassinated Abdul Ahad, in the Pakistani border city of Quetta, where the family was then based, in 1999, Populzai tribal leaders elected Hamid to succeed him.) The family's ancestral home is in the hamlet of Karz, in the parched flatlands just outside the southern city of Kandahar. Ahmed Wali Karzai, who was assassinated Tuesday, apparently by a long-trusted aide and

---

"I. Ahmed Wali Karzai (July 13, 2011)" was originally published as "Ahmed Wali Karzai's Treacherous Circle," *The New Yorker*, July 13, 2011.

member of his inner circle, was the sixth son. At the time of his death, he was the boss of Kandahar and, in the past few years, widely reputed to be deeply involved in Afghanistan's opium trade—something that not even American officials denied, while he was also (allegedly) on the CIA payroll.

When I visited Kandahar in early 2002, just a few weeks after the rout of the Taliban, "AWK" (as the Americans and other Westerners involved in the NATO war effort in Afghanistan came to refer to him) had clearly emerged as the regional power broker. He was in charge of the tribal town council, and, in that guise, and as his American-backed brother's personal representative, held the balance of power between Kandahar's several dueling tribal warlords. He was serious, opaque, but polite; a difficult man to read, but quite willing to speak his mind about the power dynamics of Kandahar into which he had become a new and potent player.

On a return visit to Kandahar, in late March 2005, I paid a call on Ahmed Wali Karzai. His house was a large one, decorated with gray and white marble, and sat at the end of a residential street a mile or so from the city center. Its approaches were guarded by a small gauntlet of road barriers. A number of sentries stood around in front of the house, where twenty or more Toyota Land Cruisers and other vehicles were parked. I noticed some changes since I had last been there. Two new, imposing houses had been built next door, and, so I was told, also belonged to Ahmed Wali. In the intervening years, clearly, his power had deepened and intensified, and yet it was not visible in the conventional sense. It was as if Kandahar were an Afghan Chicago, and AWK was its unofficial Mayor Daley, who did not go to an office, but whom people—and, in his case, especially tribal elders and other traditional leaders—came to see.

Ahmed Wali emerged to introduce me to his older brother, Qayum, who happened to be visiting from the United States, where he ran a number of Afghan restaurants. Qayum was an older, slightly fleshier version of his brother Hamid, and spoke uncannily like him, in the same carefully articulated, American-accented English. Qayum took me to visit the family's village of Karz. We drove out of Kandahar in one of Ahmed Wali's Toyota Land Cruisers. Along the way, I inquired about an attack that had occurred in the city the night before. The noise had resounded through the city center and awakened my fellow guests in the small hotel where I was staying. That morning, I had heard that the Taliban had shot up a police station. Qayum told me that an office of the Afghan intelligence services had been targeted by an antitank rocket, but that he did not believe the Taliban had been involved. He said it was thought to have been carried out by gunmen associated with Khan Muhammad Mujahid, who had recently been ousted as Kandahar's chief of police.

"I think it is part of this struggle for stability . . . with warlordism," Qayum explained. "You know, these people that have been removed together with the police chief. It seems like it. That is what people are saying. They found that the rocket that had been fired had come from the stocks of the police station."

WHEN I EXPRESSED MY SURPRISE AT THE IMPLICATIONS OF what Qayum was saying, he replied dryly, "Well, you know the nation-building process is much more difficult than it is perceived in the framework of the United Nations."

Indeed it is. The regional clans—Populzai, Alokozai, and Barakzai, chiefly—are involved in an age-old competition for power and patronage, and there have been many times in history when their rivalries have played out bloodily, as they do today. Shifting alliances are continuously being forged and broken between players who have taken sides in the NATO vs. Taliban conflict.

Last April, in a foretelling of AWK's own assassination, Kandahar's police chief was killed by a suicide bomber wearing a police uniform. The chief was Khan Muhammad Mujahid—the same man who had been ousted from the job in 2005, and whom Qayum had suspected of exploding a bomb as an expression of his displeasure. He had recently returned to Kandahar and been reinstated. In the killing of Khan Muhammad, the Taliban were blamed, but few believed it, nodding instead to the murky underworld of Afghan political intrigue where power alliances are struck and later undone in betrayals—the milieu in which Ahmed Wali Karzai spent his life. In a treacherous environment in which the rule of the game is to keep your friends close and your enemies closer, proximity to sudden death is always a real prospect.

As for AWK's killing, an Afghan friend of mine, the journalist Habib Zohori, told me that one theory was that it may have just been a case of explosive temper: Ahmed Wali was abusive, and had yelled at his aide, Sardar Muhammad, who then killed him. "He had worked with Ahmed Wali for seven years," said Zohori. "If he had been a Taliban infiltrator he could have killed him a long time ago." Like most political murders in Afghanistan—the traditional method by which most Afghan leaders have left office—there is mystery in the aftermath, even if a glimpse of the truth emerges after a time.

## II.

### Jan Muhammad Khan (July 19, 2011)

In Afghanistan, political retirement is increasingly a matter of murder. A week ago, it was Ahmed Wali Karzai, President Hamid Karzai's brother and the strongman of Kandahar. On Sunday, it was another

---

"II. Jan Muhammad Khan (July 19, 2011)" was originally published as "Will Hamid Karzai Have the Chance to Retire?," *The New Yorker*, July 19, 2011.

Karzai ally: Jan Muhammad Khan, an ex-warlord and ex-governor of Uruzgan, a southern, insurgent-and-opium-rich Afghan province. He was brazenly murdered when his Kabul home was attacked by two gunmen. (The Taliban claimed responsibility.) Jan Muhammad was a colorful character who, when I met him in 2007, had recently been removed from his governor's post by Karzai in favor of another man, an ex-Taliban official. Jan Muhammad was unhappy about it, and was openly pining to be home and running things again in restive Uruzgan; if he were there, he would, he swore, "clean out" the Islamist insurgents. He was loyal to Karzai, he told me, but proposing peace talks with the Taliban made the president look weak. He suggested, as I recall, that his replacement in Uruzgan was little more than a Taliban wolf in sheep's clothing. (When I met the new governor myself, a few weeks later, I tended to agree.)

THE TALIBAN SEEM TO BE EFFECTIVELY PURSUING A STRATEGY of assassination the length and breadth of Afghanistan. The goal, no doubt, is to further loosen the government's tenuous hold on power as the US and NATO military forces begin their long-announced drawdown and withdrawal from the country.

IN APRIL IT WAS THE TURN OF KHAN MUHAMMAD MUJAHID, the police chief of Kandahar, killed by two gunmen in police uniforms. There have been numerous attacks by Taliban infiltrators embedded within the Afghan police and army in the past year, suggesting widespread infiltration of the government's forces by the insurgents. A number of American, British, and other foreign advisers have frequently been the targets of these Trojan-horse attacks.

———

IN MAY, A SUICIDE BOMBER KILLED ANOTHER CLOSE US ALLY, Mohammad Daud Daud, the counter-narcotics minister and former Northern Alliance warlord. (He was crucial in the defeat of the last Taliban and Al Qaeda northern bastions of Taloqan and Kunduz, respectively, in 2001.) At the time of his death, Daud was the police chief of the north, and, despite private misgivings among some Western advisers about his fiscal propriety and reputed past involvement in the drug trade, he was regarded as a firm anti-Taliban asset who could be counted on in the larger battle for control of the country. When I last saw Daud, a couple of years ago, he hinted strongly that he had aspirations to higher office.

Khan Muhammad Mujahid was a longtime player in Kandahar. I first met him in 1988, when I spent a month with his boss, mujahideen warlord Mullah Naquibullah, then fighting the Soviets and their Afghan minions. He was Naquibullah's number two. After the Taliban downfall in 2001, I made contact with the two men again, and had seen them both on my various visits to Afghanistan in the decade since. Naquibullah was badly injured in an IED explosion against his vehicle in 2007 near his home, and died a few months later; the culprits were not the Taliban, said his son and successor Qudratullah, leader of the southern Alokozai tribe, when I saw him last December. He suggested it had been ordered by a political rival of his father's, a government insider, but he would not say whom he suspected. Like Jan Muhammad, Khan Muhammad, too, had been the subject of political chess moves by Karzai: Removed from his first stint as Kandahar police chief in 2005, he'd been sent to the far northern city Mazar-i-Sharif, and eventually been replaced in that post. When I tracked him down in a large villa in Kabul several months ago, he was unhappily unemployed, looking for new leverage with Karzai to return to Kandahar and take on his resurgent Taliban foes. He didn't have to wait long to be reinstated, but he did not long survive.

IN AFGHANISTAN'S POLITICS, THE QUESTION IS NOT IF, BUT when your killers come for you. At the rate things are going, Hamid Karzai himself will be fortunate to survive his presidency. A few days back, a suicide bomber exploded himself at his brother's funeral. Four mourners were killed and several wounded, but luckily for Karzai, he and his other family members were unhurt.

In fact, homicide is the odds-on likeliest way to leave office for Afghanistan's president. Four out of Afghanistan's last six leaders have been murdered, three of them in office. The other, the last Communist leader, Najibullah, who had stepped down but not fled the country when the mujahideen seized Kabul and engulfed it in civil war, was dragged out of his sanctuary in Kabul's UN compound by the Taliban, who beat him, castrated him, shot him, and finally hung him by the neck from a pole on a traffic circle. It is somewhat lost amid the clamorous chatter nowadays about "dialogue," and "moderate Taliban," but Najibullah's murder was, in fact, the first public action taken by the Taliban when they seized power the first time around, in 1996.

## III.

### Burhanuddin Rabbani (September 20, 2011)

Burhanuddin Rabbani, the former Afghan president, who was assassinated today in Kabul, was a patrician figure who had played many crucial roles in his nation's politics over the past forty years, and who never

---

"III. Burhanuddin Rabbani (September 20, 2011)" was originally published as "Rabbani Assassination: An Afghan Understanding," *The New Yorker*, September 20, 2011.

gave up wanting to return to the driver's seat. His latest role was as head of Afghanistan's so-called High Peace Council, a creation of President Hamid Karzai's to broker talks with the Taliban and other insurgent groups, including several led by characters well known to Rabbani (the Haqqanis and Gulbuddin Hekmatyar are old acquaintances). In a meeting I had with him in his Kabul home around this time last year, Rabbani spoke disparagingly of the faltering US-led counterinsurgency campaign, and confidently about his effort to reach "an Afghan understanding" with the government's foes. Sadly, and for the last time, Rabbani was mistaken about his enemies.

Long before the Taliban, in the seventies, Rabbani was an early leader of Afghanistan's Islamist movement. A teacher of Islamic law at Kabul University who founded an Islamist party, Jamiat-e-Islami, in 1971, he was a mentor to politicized students like Ahmad Shah Massoud, who became a legendary guerrilla leader known as Lion of the Panjshir. Massoud and others followed Rabbani into exile in Pakistan after Afghanistan's monarchy was overthrown, in 1975, by Mohammad Daoud, who established a coalition government with Afghanistan's Communist party. Massoud then led Rabbani's followers in a series of armed attacks against the new regime. Their increasingly violent and ideological confrontation resulted, in 1979, in the Soviet invasion of Afghanistan. In the decade of warfare that followed, Rabbani's party was a leading mujahideen faction. After the Soviet withdrawal in 1989, followed by more fighting, and the mujahideen takeover of Kabul in 1992, Rabbani became the president of the new Islamic State of Afghanistan. Rabbani presided over the tragic destruction of much of Kabul in the ensuing civil war between competing mujahideen factions. In 1996, the fighting culminated in his, and his protégé Massoud's, flight into northern Afghanistan as the Taliban, newcomers to the Afghan jihad, conquered the capital and began consolidating their power.

From then until September 9, 2001, when Massoud was assassinated by Al Qaeda suicide bombers, Rabbani fought off the Taliban's advances from an ever-shrinking swatch of Afghan territory—a rump state he ruled from his remote birthplace of Faizabad on behalf of the Northern Alliance. In our first meeting, in Faizabad, Rabbani struck me as an ineffectual figure in some ways, but at the same time as a cunning politician and master of the artful dodge. He was determined to return to power. When I challenged him to define his own brand of Islamism vis-à-vis the Taliban's, he responded vaguely that their form of Sharia was an extremist application of Pashtun tribal code, while his was more in keeping with Islamic tradition. The Afghan civil war, sadly, had prevented him from "enforcing Islamic law in a way that could benefit and advance Afghan society."

RABBANI'S FORTUNES HAD BEEN REVERSED ONCE AGAIN IN the wake of 9/11, when the US went to war with the Taliban and forged a partnership with the Northern Alliance. In November 2001, a few weeks after I met him and following the ouster of the Taliban from Kabul, Rabbani reinstalled himself in the old royal palace as Afghanistan's still-titular president. This move resulted in several weeks of uncomfortable maneuvering with Hamid Karzai, the man who, weeks earlier at a conference in Bonn, had been picked by the US and its allies to lead Afghanistan. Eventually, Rabbani vacated the palace and assumed a role as elder statesman, in his residential complex, not far from the present US embassy.

In the years that followed, Rabbani and I had many meetings—they were audiences, really. Rabbani was an aloof, courtly man used to being treated with abject deference by his retinue, and by visitors. (Rabbani liked it when I addressed him, as Americans do their former leaders, as "Mr. President.") I usually approached these as courtesy calls on a man who, in large measure, had been temporarily sidelined by events, but who nonetheless remained in the mix. An Afghan politico through and through, he had lived long enough and outlasted enough friends and rivals to know that endurance, and indeed, survival itself, was a possible route back to power. The wheel could always turn in his favor again—just as, for instance, it has for the Taliban.

In his desire to play a vital role again, Rabbani may well have overestimated his own utility, and fatally underestimated the ferocity and the cunning of the insurgents seeking power in Afghanistan today. Meanwhile, with his passing—the latest and most notable in a string of murders of Afghan "moderates" at the hands of the Taliban and their allies—the playing field is being cleared of political rivals who carry any clout locally, regionally, and nationally. "Reconciliation," as things stand today, would appear to be a concept that the Taliban either doesn't understand or for which they wish to dictate the terms.

# 14

## AN AMERICAN
## WAY OF KILLING

### (March 11, 2012)

All the signs are that the United States military and its NATO allies have not only outlived their welcome in Afghanistan but also passed the point at which their presence is anything other than toxic. While the exact details of the incident are still unclear, it's known that early Sunday morning, an American soldier in Kandahar Province's Panjwai district apparently murdered up to sixteen Afghan civilians in cold blood. Nine of the victims were reportedly children. This is merely the latest in a string of episodes in which American soldiers—in spite of the positive intentions of an overwhelming majority of the troops there—have shown scorn, disrespect, and, increasingly and tragically, hatred for the people of the country hosting them.

Two weeks ago it was the accidental burning of Korans and other sacred texts on an American military base—the news of which led to angry riots across Afghanistan and the deaths of at least thirty people,

---

This chapter was originally published as "Massacre in Kandahar," *The New Yorker*, March 11, 2012.

including six American soldiers. In January, it was the posting of a video, shot by American troops themselves, showing four marines urinating on the corpses of several dead Afghans, suspected Taliban, whom they had killed. In 2010, in Maiwand Province in southern Afghanistan—not far from Panjwai district—a group of American soldiers carried out the "sport killings" of Afghan civilians; they took pictures of themselves posing with their victims, and also collected parts of their bodies as trophies.

Such incidents are not unfamiliar to Americans—or should not be. They happened in Iraq, too. There were the Abu Ghraib ignominies, and the Haditha massacre, and there were a thousand lesser, sometimes unreported incidents, in which soldiers humiliated, abused, or killed Iraqi civilians for reasons that had less to do with the Iraqis' possible hostile intentions and more to do with the Americans' fears and hatreds.

In the summer of 2003, in Fallujah, I met an American soldier who boasted to me of having "lit up" approaching civilian vehicles on the road between Basra and Baghdad, because he wasn't sure who was in them. At the time, he said, it had seemed wiser to kill them than leave them alive, because of the possibility that they might be hostile. The way he told me of his experiences, though, hinted at a reality that few soldiers like to discuss: that sometimes they kill because the opportunity is there, and because, at the time, for some of them, it seems fun. Seven years later, that same soldier got in touch with me in a letter to say, ruefully, that he was a different person from the young man I had met. I had the sense that he sought some kind of atonement for the things he had done, but also wanted my understanding. He expressed a stark sense of self-awareness, and I wondered where it would lead him.

Two generations ago, pre-Twitter, pre-YouTube, and pre–camera phone, American soldiers in Vietnam routinely showed their hatred toward the people of their host country, often in far worse ways, and much more frequently than has been the case lately in Afghanistan. In those days, it took much longer for the American public to learn about each of the episodes—more than a year, in the case of the 1968 My Lai massacre. "No one wanted to be the first to publish," Seymour Hersh, who brought the story to light, recently wrote.

AT MY LAI, SOMEWHERE BETWEEN 370 AND 520 VIETNAMESE civilians, mostly women and children, were slaughtered in cold blood by American soldiers, who then, for the most part, kept quiet about it. It was after Hersh's first article appeared that graphic photographs of the massacre—shot while it was taking place by an American army photographer who was at the scene—appeared in newspapers and *Life* magazine. Given today's technology and feverishly up-to-the-minute media culture, it seems unlikely that anything on that scale could occur today and be covered up.

But the fact that fewer civilians—and soldiers, too—are dying in today's wars does not mitigate the sickening horrors of their actions, or reduce their political damage in Afghanistan. The NATO allies are seeking to extricate themselves with a modicum of grace and dignity from a situation that has turned foul, and in which their assigned enemy, the Taliban, has not only gained ground but appears likely to regain power when the final exit is made.

In the fall of 2010, I paid a visit to Mullah Zaeef, a former senior Taliban envoy and post-9/11 Guantánamo inmate, who, since his release and return to Afghanistan, has lived in a Kabul villa with guards provided by President Hamid Karzai. Although he formally eschews any ongoing links with his former Taliban comrades still in the field, Zaeef clearly retains a role of an intermediary; Karzai and many Americans and senior NATO military and intelligence officials certainly viewed him as a possible liaison to moderate Taliban.

Zaeef said he was amused at having become the object of attention of so many Western officials. But he, for one, was not sure who these "moderate" Taliban might be. As for the value of future negotiations, he smiled tartly, and said that the only possible thing that the Taliban might be willing to talk about with the Americans and their allies were the terms of their complete withdrawal from the country. Such an agreement could determine whether they were able to leave Afghanistan with some semblance of dignity, or not, he said.

The sense of inevitability has only intensified since then. Lately, the Taliban have been rubbing the Western forces' noses in it. In dozens of incidents now, Afghan government soldiers, and sometimes officers, have increasingly turned their guns on their unsuspecting American and European military allies. Usually, after the fact, the Taliban claim that the assailants were their members, secretly embedded with the enemy, waiting for the moment to strike, and it is possible that some of them are—but not all of them. Just as there are Americans who—perhaps overwhelmed by the futility of their mission and their own inability to comprehend it, and their hatreds, too—"lose it" and kill Afghan families in the dead of night, there are Afghans who kill Americans in what they conceive of as an act of self-respect. War has a way of making all kinds of killings possible.

# 15

## THE BALLAD OF
## MULLAH OMAR

### (July 30, 2015)

Mullah Omar, whose death Afghan authorities announced on July 29, 2015, was the charismatic spiritual leader of the Taliban, and symbolically a man of great significance. This was so even though he was rarely seen and, according to Afghans, has actually been dead since 2013. (The White House said that the Afghan announcement was "credible.") In the wake of the September 11 terrorist attacks, Mullah Omar refused to hand over Osama bin Laden, his honored "guest" at the time, to the United States government, triggering the invasion of his country.

The international conflict that Mullah Omar helped to start in 2001 is still going on, having cost, thus far, the lives of an estimated ninety-one thousand Afghans, twenty-six thousand of them civilians. Three thousand three hundred ninety-three soldiers from twenty-nine

---

This chapter was originally published as "The Ballad of Mullah Omar," *The New Yorker*, July 30, 2015.

different countries died, too, the majority of them—2,316—Americans. The financial cost to US taxpayers alone has been around a trillion dollars, with billions more to come in the years ahead, in medical bills and other long-term costs for Afghan war veterans. Although the American combat role in the Afghan war officially ended last December, about ten thousand troops have stayed on as advisers and as a counterterrorism quick-reaction force within a reconstituted NATO mission, and will remain at least through the end of 2016.

Mullah Omar's Taliban survived NATO's extended presence in Afghanistan. In some ways, it can be argued that it defeated it. After being dislodged from power by the initial US military assault launched in 2001, the Taliban eventually revived and now has an increasingly robust presence in many parts of the country, leaving Afghanistan in a chronically precarious state. In the past few years, they have carried out suicide attacks (a new tactic for the group) aimed at killing foreigners in Kabul's hotels and restaurants. The Taliban have also launched frequent assaults on Afghan soldiers and policemen around the country, more than four thousand of whom have been killed in 2015, according to a recent *New York Times* report, putting this on track to be the deadliest year for government forces since the conflict began, in 2001. Along the way, the Taliban spun off a lethal franchise in neighboring Pakistan. Among their targets: the schoolgirl Malala Yousafzai, who survived a bullet in the head in 2012.

If he is dead, Mullah Omar joins the growing ranks of his jihadist comrades who have been killed, not least among them bin Laden himself. Pakistani authorities have also reported the death, in a shoot-out, of Malik Ishaq, a notorious Pakistani jihadist and the leader of Lashkar-e-Jhangvi, a murderously sectarian group. Earlier this month, it was the turn, in a US drone strike in Libya, of a Tunisian terrorist called Abu Iyadh, who also spent years in Afghanistan at bin Laden's side, thanks to Mullah Omar's peculiar notion of hospitality. But Mullah Omar's death is being confirmed at the same moment that ISIS—which, in its viciousness and its ability to spread, is something like the perfect storm of jihadism—has begun to make attempted inroads onto the Taliban's turf in Afghanistan, and has established a presence in a strategic province bordering Pakistan.

Despite Taliban warnings to ISIS not to interfere in Afghanistan, the group is believed to be recruiting and planning for an expansion there. A few weeks ago, Gulbuddin Hekmatyar, a veteran Islamist and a Taliban rival, proclaimed his group's allegiance to ISIS, and urged his fighters to attack the Taliban. (Coincidentally or not, the Afghan government and the Taliban recently held a round of face-to-face peace talks.)

The secretive Mullah Omar was a veteran of the Afghan mujahideen's anti-Soviet jihad of the 1980s. He was missing an eye from a battle wound, and had become a self-taught religious scholar. He became a more widely known figure only in the early 1990s, when the mujahideen were fighting among themselves for power, and he was named as the leader of the obscure Taliban. The Taliban were an army of religious students who stormed out of Pakistan and into southern Afghanistan in 1994, vowing to do battle against "immoral and corrupt" mujahideen commanders. They quickly conquered the southern city of Kandahar, and two years later seized the country's capital, Kabul. By then, Mullah Omar—who was rarely photographed—had appeared outside Kandahar's venerable Ahmed Shah Mosque wearing a sacred cloak that was said to have belonged to the Prophet Muhammad. He was proclaimed Keeper of the Faithful by his gaggle of devout armed followers, most of whom, like himself, were ethnic Pashtuns and Sunni Muslims. They were also characterized by their lack of formal schooling, their xenophobia, and their fervent insistence on a strict interpretation of Sharia law. When his followers went to Kabul, Mullah Omar stayed behind in

Kandahar, taking up residence in a rambling walled compound outside the city center, where he held forth in oracular fashion and otherwise spent his time with his several wives, children, and a favorite cow that he would reportedly spend hours with, petting it fondly.

In one of their very first acts in Kabul, Taliban fighters stormed the United Nations compound in Kabul and seized the former Afghan president, Mohammad Najibullah, who had taken refuge there since his overthrow, in 1992. The Taliban beat him, castrated him, dragged him behind a jeep, shot him, and then hanged him. This act set the tone for the Taliban's subsequent rule: They massacred members of the Hazara minority for being Shiites, banned women from working in hospitals or any public offices, and kept girls out of schools; they banned public music, the sale of CDs, and kite flying. Kabul's sports stadium became an execution ground. In March 2001, Mullah Omar's men blew up the two giant stone Buddhas of Bamiyan, archaeological treasures that were fifteen hundred years old.

Mullah Omar had allowed the wealthy Saudi terrorist Osama bin Laden to return to Afghanistan in 1996—he had earlier been a presence during the Soviets' Afghan war—and establish training camps and bases for jihadists from around the world. The two established a terrorist alliance that culminated in the 9/11 attacks. Mullah Omar's house in Kandahar was targeted and mostly destroyed by American bombing raids in the autumn of 2001, but he had escaped and gone into hiding. On a visit there a few weeks after the Taliban fled Kandahar, I visited his home and noticed that, while much of it had been pulverized, there was a core of the flat-roofed house that was untouched. The intact rooms had twelve-foot-thick concrete walls. Just outside the home stood a smaller house, which had a similar roof. It, too, was intact. Local residents told me that they believed it had been built especially for visits to Mullah Omar by "the Sheikh," as bin Laden was known.

On that same trip, I revisited a mujahideen commander with whom

I had spent time during the war against the Soviets. His name was Mullah Naquibullah, and his compound turned out to be right next to Mullah Omar's. When I remarked on his close proximity to the fugitive leader, Naquibullah, a big, hale man, winked and led me to a yard. There were a pair of luxurious pearl-colored Toyota Land Cruisers—XV Limited Editions—and he said, confidingly, "They're Mullah Omar's." He suggested we go see where his old mujahideen camp had been. We drove off in one of Omar's cars, with Naquibullah at the wheel. He popped a CD, which he said he'd found in the car, into a player, and the sound of Afghan music instantly surrounded us. "But Omar banned music!" I said. Naquibullah shrugged. He explained that the song was a diatribe against a particularly despised Taliban foe, a notorious Uzbek warlord named General Rashid Dostum; its main refrain was: "O murderer of the Afghan people."

Smiling, Naquibullah turned to me and said, "What would life be without music?"

# 16

## KUNDUZ FALLS AGAIN

### (October 6, 2015)

Fourteen years ago, on November 25, 2001, I watched the Taliban surrender Kunduz to Northern Alliance forces. It was a tense and dramatic day. I entered the city, on foot, before dawn, with a column of mujahideen fighters, and, like them, was confused by the noise of aircraft taking off from the city's airport. After daybreak, at a mustering point in the city, enraged mujahideen commanders told me that what we had heard was an exodus, by airplane, of large numbers of Pakistani and Al Qaeda fighters, as well as some senior Taliban figures, whom, they claimed, the Americans had allowed to leave the city.

At the time, the accusations struck me and other colleagues as unlikely: Why would our government allow Al Qaeda's allies to escape its dragnet? Later on, however, my Washington-based colleague Seymour Hersh confirmed that the US government had allowed Pakistan, which had secretly fostered the Taliban and Al Qaeda alliance, a face-saving

---

This chapter was originally published as "The Fall of Kunduz," *The New Yorker*, October 6, 2015.

retreat from Kunduz. It was one of the many murky episodes that made
the US military's "defeat" of the Taliban seem less of one in those tu-
multuous early days of the "war on terror." Deals were often cut between
surrendering forces and the Northern Alliance, as we had previously
seen in the northern city of Taloqan, where hundreds of well-armed
Uzbek fighters for the other side were allowed to cross the battle lines,
harbored by commanders who had come to agreements with them,
given them safe refuge, and allowed them to keep their guns. Many, apparently, later made their way to the tribal territories of Pakistan, where
they have fought on as Islamist extremists, in alliance with the Taliban, to this day.

The fall of Kunduz was a messy thing, and took place throughout
the day. There were continuing firefights, as some Taliban units refused
to stand down and others surrendered. Bodies lay here and there. We
heard that, on the other side of the city, a large number of Taliban were
surrendering to forces commanded by the redoubtable Uzbek Northern
Alliance warlord Abdul Rashid Dostum. In the coming days, the news
trickled out that many hundreds of those Taliban prisoners had died
from asphyxiation after being locked in shipping containers by Dostum's men.

Western reporters moved on from Kunduz, and few ever returned.
In the coming years, as NATO moved into the country to help pacify it
and protect it from the resurgent Taliban, Kunduz was assigned to a
contingent of German peacekeeping troops. By the late 2000s, as the
Taliban became increasingly strong throughout Afghanistan, they reappeared in the Kunduz countryside as well. American and British
NATO commanders grumbled about the unwillingness of their German counterparts to engage the enemy, and claimed, apparently credi-
bly, that one of the Germans' initial stipulations for their Kunduz
deployment was that they would not patrol outside their bases at night.

To them, this policy amounted to a tacit green light from the Germans for the Taliban to roam throughout the province.

BY 2010, SECURITY HAD SO DETERIORATED IN KUNDUZ THAT the US military bolstered the German presence there with an additional twenty-five hundred troops. This was only a holding tactic, however, because by 2013 most of the NATO drawdown had taken place, and the Germans handed off Kunduz to the Afghan government forces, which, as we have seen this past week, have proved unable to hold the city without US assistance.

First, on September 28, Kunduz fell to the Taliban, making it the first Afghan provincial capital to revert to the militia's control. The Taliban did what might have been expected: They roared around the streets in pickups, celebrating their victory; freed hundreds of prisoners, including many militants; and declared Sharia law. Executions and abductions were also reported. Then, on October 1, Kunduz was retaken by Afghan government forces, which had regrouped outside the city after failing to defend it. US military aircraft helped by bombing the Taliban from the air, and American Special Forces assisted the Afghans on the ground. (NATO's military forces ended their combat role in Afghanistan last year, but reduced numbers of troops have remained to train and assist the Afghan Army.)

On October 4, a US air strike resulted in the deaths of twenty-two civilians, including doctors and patients, at the Médecins Sans Frontières hospital in Kunduz. The Pentagon has acknowledged that its warplanes carried out the attack, but said that the Afghan military requested "air support" because it was taking fire from the hospital. Tragic as it is, the attack seems unlikely to have been an intentionally criminal action— or, for that matter, a war crime—as some have alleged.

The fact is that, in the aftermath of the drawdown in Afghanistan, US forces have had to intervene to save a city that has fallen to Islamist extremists, much as they have had to intervene in the aftermath of the withdrawal from Iraq. And although Kunduz has been retaken for now, the outlook there, and throughout Afghanistan, is not promising. The Kunduz Province is a bastion of ethnic Pashtuns—the Taliban's main constituency—in the otherwise predominantly Tajik and Uzbek north. Within Afghanistan, it has strategic importance on par with Mosul in Iraq. In 2001, Kunduz was not only the Taliban's last stand, but also one of Al Qaeda's. The city fell to the Northern Alliance only on November 26, weeks after the Taliban retreated from the capital, Kabul, and from Kandahar, the ultimate Taliban stronghold, in the deep south.

In a sense, however, the current situation raises the question: Did Kunduz—or much of the rest of Afghanistan, for that matter—ever really fall? And if it didn't, what does that say about the decade-and-a-half-long American-led counterinsurgency campaign that has cost so much "in blood and treasure"—as American generals and politicians like to call the thousands of lives sacrificed and the trillions of dollars spent? The victims of the hospital air strike are only the latest casualties in an ongoing Afghan war in which the Taliban, once again, are major players, and now seem as likely to win back power as they once appeared to have lost it.

# 17

---

# THE RETURN OF
# THE TALIBAN

## (August 13, 2021)

Watching Afghanistan's cities fall to the Taliban in rapid succession, as the United States completes a hasty withdrawal from the country, is a surreal experience, laced with a sense of déjà vu. Twenty years ago, I reported from Afghanistan as the Taliban's enemies took these same cities from them, in the short but decisive US-backed military offensive that followed the 9/11 attacks. The war on terror had just been declared, and the unfolding American military action was cloaked in purposeful determinism in the name of freedom and against tyranny. For a brief moment, the war was blessed by that rare thing: public support, both at home and abroad.

In the wake of the horror of Al Qaeda's attacks on the United States, most Americans polled believed that the country was doing the "right thing" in going to war in Afghanistan. That level of support didn't last

---

This chapter was originally published as "The Return of the Taliban," *The New Yorker*, August 13, 2021.

long, but the war on terror did, and so did the military expedition to Afghanistan, which stretched on inconclusively for two decades and now ends in ignominy. Donald Trump set this fiasco in motion, by announcing his intention to pull out the remaining American troops in Afghanistan and begin negotiations with the Taliban. In February 2020, an agreement was signed that promised to withdraw all US military forces in return for, among other things, peace talks with the US-backed Afghan government. The American troops were duly drawn down, but, instead of engaging in real discussions, the Taliban stepped up their attacks. In April, President Joe Biden announced his intention to carry on with the withdrawal, and pull out forces by September 11. However much he says that he does "not regret" his decision, his presidency will be held responsible for whatever happens in Afghanistan now, and the key words that will forever be associated with the long American sojourn there will include hubris, ignorance, inevitability, betrayal, and failure.

In that regard, the United States joins a line of notable predecessors, including Great Britain in the nineteenth century, and the Soviet Union in the twentieth. Those historic precedents don't make the American experience any more palatable. In Afghanistan—and, for that matter, in Iraq, as well—the Americans did not merely not learn from the mistakes of others; they did not learn from their own mistakes, committed a generation earlier, in Vietnam.

The main errors were, first, to underestimate the adversaries and to presume that American technological superiority necessarily translated into mastery of the battlefield, and, second, to be culturally disdainful, rarely learning the languages or the customs of the local people. By the end of the first American decade in Afghanistan, it seemed evident that the Western counterinsurgency enterprise was doomed to fail, and not only because of the return of the Taliban in many rural parts of the country: The Americans and their NATO allies closed themselves off from Afghans in large regional bases, from which they operated in smaller units out of combat outposts, and distrust reigned between them and their putative Afghan comrades. "Green-on-blue attacks," in which Afghan security forces opened fire on their American and European counterparts, became alarmingly frequent. The Taliban, meanwhile, grew inexorably stronger.

Ten years on, as Afghanistan's provincial capitals are falling to the Taliban and Kabul itself becomes encircled, the litany of exotic place names—Sheberghan, Taloqan, Kunduz, Kandahar, Herat—must mean little to most Americans, except for those who were once deployed in them. But a generation ago, as Afghan mujahideen, or holy warriors, of the so-called Northern Alliance (an anti-Taliban coalition commanded by warlords) battled alongside American Special Forces to free these same towns from the Taliban, they were in the news constantly, as commonplace to Americans then as Benghazi or Raqqa became in later years. (In war, as in life, perhaps, people and places can become briefly and often intensely familiar, only to be discarded from memory when their apparent relevance has ceased. Who today remembers Hamid Karzai? Or Mullah Omar?)

When Kunduz and Sheberghan, adjacent cities in northern Afghanistan, fell within a day of each other last weekend, I wondered how many Americans recalled that these were the sites of some of the bloodiest early episodes of the war, in 2001. In the desert outside Kunduz, hundreds and possibly thousands of Taliban and suspected Al Qaeda prisoners of war, who had surrendered to the Northern Alliance after the fall of the city that November, were locked in shipping containers and shot or left to die by forces led by the Afghan warlord Abdul Rashid Dostum, who was working with the CIA and with Special Forces commandos. Some of the survivors of that ordeal were selected for rendition by American agents on the ground, and ended up as prisoners in Guantánamo, beginning a controversial new chapter in American judicial history.

At the same time, an uprising by captured Taliban and foreign jihadis, at a nearby fortress named Qala-i-Jangi, resulted in the killing of Johnny Micheal Spann, an American CIA officer—the first American to die in combat in Afghanistan. After days of fighting, during which at least three hundred prisoners died, the "American Taliban" John Walker Lindh, a twenty-year-old Muslim convert from California who had become a volunteer with the Taliban forces and had been questioned by Spann, was recaptured, after Dostum flooded the compound's underground chambers. Lindh was returned to the US, tried in federal court for providing support to the Taliban, and sentenced to twenty years in a high-security federal prison. His presence at the fortress, though there is no evidence that he participated in the revolt, provoked strong feelings in the United States and led to an ongoing debate about national identity and loyalty in the modern age. In 2019, Lindh was released three years early, for good behavior, and he is on probation for the remainder of his sentence.

I was on the scene for the fall of Kunduz, in 2001, and was part of a small group of foreign journalists ambushed by Taliban fighters who had remained in hiding and attacked, even as most of their comrades were in the process of surrendering. Fortunately, none of us was killed, but the following night, after we returned to the nearby provincial capital, Taloqan, which had already been retaken by the Northern Alliance—and which also fell to the Taliban last weekend—a Swedish journalist was shot and killed by gunmen at the house where he was staying. After his death, and considering the lingering presence of numerous Taliban in Taloqan—along with that of allied Uzbek fighters, a group of whom we had seen engaged in last-minute deals with the Northern Alliance—the foreign journalists soon fled the city. I joined an armed convoy headed for Kabul, a four-day journey through the Hindu Kush mountains. Along the way, we were accosted by Afghan gunmen—perhaps Taliban, perhaps merely highwaymen—but, again, we were lucky, and arrived without loss of life.

Kabul had already fallen, supposedly. At least, the Taliban were visibly gone and, with them, their Al Qaeda friends. But, on subsequent days, as I moved around the devastated city, I had reason to wonder how genuine the Western-assisted Northern Alliance victory had been. One morning, a group of four women concealed in blue burkhas approached me on the street, and one asked if I knew of any work opportunities. I was accosted by a furious shopkeeper for daring to communicate across the gender divide. The women scattered. It was as if a malady lingered in the Afghan air, despite the Taliban's retreat.

MOST OF THE AFGHAN MEN WHOM I MET AND WHO LED BAT-tles against the Taliban two decades ago are now dead. Almost all were killed, in separate assassinations, as part of the Taliban's plan to return to action. Their comeback has taken twenty years, but it is a classic example of a successful guerrilla war of attrition, and has involved all the usual elements of guerrilla strategy: a stealth campaign of hit-and-run military attacks, selective assassinations to demoralize their adversaries, and acts of terror that both weakened the government and created an atmosphere of abject compliance from local populations. A public campaign of hearts and minds followed, accompanied by decoy negotiations with the government and its allies in order to promote the idea that, as a force, the Taliban are not really extremist and are, in fact, open to dialogue, even to internal change. But the Taliban, by their very nature, are fundamentalists, believers in a strict Koranic credo.

In the pre-Taliban days of the late eighties, when I spent time with the mujahideen of Kandahar, who were then fighting the Soviets, a pair of local Islamic scholars banned music after consulting their sacred texts; this rule was added to their list of severe prohibitions, which included death for adulterers and the amputation of hands for thieves. In a court, set up in the middle of a battlefield, the two judges explained their sentencing system and told me how many murderers and adulterers they had put to death, after which one of them said, "We adhere to the Sharia in all cases." Patting a pile of holy tracts next to him, he added, "All the answers are here."

It was this same kind of earnest devotion to Islamic law that earned early popularity for the Taliban, when they emerged in the same area a few years later, after the Soviet retreat, under the leadership of Mullah Omar, a particularly devout mujahideen commander. Various mujahideen warlords who had emerged ascendant were fighting one another for power, and some were abusive toward civilians in the areas that they controlled. Mullah Omar's Taliban presented themselves as a moralizing force and made swift headway against the warlords. Within a couple of years, they controlled most of Afghanistan, and Kabul fell to them in 1996.

With no opposition except for a rump group of Northern Alliance warlords, who held out in the northern mountains for the next few years (until the Americans came along to assist them, in 2001), the Taliban imposed their strict version of Sharia law. Afghan women were all but excluded from public life, with many girls prohibited from attending school; the freedom to work for female teachers, doctors, and nurses was drastically circumscribed. The Taliban zealotry grew so great that children were forbidden to play with dolls or to fly kites, in favor of prayer sessions, while ethnic minorities and members of religious sects other than the extreme Sunni version of Islam that the Taliban espoused were persecuted. In one incident, it is estimated that the Taliban killed at least two thousand ethnic Hazaras, who are Shiite. Public executions became a norm, as well, often of women accused of various moral offenses. The killings were often carried out on sports fields or in stadiums, with the condemned sometimes stoned to death, or summarily shot in the head, or hanged, or, in the case of homosexuals, crushed and suffocated by mud walls toppled onto them by tanks. Before ISIS, in other words, there was the Taliban, showing how to do things.

In March 2001—a few months before their Al Qaeda comrades carried out the 9/11 attacks—the Taliban, as a testament to their supposed iconoclastic purity, destroyed the Bamiyan Buddhas. These were a pair of giant, 1,500-year-old sandstone statues, regarded as one of the man-made wonders of the ancient world. Taliban officials also took sledgehammers and axes to priceless artifacts in the Kabul Museum, destroying anything that predated Islamic civilization. The outside world did little to prevent any of these crimes.

The list of atrocities that the Taliban committed while they were in power goes on and on, and in the two decades since their ouster they have murdered again and again, in a war aimed at anyone who opposes them or even represents a potential challenge to them. The other day, a Taliban spokesman took credit for the murder, in Kabul, of his government counterpart, in what he called "a special attack." Women have also been among the Taliban's most consistent victims, from schoolteachers and television presenters to female parliamentarians and judges. In March, in the eastern city of Jalalabad, the Taliban killed three young female media workers; a female journalist was killed in June, in Kabul, by a car bomb. If the Taliban do sweep back into power in Kabul in the coming weeks, which seems a strong possibility, women will again be among their foremost targets.

There is a conceit that today's Taliban is different from the Taliban of 2001. This is certainly an idea that some senior Taliban officials have sought to propagate in recent years. Facts on the ground suggest otherwise. They claim to have moved on from their old alliance with Al Qaeda, for instance, but over the years they have partnered with other jihadist groups operating, as they have done, out of sanctuaries in neighboring Pakistan, such as the Haqqani network, which is responsible for scores of suicide bombings and so-called complex attacks—involving gunmen and suicide bombers acting in tandem—and for causing hundreds of civilian deaths.

The Taliban have rendered Afghanistan unworkable as a country; unworkable, that is, without them. And the truth is that they were never really beaten. They merely did what guerrillas do in order to survive: They melted away in the face of overwhelming force, regrouped and restored themselves to fighting strength, and returned to battle. Here they are.

# 18

———

# THE END OF THE
# AMERICAN EMPIRE?

## (September 1, 2021)

How does an empire die? Often, it seems, there is a growing sense of decay, and then something happens, a single event that provides the tipping point. After the Second World War, Great Britain was all but bankrupt and its empire was in shreds, but it soldiered on thanks to a US government loan and the new Cold War exigencies that allowed it to maintain the outward appearance of a global player. It wasn't until the 1956 Suez debacle, when Britain was pressured by the US, the Soviet Union, and the United Nations to withdraw its forces from Egypt—which it had invaded along with Israel and France following Gamal Abdel Nasser's seizure of the Suez Canal—that it became clear that its imperial days were over. The floodgates to decolonization soon opened.

In February 1989, when the Soviet Union withdrew its military from Afghanistan after a failed nine-year attempt to pacify the country,

———

This chapter was originally published as "Is the U.S. Withdrawal from Afghanistan the End of the American Empire?," *The New Yorker*, September 1, 2021.

it did so in a carefully choreographed ceremony that telegraphed solemnity and dignity. An orderly procession of tanks moved north across the Friendship Bridge, which spans the Amu Dar'ya River, between Afghanistan and Uzbekistan—then a Soviet republic. The Soviet commander, Lieutenant General Boris Gromov, walked across with his teenage son, carrying a bouquet of flowers and smiling for the cameras. Behind him, he declared, no Soviet soldiers remained in the country. "The day that millions of Soviet people have waited for has come," he said at a military rally later that day. "In spite of our sacrifices and losses, we have totally fulfilled our internationalist duty."

Gromov's triumphal speech was not quite the equivalent of George W. Bush's "Mission Accomplished" following the 2003 Iraq invasion, but it came close, and the message that it was intended to relay, at least to people inside the Soviet Union, was a reassuring one: The Red Army was leaving Afghanistan because it wanted to, not because it had been defeated. The Kremlin had installed an ironfisted Afghan loyalist who was left to run things in its absence, a former secret-police chief named Najibullah; there was also a combat-tested Afghan Army, equipped and trained by the Soviets.

Meanwhile, the mujahideen guerrilla armies that had been subsidized and armed by the United States and its partners Saudi Arabia and Pakistan were in a celebratory mood. Their combat units were massed outside Afghanistan's regime-held cities, and there was an expectation that it would not be long before Najibullah succumbed, too, and Kabul would be theirs. In the end, he held out for another three years, with his downfall merely leading to a new civil war.

For all the talk of internationalist duty, the Afghanistan that the Soviets left behind was a charnel ground. Out of its population of twelve million people, as many as two million civilians had been killed in the war, more than five million had fled the country, and another two million were internally displaced. Many of the country's towns and cities lay in ruins, and half of Afghanistan's rural villages and hamlets had been destroyed.

Officially, only fifteen thousand or so Soviet troops had been killed—although the real figure may be much higher—and fifty thousand more soldiers were wounded. But hundreds of aircraft, tanks, and artillery pieces were destroyed or lost, and countless billions of dollars diverted from the hard-pressed Soviet economy to pay for it all. However much the Kremlin tried to gloss it over, the average Soviet citizen understood that the Afghanistan intervention had been a costly fiasco.

It was only eighteen months after the Soviet withdrawal from Afghanistan that a group of hard-liners tried to launch a coup against the reformist premier Mikhail Gorbachev. But they had miscalculated their power, and popular support. In the face of public demonstrations against them, their putsch soon failed, followed by the collapse of the Soviet Union itself. Of course, by then, much beyond the Soviet Union's Afghan quagmire had conspired to fatally weaken the once powerful empire from within.

While the two events are humiliatingly comparable, only time will tell whether the old adage about Afghanistan's being the graveyard of empires proves as true for the United States as it did for the Soviet Union. My colleague Robin Wright thinks so, writing in *The New Yorker* on August 15, "America's Great Retreat [from Afghanistan] is at least as humiliating as the Soviet Union's withdrawal in 1989, an event that contributed to the end of its empire and Communist rule. . . . Both of the big powers withdrew as losers, with their tails between their legs, leaving behind chaos." When I asked James Clad, a former US deputy assistant secretary of defense, for his thoughts on the matter, he emailed me, "It's a damaging blow, but the 'end' of Empire? Not yet, and probably not for a long time. The egregious *defeat* has hammered American prestige, however, delivering the geopolitical equivalent of egg on our face. Is that a fatal blow? In the wider world, America still retains its offshore power-balancing function. And despite some overheated journalism, no irreversible advantage has passed to our primary geopolitical opponent—China."

It is true that, for the time being, America retains its military prowess and its economic strength. But, for two decades now, it has seemed increasingly unable to effectively harness either of them to its advantage. Instead of enhancing its hegemony by deploying its strengths wisely, it has repeatedly squandered its efforts, diminishing both its aura of invincibility and its standing in the eyes of other nations. The vaunted global war on terror—which included Bush's invasion of Iraq for the purpose of finding weapons of mass destruction that did not exist, Barack Obama's decision to intervene in Libya and his indecisiveness about a "red line" in Syria, and Donald Trump's betrayal of the Kurds in the same country and his 2020 deal with the Taliban to withdraw US troops from Afghanistan—has effectively caused terrorism to metastasize across the planet. Al Qaeda may no longer be as prominent as it was on 9/11, but it still exists and has a branch in North Africa; ISIS has affiliates there, too, and in Mozambique, and, of course, as the horrific attacks last Thursday at Kabul's airport underscored, in Afghanistan. And the Taliban have returned to power, right where it all began twenty years ago.

Rory Stewart, a former British government minister who served on Prime Minister Theresa May's National Security Council, told me that he has observed the events in Afghanistan with "horror":

Throughout the Cold War, the United States had a consistent world view. Administrations came and went, but the world view didn't change that much. And then, following 9/11, we—America's allies—went along with the new theories it came up with to explain its response to the terrorist threat in Afghanistan and elsewhere. But there's been a total lack of continuity since then; the way the United States viewed the world in 2006 is night and day to how it views it today. Afghanistan has gone from being the center of the world to one in which we are told that such places pose no threat at all. What that suggests is that all of the former theorizing now means nothing. To see this lurch to isolationism that is so sudden that it practically destroys everything we've fought for together for twenty years is deeply disturbing.

STEWART, WHO COFOUNDED THE TURQUOISE MOUNTAIN Foundation—which has supported cultural heritage projects, health, and education in Afghanistan for fifteen years years—and is now a senior fellow at Yale's Jackson School of Global Affairs, was skeptical of Joe Biden's assertion that the strategic priorities of the United States no longer lie in places like Afghanistan, but in countering China's expansion. "If this were true," he said, "then clearly part of the logic of the American confrontation with China would be to say, 'We're going to demonstrate our values with our presence across the world,' just as it did in the Cold War with the USSR. And one way you'd do that is to continue your presence in the Middle East and other places, because removing yourself is counterproductive. In the end, I think all of this talk about a China pivot is really just an excuse for American isolationism."

Back to the nagging question: Does the return of the Taliban in Afghanistan represent the end of the American era? On the heels of what appears to have been a disastrous decision by Biden to adhere to a US troop drawdown that was set in motion by his feckless predecessor, it can certainly be said that the international image of the United States has been damaged. It seems a valid question to ask whether the United States can claim much moral authority internationally after handing

Afghanistan, and its millions of hapless citizens, back to the custody of the Taliban. But it remains unclear whether, as Stewart suggests, the US retreat from Afghanistan represents part of a larger inward turn, or whether, as Clad believes, the US may soon reassert itself somewhere else to show the world that it still has muscle. Right now, it feels as if the American era isn't quite over, but it isn't what it once was, either.

# 19

## AFTER THE FALL

For fifteen years, Zabihullah Mujahid was the Tokyo Rose of the Taliban: a clandestine operative who called reporters to claim responsibility for his fighters' attacks and to exult in their victories. Sometimes the victims were American soldiers or their coalition allies. Sometimes they were Afghan government troops. Often, civilians were killed. For reporters, Mujahid was a kind of phantom, a disembodied voice on the phone. No one ever saw his face, and, when one journalist claimed to have encountered him, Mujahid fiercely denied it. But he seemed to talk to everyone, all the time, and a rumor spread to explain his output: Zabihullah Mujahid was a composite identity, assumed by a rotating group of Talibs, who perhaps weren't even living in Afghanistan. He denied this, too.

Last summer, Mujahid appeared in public for the first time. After years of steady gains in the countryside, the Taliban had swarmed into

---

This chapter was originally published as "After the Fall," *The New Yorker*, February 28, 2022.

Kabul as President Ashraf Ghani fled to Abu Dhabi. While the Taliban asserted their authority, Mujahid held a press conference to announce that he was the new government's acting deputy minister of information and culture. With the fall of Kabul, he had been transformed from the covert spokesman of a long-running insurgency to the face of a national administration. He was, it turned out, a lean, sharp-featured man in middle age.

In September, after the US military's last humanitarian-evacuation flight left Kabul's airport, Mujahid introduced the interim government of the Islamic Emirate of Afghanistan. This was the same name that the Taliban had adopted during their previous stint in power, a brutal period that extended from 1996 to 2001. But Mujahid offered a vision of a more ecumenical Afghanistan, with an "inclusive" government that protected the rights of women and ethnic minorities. He maintained that the Taliban weren't after revenge, and would offer amnesty to their former enemies. This was hard to believe. A few weeks earlier, Mujahid had issued a press release rejoicing in the assassination of the previous government's spokesman, a man named Dawa Khan Menapal. He didn't say what his predecessor's offense was, only that he had been "punished for his misdeeds, killed in a special operation carried out by the mujahideen."

One December evening, I met with Mujahid in an unheated corner office at the Afghan Media and Information Center, the mostly empty ministry that he now ran. Wearing a black turban with white stripes, he sat very still, his eyes watchful.

I asked how his new position compared with his old one. "In the past, it was a military situation, and it wasn't very pleasant," he said. "We had to announce how many people were killed. That in itself was painful. The second really painful aspect was the civilian casualties. We had to gather information and publish it. It was heartbreaking. It is three months now that we do not have such heartbreaking news."

The Taliban had achieved an astonishing victory: After years of guerrilla warfare, they had seized power from an established government backed by some of the world's best-equipped militaries. Afghanistan is now in the hands of an insurgent force, fervently committed to bringing about a truly Islamic state. The country seems to be at the beginning of a revolution just as sweeping as the Communist victory that remade China in the 1940s, or the Islamist takeover of Iran in 1979. But when I asked Mujahid if the Taliban were imposing a revolution, he seemed taken aback. "This is a soft revolution," he said. "Revolutions are sharp and problematic, causing bloodshed, destruction of foundations. That is not what has happened." He added, "This was a change that was needed. We fought for twenty years to free Afghanistan from the foreigners, so that the Afghans would have a government of their choice." Now that the Americans were gone, Mujahid suggested, Afghanistan could begin anew. "The foreign forces were the cause of the casualties, and when they left the war ended," he said. "There were also some authorities who were pocketing the public wealth. They were corrupt. The country is free of them, and now we will try to lead the country toward a positive change."

During several weeks I spent talking with Taliban officials, they all expressed a desire for good relations with the United States. Some even argued that the US should reopen its embassy and lead international efforts to rebuild Afghanistan. But had the Taliban really changed, or were they just saying what they needed to say in order to stabilize the economy and keep themselves in power? Until August, some 80 percent of the Afghan government's budget had come from the United States, its partners, and international lenders. That support had disappeared. The Biden administration also froze all Afghan government funds in US banks—some $7 billion. The Afghan banking system, without access to overseas assets, risks collapse. "Our message to the world, especially to the American public and the American politicians, is that they should choose a different path, different from the path of war," Mujahid told me.

"Sanctions, pressures, and threats have not resulted in anything positive in the past twenty years. We can go forward through positive interactions."

The Taliban seemed assured that their victory allowed them to reshape the story of the country's future, and of its past. I asked Mujahid if he felt any regrets over the killing of his predecessor. "You mean Dawa Khan Menapal?" he said, and laughed for the first time in our talk. He waved his hands dismissively. "It was war," he said. The Americans had tried to kill him "more than ten times," he claimed. "I was just a spokesman, too. Was *I* a justifiable target?"

To most of the Taliban, Kabul is terra incognita—a cosmopolitan enclave in an otherwise rural, and deeply traditional, country. To the city's residents, the Taliban are interlopers, as out of place as Texas militiamen on the Upper West Side. Three months after the takeover, the residents of Kabul were uneasily adapting to the new reality. Just about all the foreigners had left the country, but the Taliban were ubiquitous, manning roadblocks and access points, riding in Humvees and pickup trucks with guns at the ready. Some kept their hair long and wore the traditional *shalwar kameez*—occasionally in incongruously bright blues, oranges, or yellows—with their eyes lined with black kohl. Others borrowed the style of US Special Forces, wearing camouflage uniforms, boots, and wraparound sunglasses, and carrying weapons left behind by American troops. For the most part, the civilians pretended the Talibs weren't there.

In 2001, when the American-led invasion forced out the Taliban, the Afghan capital was a forlorn place, much of it in ruins after more than two decades of Soviet occupation and civil war. By the following spring, it had begun to revive, as more than a million refugees returned from abroad. Since then, Kabul's estimated population has nearly doubled, to almost five million; the country has grown from some twenty-one million citizens to forty million. The median age is just eighteen.

Kabul is now a bustling commercial city, with new apartment buildings rising above the skyline. Its endemic inequities remain: There are beggars in the streets, and the slums on the surrounding hills have expanded. But there are gaudy wedding palaces and dress shops for the middle class, along with pool halls, gyms, and hairdressers for young men. Billboards advertise a startling variety of imported energy drinks.

In the nineties, the Taliban forced Afghans to conform to their stringent interpretation of Islam. Violators could have limbs amputated, or be publicly stoned to death. Women were made to wear all-concealing

Taliban fighter seen in a car's rearview mirror, moving through Kabul, December 2021.   MOISES SAMAN/MAGNUM PHOTOS

burkhas and prevented from holding jobs or attending school. Morality commissars hunted down graven images; in shops, men with markers blacked out illustrations on packages of baby soap. Even road-crossing signs for livestock were painted over.

The current residents of Kabul clearly feared that the terror of those days would return. But, aside from a few incidents, the Taliban had subjected them to little visible repression. Signs on dress shops still showed Bollywood-style images of glamorous women, which in the nineties would have brought their proprietors a beating, or worse. The battle over graven images was effectively lost: Just about everyone has a smartphone, with access to Instagram. Although women and girls had been provisionally banished from workplaces and high schools, they were still out on the streets. All wore headscarves, but few had on burkhas. Some even wore makeup, without evident harassment from soldiers.

One afternoon, I spoke about the new regime with Sayed Hamed Gailani, a prominent former politician and an astute observer of his country. We met at his home, in a wealthy section of Kabul, where a servant brought fresh pomegranate juice and pastries on delicate porcelain plates. Gailani, a onetime mujahideen fighter against the Soviets, is now a rotund, urbane man in his sixties. His father was Pir Sayed Gailani, a Sufi spiritual leader who also controlled a mujahideen faction—known, in tribute to its leader's elegant taste, as the Gucci Muj. When I mentioned it to Gailani, he laughed good-naturedly and said, "I must point out that my father much preferred Hermès."

Gailani was among a handful of politically connected Afghans who had remained in the country after President Ghani fled, hoping to persuade both the Taliban and the international community that there was a viable way forward. He didn't pretend that the conflict was over in Afghanistan. "I don't think my life will be long enough to see the end of this drama," he said, laughing. "It's like one of those Turkish TV series that never end." But he professed guarded optimism. Unlike most revolutionaries, he argued, the Talibs had not killed a lot of people in their return to power; they had behaved themselves this time. When the Taliban seized power twenty-five years ago, he said, "you couldn't go out without a beard, and the women couldn't leave the house." But, he suggested, the reason the Taliban hadn't moved faster to reshape the country was that Ghani's flight and the quick fall of Kabul had taken them by surprise. "They weren't really ready for it," Gailani said. "They still have problems to work out among themselves."

Near Kabul's Bird Market, an ancient bazaar where poultry, fighting birds, and songbirds are sold, is a twenty-foot obelisk, topped with a red clenched fist. It was erected in honor of Farkhunda Malikzada, a young woman who was beaten and burned to death by a jeering mob of men in 2015, after being falsely accused of burning a Koran.

The question of women's rights is perhaps the greatest unresolved issue in the new Afghanistan. After taking power, the Taliban leadership announced that girls up to the sixth grade could resume schooling, but for the most part older girls had to wait until "conditions" were right. When I talked with Mujahid, the spokesman, he was vague about what those conditions were, and about whether women would be allowed to work. The impediment was funding, he said. "For education and work, women need to have separate spaces," he explained primly. "They would also require special separate means of transportation." But, he added, "the banks are closed, the money is frozen."

Mujahid didn't answer when I asked about plans for women in government. Instead, he pointed out that there were still women working in various ministries, including health, education, and the interior, and also at the airports and in the courts. "Wherever they are needed, they come to work," he insisted.

But some of these women were being forced to sign in at their jobs and then go home, to create the illusion of equity. The Taliban had also closed the Ministry of Women's Affairs, which was created soon after the US invasion; the building was repurposed as the new headquarters of the religious police, the Ministry for the Promotion of Virtue and Prevention of Vice. In September, on the day that Mujahid announced the new government, a group of women gathered on the street to protest. Taliban fighters pushed their way into the crowd, striking some of the demonstrators and firing weapons into the air.

Senior Taliban officials tended to deflect concerns about the future of women in Afghanistan. When I asked Suhail Shaheen, the Taliban nominee for ambassador to the UN, whether his government would allow women in schools and in the workplace, he shot back, "If the West really cares about girls, they should attend to their poverty. Sanctions are punishing the fifteen million girls in this country."

Shaheen was in Kabul, rather than at the UN headquarters, in New York, because the Taliban regime has not been granted diplomatic recognition. I met him in the garden of the Serena Hotel, an old haunt of journalists and politicians. Shaheen was happy to talk about America's failings but grew testy when pressed on sensitive matters. I asked about the Hazaras, a predominantly Shiite minority that has historically been persecuted by the Taliban, who are mostly Sunnis from the Pashtun ethnic majority. Shaheen replied that the new government had no intention of harming them. I noted that, in the nineties, his comrades had slaughtered thousands of Hazaras, whom they regarded as apostates. He stared stonily at me. Finally, he said, "The Hazara Shia for us are also Muslim. We believe we are one, like flowers in a garden. The more flowers, the more beautiful." He went on, "We have started a new page. We do not want to be entangled with the past."

DESPITE THE TALK OF INCLUSION, THE HIGHEST RANKS OF THE Taliban government initially contained no Hazaras, and no women. In late September, amid international criticism, the Talibs added an ethnic Hazara, as the deputy health minister, and an ethnic Tajik, as the deputy trade minister. The additions struck many Afghans as tokenism. As an adviser to the Taliban told me, "Calling their government inclusive is not a help—because it's *not*."

The government is also said to be profoundly divided. On one side is the Kandahar faction, named for the southern city where the late Mullah Muhammad Omar founded the Taliban. It includes the country's supreme leader, an enigmatic scholar of Islam named Mawlawi Haibatullah Akhundzada, and the acting defense minister, Mullah Mohammad Yaqoob, who is Mullah Omar's son. Its public face is Abdul Ghani Baradar, the acting deputy prime minister, who played a crucial role in negotiations with the Americans.

On the other side is the Haqqani network, a clan of militants closely linked to Pakistan's secret services. Where the Kandahar faction began as an insular, rural force, primarily concerned with ruling its home turf, the Haqqanis were interested in global jihad. It was the clan's founder, the late Jalaluddin Haqqani, who connected the Taliban with Osama bin Laden. For some members of the Kandahar faction, this is a kind of original sin in modern Afghan history—a crucial miscalculation that led to the attacks of September 11 and to the foreign intervention that forced the Taliban from power.

The Haqqanis led the military takeover of Kabul this summer, and their leader, Sirajuddin Haqqani, is the acting interior minister. The US government has offered a $10 million bounty for Haqqani's arrest, in connection with a series of terror attacks. One occurred in 2008 at the Serena Hotel, where I'd met Shaheen; a US citizen and five other people were killed. Haqqani is thought to be responsible for at least two other hotel attacks, and for two attacks on the Indian Embassy, in which dozens of people died. He and his clan now control a preponderance of security positions in Afghanistan. As interior minister, he has authority over the police and the intelligence services. His uncle Khalil

Haqqani, who is also wanted for terrorism, leads the Ministry of Refugees. Elite Haqqani commandos run military bases in and around Kabul.

Mawlawi Mohammad Salim Saad, a former head of suicide bombers, is in charge of security at Kabul's airport. I met him one evening at his office, surrounded by a dozen of his men. They had just come from their prayers, and Saad, a tall, severe-looking man, told me that he was fasting. When I asked how he had felt sending men to their deaths, he said, "You should ask what it is that makes people become willing to give up their lives. These were oppressed people, willing to sacrifice themselves against a much larger army."

For the Haqqani faction, it was the suicide missions and other "complex attacks" that secured victory over the foreign occupiers. For Baradar, the war was won at the negotiating table, where Trump's envoys agreed to lenient terms for a withdrawal. I asked Shaheen, the diplomat, "Are there two Talibans?" Shaking his head, he said, "There is *one* Taliban. They have different viewpoints and different angles on how to proceed, but there is one Islam." Mujahid went further, insisting, "There is no Haqqani network."

The government remains opaque to many Afghans: Its major figures, after decades as secretive insurgents, avoid appearing in public. The supreme leader has never been seen. The single known image of Sirajuddin Haqqani is a silhouette. Officials like Yaqoob, the defense minister, typically appear in carefully controlled videos. Among the top leaders, the most familiar face belongs to the acting prime minister, Mullah Mohammad Hassan Akhund. He was the Taliban's foreign minister in the nineties, and remains under sanction by the UN Security Council.

The rumors of internal conflict persist. In mid-September, Baradar vanished from view, as reports circulated that he had been wounded in a brawl with Haqqani men at the presidential palace. The fight was ostensibly set off by a dispute over which faction had done more to secure Kabul. Baradar, after an absence of several days, released a video denying the reports; his office explained that he had traveled to Kandahar, because he needed "rest."

During my visit, I went to Wardak, a rural province west of Kabul. It was one of the last major battlefields in the country; many of its villages had been partly destroyed, and the crude stone graves of war dead were everywhere, marked with martyrs' flags. As we drove through a roadside village, there was a commotion just ahead of us: Gunmen were yelling and waving their weapons as frightened civilians hustled past them. An elderly man explained that the Taliban were having an armed standoff. No one seemed to know what the men were fighting over; it was just another fight.

IN KABUL, STREET MARKETS HAVE SPRUNG UP, WHERE DESPERate people sell off their possessions, everything from rugs and heaters to pet birds. There are beggars everywhere: young children, elderly women, men pulling carts from straps around their foreheads. On the city's outskirts, women in burkhas sit in the middle of the road with their children around them, hoping that people in passing cars will toss them some food or some money.

Without financial backing from the US and from international lending institutions, Afghanistan's economy has all but evaporated. Hundreds of thousands of government employees have not received a salary for months. In the cities, there is food for sale in the bazaars, but prices have risen so steeply that Afghans find it difficult to sustain their families. In the countryside, drought has caused widespread hunger, worsening during the cold winter months. The UN World Food Program country director, Mary Ellen McGroarty, told me that the situation was dire. "Twenty-two-point-eight million Afghans are already severely food-insecure, and seven million of them are one step away from famine," she said. "You have the drought banging into the economic crisis, and it's been one of the worst droughts in thirty years." She concluded, "If this trajectory continues, ninety-five percent of the Afghan population will fall below the poverty line by mid-2022. It's just devastating to watch. If I were an Afghan, I'd flee."

As the economic crisis intensifies, there is a threat of deepening anti-Western resentment among citizens. In a curious reversal, Taliban officials I met with often made overtures of friendship with the US, while former US allies expressed bitterness about America's failure in their country. Gailani recalled warmly how President George W. Bush had invited him to the 2006 State of the Union address and told him, during a photo op, "Hamed, buddy, we're proud of you!" But he was shocked at the money that the US had expended in Afghanistan. "They say as much as two and a half *trillion* dollars was spent here since 2001," he said. "No doubt some great things were achieved in Afghanistan in that time, but you don't see any big changes in the country's infrastructure, do you?" Gailani shook his head. "The fact is, most of the money that supposedly came to Afghanistan—probably eight and a half dollars out of every ten—went back to the US, and meanwhile the corruption here was out of control. Afghan society became corrupted, and it was that corruption which brought about this day, with the Taliban back in power." With a smile, Gailani said, "The Americans spent two and a half trillion dollars to clear this country from the Taliban, only to give it back to them again. I will go to my grave trying to figure out this riddle."

Hamid Karzai, who served as president from 2004 to 2014, was also deeply critical of America's occupation. He received me in his private library, in a residential compound in Kabul. It is surrounded by high concrete blast walls and situated in the Green Zone, a highly fortified area around the former US Embassy.

An elegant, ceremonious man, Karzai urged green tea on me and spoke about poetry. He especially loved Emerson. Kipling was fine, except for "The White Man's Burden," he said, shaking his head. In a marveling tone, Karzai mentioned that he had been "greatly impressed" by the poem Amanda Gorman had recited at Biden's inauguration.

Karzai would not have been president without US support, but while in office he became increasingly frustrated by America's counterinsurgency tactics. In 2013, he visited Washington and, in a tense meeting with Obama in the Oval Office, raised the issue of civilian casualties. Karzai told me that he had shown Obama a gruesome photograph: An American soldier stood with his boot on an elderly Afghan man's severed hand, while a terrified woman and children looked on. "I asked Obama, 'How can you expect me to be your ally and to go along with such actions when I am the Afghan president and am supposed to protect my people?'" Karzai waved his arms in a wide arc: "And here we are."

Karzai's government, built on uneasy alliances, accommodated a range of aggressive warlords and corrupt officials. Hoping to end the war, he made strenuous efforts to start a dialogue with the Taliban. These had served mostly to compound his image as a hapless leader, trapped in a toxic relationship with his American patrons, but he hadn't given up. "I've been saying for years that the Taliban are our brothers," he told me. "Let's work together for a common future."

Karzai's status in the new Afghanistan is tenuous; he is not in power, but neither is he entirely out. A well-connected Afghan suggested that Karzai was a "sort of hostage" of the Taliban, who had prevented him from leaving because they needed him as an interlocutor with the West. (Karzai and Mujahid both deny this.) Karzai had reason to be wary of the new government. Sirajuddin Haqqani had once tried to assassinate him. But Karzai told me that he had been meeting regularly with Taliban ministers, and insisted that they had "an absolute conviction that the government needs to be inclusive." He emphasized that Afghan society had changed in the previous two decades. "There were downsides to the American experience, but there were positives, too," he said. He mentioned increased education, especially among women, and the improved roads.

The question of how Afghanistan would be governed remained open, he conceded. A provisional constitution had to be enacted; a commission would then draft a permanent constitution and submit it to a national Loya Jirga, or grand council. "The future state should present the will of the people," Karzai said. "I will be pushing for a democracy, of course." He laughed. "But there will be those who oppose it, who will say, 'Look at the sham of a democracy that was here before.'"

On a road east of Kabul is Camp Phoenix, a military base erected by the US. In 2014, the Americans handed it over to the Afghan military, and it was turned into a rehabilitation center for a burgeoning population of drug addicts. The Taliban, during their first tenure, virtually stamped out opium-poppy cultivation. But, after the Americans invaded, several prominent warlords allied with the US reportedly became involved in the heroin trade. Opium farming expanded hugely, and Afghanistan reemerged as the world's primary supplier. There are now believed to be more than three million addicts in the country.

When the Taliban returned in August, about a thousand addicts were housed on the former base, where a six-week rehabilitation program had been instituted under the auspices of the Ministry of Public Health. By December, the Talibs had picked up some two thousand more on the street and brought them to the center. But the program's staff, like other civil servants in Afghanistan, had not been paid for months. There was no budget for food, and the patients were starving.

I toured the center with a young social worker named Mohammad Sabir. The patients, most of them wearing dirty hospital smocks, were shuffling around the grounds, or sprawled in an unkempt yard. All were painfully thin. Many pantomimed hunger, rubbing their bellies or gesturing as if eating an imaginary meal.

Sabir acknowledged that the only food the camp had was what remained in its stores from before the government fell. The patients were given a cup of watered-down milk and a piece of naan for breakfast, rice for lunch, and beans and a half piece of naan for dinner. As we approached a garbage bin, Sabir chased away a man who was scrounging for food. "Two nights ago, they ate the camp cat," he said. "They tore it apart and ate it raw."

In the yard, one man was carrying another on his back. They were Amanullah and Abdul Rahman, two friends in their early thirties. They had grown up in the farm country near Kunduz, and had joined the Afghan Army when they were in their late teens. Amanullah explained that he was being carried because he had lost a leg when he stepped on a mine in Helmand. Abdul Rahman's arm had been wounded in the same explosion; he wore a metal vise, with pins going into his humerus. They had both started using heroin to ease their pain.

Abdul Rahman sat by silently, wearing a vacant look. Amanullah told me that the explosion had affected his friend: "He was different before." Amanullah said that his greatest wish was to return to his wife and three children. He believed that his addiction was cured, and he was determined never to use heroin again. In his hand, he carried what remained of a broken prosthesis. Holding it up, he declared, "I am still ready to sacrifice for my country."

Many Taliban I spoke to suggested that the viciousness of the war was an inevitable response to the presence of foreigners. One senior leader complained, "When there were forty-five countries present in Afghanistan, and hundreds of people were being killed a day, that was called security." Now that the Taliban were in charge, he argued, there was no need for further unrest. "Not one person a day is killed," he said, without apparent irony. "Is this not called security?"

In some ways, though, the Taliban's rejection of the previous order has increased the chaos in Afghanistan. On the day that they took

Kabul, they opened the gates of the city's main prison, at Pul-e-Charkhi, and of Bagram prison, on a former US air base outside the capital. More than twelve thousand inmates rushed out. They included senior leaders of Al Qaeda and at least a thousand members of IS-K, the Afghan affiliate of ISIS. On August 26, one of the IS-K fighters blew himself up outside the gates of Kabul's airport, killing thirteen American soldiers and nearly two hundred Afghans seeking evacuation.

During my visit, there were "sticky bomb" explosions every few days in Kabul: Bombs attached to a magnet were slapped onto the exterior of a car and set off with a signal from a cell phone. I came upon the site of an attack just a few blocks from the police headquarters. The bombed vehicle had been removed, and Taliban were directing traffic around strewn debris and a large scorch mark in the road. Down the street, gunmen moved in pairs, scanning rooftops and searching in alleyways. The civilians passing by kept their eyes averted, determined not to reveal any interest.

The sticky-bomb attacks were reported on social media, but with no information about who had carried them out or why. Last summer, IS-K claimed responsibility for two such attacks on vans carrying Shiite "disbelievers." The group has slaughtered hundreds of Shiites, in schools, hospitals, and mosques. It has also targeted the Taliban, whose members it regards as apostates. Not long after the fall of Kabul, Zabihullah Mujahid, the spokesman, held a wake for his mother, who had died of an illness. While he and other officials were at the mosque, an IS-K suicide bomber struck. Mujahid survived, but several people were killed and many others were wounded—victims of the kind of attack that he had once applauded.

Taliban officials mostly brushed aside the dangers of IS-K. At a military base in Logar, a strategic hill town outside Kabul, a senior Haqqani commander named Mawlawi Deen Shah Mokhbit assured me that IS-K had "already been defeated, by God." In the manner of someone unused to being interrupted, he intoned, "When we were fighting the Americans and their Afghan mercenaries and slaves, doing jihad against them, we were also fighting the Daesh, the Khawarij"—those who fight other Muslims in the name of Islam. "But God defeated them, God obliterated and finished them." Noting that the country had endured forty years of war, Mokhbit added a caveat: "Afghanistan is full of weapons and of people who grew up in war, so there may be small incidents. But they cannot pose a threat to our nation and system of government." As we talked, a bodyguard stood at his side, staring at me with a finger on the trigger of his weapon. At the end of the interview, Mokhbit, evidently in an abundance of caution, ordered a group of his gunmen to escort me down the mountainside. About halfway, they handed me off to another armed convoy, which accompanied me to the edge of the city.

IN LARGE SWATHS OF THE COUNTRYSIDE, AS THE TALIBAN TOOK territory over the past decade, they became a kind of shadow government. The Talibs were popular among some locals; they were, after all, sons of the same soil. As the Americans withdrew, many people surrendered to the Taliban without a fight—some of them motivated by survival, others by genuine affinity. In the town of Bamiyan, eighty miles west of Kabul, the new governor, Mullah Abdullah Sarhadi, told me that he had taken the territory peacefully. "There was no fighting, praise be to God," he said.

In Bamiyan, the Taliban occupy a fortified complex on a high hilltop. Governor Sarhadi, a spare-looking man with a gray beard, wore a black turban and a short umber shawl, called a *patou*. He told me that he had joined the jihad during the Soviet invasion, and had been a fighter ever since. "I have many scars on my body," he said. He had lost an eye in a firefight outside Kabul, he explained: A bullet had entered his head and come out through his eye socket.

In 2001, during the Taliban's last stand, at Kunduz, Sarhadi had been taken prisoner, and militiamen had locked him in an airless shipping container, along with hundreds of other fighters. Many asphyxiated, but Sarhadi was saved by a fluke: His captors fired into the container, and he survived by breathing through the bullet holes. Afterward, he was handed over to the Americans and held for four years in Guantánamo. Following his release, he returned to the battlefield and was captured again; he spent eight more years in prison, this time in Pakistan.

In Bamiyan, though, he and his men felt at home. "We have no concerns," he told me. "This is part of our nation, and we all belong to the same nation." He had been there before the Americans came, he said, and it had been fine then, too.

This was a strikingly revisionist view. If there is a single place that embodies the Taliban's abuses, it is Bamiyan. The small town, set in a beautiful mountain valley, is inhabited mostly by Hazaras. Distinguished by their Mongol features, the Hazaras are said to be descendants of Genghis Khan's army, which invaded in the thirteenth century.

Many Hazaras live in caves hewed into the valley's vast wall of sandstone cliffs. The caves were first excavated by Buddhist hermits—monks who had made their way along the ancient Silk Road, which connected China with the Middle East and Europe. About fifteen hundred years ago, the monks carved two statues of the Buddha, each as big as a jetliner, into the porous stone.

The Bamiyan Buddhas became Afghanistan's greatest tourist attraction. But, in 2001, Mullah Omar decreed that they were un-Islamic idols and had to be destroyed. As archaeologists and world leaders pleaded for restraint, militants demolished the statues with explosives and artillery. Around the same time, Taliban entered the Kabul Museum and took sledgehammers and axes to thousands of years' worth of artifacts.

On my recent visit, when I brought this up with officials in Kabul, they generally tried to change the subject.

Sarhadi had been in Bamiyan when the Buddhas were destroyed, and I asked if he thought that it had been a mistake. His aides looked upset, but he waved a hand dismissively. "This was a decision by the leadership," he said. "Whatever the leaders and the emirs of the Islamic Emirate decide, we follow."

According to reports, Sarhadi was also linked to killings of Hazaras, including a massacre in 2001 that Amnesty International said took the lives of "over three hundred unarmed men and a number of civilian women and children." Sarhadi denied any involvement. His aides protested that I had no right to question him. "Have you ever asked officials in the West about the atrocities they have committed in the Islamic world?" one asked. Sarhadi added that the West had nothing to teach Muslim countries about human rights. "We challenge the whole world!" he said. "In Islam, even when you slaughter a sheep, the first condition is that you should not sharpen your knife in front of it, and the second condition is that the knife should be very sharp, so that the sheep does not suffer."

Sarhadi told me that he had brought peace to the area. "By the grace of God, there are no problems now, and there will be none in the future," he said. If I wanted to know how the local people felt about his leadership, he said, I should go ask them: "We serve the people day and night."

Later that day, I met some of the local people. Near the base of the cliff where the Buddhas once stood, some young men had dug a hole and set a fire to bake potatoes. There was no work, they explained, and so they were trying to stave off hunger.

At the great gash where the smaller Buddha had been, I found Hazara men and boys staring into the dark recess. They explained that they had come from a neighboring province, after hearing that the new authorities were handing out food coupons. At the governor's compound, they had joined a crowd that gathered to plead for help. The Taliban guards had said that they had nothing to give, and ordered them to leave.

The Hazaras decided that, before returning home, they would visit the site of the Buddhas. They had never seen them, and now they had come too late. I asked what they thought about their destruction. The oldest man said, cautiously, that he thought it was a pity, since the statues had been "a part of history." When I asked what he thought about the Taliban, he looked away, pretending not to hear me.

SPRAWLED ON AN ARID PLAIN FOUR HUNDRED MILES WEST OF Kabul is Herat, an elegant oasis city distinguished by an immense mosque with exquisite blue-and-yellow tile work. It has been fought over many times in its long history. The latest battle ended on August 13, when, after weeks of fighting, government forces surrendered to the Taliban. Kabul's collapse came just forty-eight hours later.

Herat's defense was led in part by its former governor Ismail Khan, a tough-as-nails warlord in his late seventies. Khan is renowned in Afghanistan as a mujahideen leader, a minister in Karzai's government, and a longtime enemy of the Taliban. He spent some three years as their prisoner before escaping, and he later survived a suicide bombing that killed several civilians. Zabihullah Mujahid claimed responsibility for the attack.

When Herat fell, the Taliban captured Khan, but he managed to flee to Iran. It is not clear that he poses less risk from afar. Along with other political figures—including two of Ghani's vice presidents, Amrullah Saleh and the warlord Abdul Rashid Dostum—Khan may attempt to raise an armed insurrection if the new government appears weak.

In Herat, the Taliban announced their presence by hanging the bodies of four alleged kidnappers above the city from construction cranes. Since then, things have mostly been quiet, but during the autumn the city began filling with displaced people, as thousands of peasant farmers and their families fled the drought-stricken provinces of Badghis and Ghor. According to Mary Ellen McGroarty, the WFP director, the refugees were in a desperate state; on a recent visit, she had nearly been taken hostage by a mob of them.

I found the refugees along a road that leads through the desert from Herat to Badghis. On a patch of treeless dirt, a few dozen families had cobbled together shelters from rocks, plastic sheeting, and discarded tin. Most of the men had worked as day laborers, paid with a portion of whatever crops they helped plant. With the drought, though, there had been no harvest, and no pay.

Two of the women had tuberculosis, and two others were pregnant. Zainab, one of those with TB, had four children. She squatted in the dirt and explained that she couldn't sleep well; she coughed constantly and had pain in her hands and her head.

An elderly man named Ibrahim lived nearby, with his sister Guljan. As Guljan spoke, Ibrahim stood silently, leaning on a stick. She explained that he had been beaten by militiamen in their village three years earlier. "He hasn't been the same since," she said. "He talks nonsense and swears and sometimes breaks things." The other refugees stood and listened, nodding sympathetically. They seemed distressed that their elders had no one to help them. When I asked their ages, Guljan looked uncertain and said, "Ibrahim may be seventy or eighty, and I am fifty or sixty." (Most Afghans do not know their precise age, because they don't traditionally celebrate birthdays.)

Down the road, I stopped at a field where a larger group had camped out. Men and boys crowded around, jostling and talking, until their elders managed to calm them down. One elder, Jan Muhammad, told me that he had led about a hundred people to Herat, because there had been no rain where they lived: "We had nothing to eat, so we left." He had no plan, he said. "We are hoping for some aid from the UN after some of

its officials visited." No one from the Afghan government had come to
see them yet. A wealthy businessman had arrived a few days earlier and
distributed tents, but there had not been enough for everyone.

A man carried a young boy over to me, pulling aside his smock to
show his back and left arm, where the skin had been burned to a livid,
bubbled mass. The Americans had bombed his village the previous
year, he explained. His older son was killed, and this boy, who was six,
had sustained these burns. "It itches him," the man said. "He can't sleep
at night."

Everyone there had a story of privation and despair. A young man
who worked in a roadside eatery next to the encampments told me that
at night, from his adjoining bedroom, he could hear the children crying
of cold and hunger. With a despairing look, he said that he hoped something could be done.

The most important local authority was the governor of Herat,
Noor Mohammad Islamjar, a scholar of Islam whom the Taliban had
drafted into office. When I visited the governor's palace, there was a
kind of coat check, where visitors could leave their Kalashnikovs, and
an armed guard posted by the door. Inside, Islamjar had set up an office
in an elegant sitting room, a legacy of the days of the Afghan monarchy.

Islamjar, wearing glasses and a white *shalwar kameez*, spoke about
the refugees with scholarly detachment. "The security problems are over,
but the economic problems are not," he said. "Part of this is climate
change. Other factors include the unfair sanctions." He gave me a scold-
ing look. "The Islamic Emirate of Afghanistan will not suffer much," he
added. "But the women and old people will."

I reminded him that there was a humanitarian crisis on his city's
outskirts. "I hope that climate change and the drought will end," he replied. There was also a plan to send people back to their villages, "with
the help of NGOs." But what could he do *now*? Many of the people I
had met had nothing to eat. Islamjar assured me that he had "instructed

the Red Crescent and others to give them some assistance." He added, "But we're trying not to give them free food, because it creates a pattern of more people coming and establishing themselves here just to receive assistance. The main problem we have is that our assets are frozen. The situation of these people is the responsibility of those who have frozen our assets."

JUST ABOUT EVERYONE I SPOKE TO IN AFGHANISTAN BELIEVED that the US and its allies should release funds for humanitarian assistance. Withholding them would be cruel, and would also likely deepen anti-Western resentments. "Punishment is not the answer," Gailani told me. "Sanctions don't hurt the leaders, only ordinary people."

The public relations disaster of the US withdrawal left Joe Biden with a conundrum: Ignoring the desperate situation in Afghanistan would make him look callous, but cooperating with the Taliban would make him look weak. Zalmay Khalilzad, who led the American team in negotiations with the Taliban, told me, "I thought after the overthrow that we should use the leverage we had to get the Taliban off the terror list, gradually release funds, and reopen the embassy—so we could get what we wanted from them in exchange, which is counterterror cooperation, women's rights, and an inclusive government." But, he said, "it's a problem for the Biden people, politically. How do you talk about a grand bargain with the Taliban if the American people think they're a terrorist group? Especially when the Talibs have not done enough to dispel that perception."

Since last fall, the administration has been working to provide relief without giving the regime access to funds. It granted licenses for hundreds of millions of dollars in US aid, and has backed a "humanitarian exchange facility" that would allow aid organizations to help pay doctors, nurses, and other workers. The administration has also encouraged the World Bank to release hundreds of millions of dollars from its Afghanistan Reconstruction Trust Fund. During my visit, I saw cash, food, and winter clothing being handed out by people working under the aegis of international agencies.

In February, Biden announced a plan for handling the $7 billion in Afghan money held in US banks. Half would be set aside to potentially pay damages to a group of relatives of 9/11 victims who are suing the Taliban and Al Qaeda; the other half would go into a trust fund for humanitarian aid in Afghanistan. This plan provides continued relief, but it leaves the Taliban almost unable to govern, with a teetering central bank and no diplomatic recognition from the West. "The Americans need to engage with the current Afghan government through official channels, to recognize the Afghan government and cooperate with it," Mujahid, the spokesman, told me. "Like the good relations the United States has had with Saudi Arabia, an Islamic country—they can have the same with us."

In recent years, though, Saudi Arabia has made at least token gestures at making its version of Islamic law more palatable to the West (notwithstanding its persecution of political dissidents). In Herat, Governor Islamjar suggested that the Afghans, too, were pursuing a "softer" Sharia. The new appointees to the Ministry for the Promotion of Virtue and Prevention of Vice were "just encouraging people to behave," he said. Under updated rules, "criminals will be tried three times." In the case of a death sentence, he said, the supreme leader would have to sign the authorization; no one else would have the authority to order people killed. When I asked about the men who had been hanged from cranes in his city, Islamjar looked chagrined. "They don't plan to do this in the future," he said quietly.

In Kabul, I spoke with Mullah Abdul Salam Zaeef about the difficulty of reconciling these disparate visions of Islamic governance. A leg-

endary figure, Zaeef is a big, broad-faced Pashtun in his mid-fifties. He
grew up in Kandahar, went to a Pakistani madrasah, joined the war
against the Soviets, and helped create the Taliban. A close friend of
Mullah Omar, he served for a time as the Taliban's defense minister
and, after their fall, spent four years at Guantánamo.

Zaeef, dressed in a white *shalwar kameez*, told me that he was still
a Talib but had not joined the government because he wanted to "be
free." (An Afghan who knows him well told me that his real motivation
was concern about the Haqqanis, though Zaeef denies this.) In the
meantime, he had an NGO, which helped war orphans, and ran a radio
station, with broadcasts to "explain Islam to people" in the countryside;
he also had a madrasah, with fifteen hundred students. Zaeef seemed
most enthusiastic about farmland he owned in Kandahar, where he
grew pistachios, pomegranates, and grapes. "They are good for the birds,
and nature," he said.

The Taliban's laws are being applied inconsistently across the country, and some abuses are clearly occurring. During my visit, reports circulated of Hazara farmers being forced from their land by ethnic
Pashtuns, of raids on activists' homes, and of extrajudicial executions
of former government soldiers and intelligence agents. Zaeef acknowledged that the criminal justice system remained slow and uneven, because the new authorities were not up to speed on the laws; it would take
time. "Afghanistan will not be a democracy," he said. "But it won't be a
complete dictatorship, either. For at least fifteen years, we need a system
that will not allow the people to do wrong."

His dream was for Sharia to be implemented in a way that benefited
all Afghans. He conceded that the Taliban, like the Americans, had
made mistakes, but he hoped they would get it right this time. "Islamic
law should not be *hard*. For the Muslim, it is a good life," he said. "The
problem is that there is not a model for Islamic law in the world today.

Even I cannot explain it. It is like an ocean when you enter. But a way must be found."

IBRAHIM HAQQANI, THE UNCLE OF THE TALIBAN'S INTERIOR minister, met me in his fortified residence in Kabul. Armed men guarded the approaches; at the end of a long driveway lined with blast walls, more gathered outside. Haqqani received me in a room with long yellow curtains, drawn against the sunlight. Apparently in his sixties, he had a long dyed-black beard and a turban flamboyant enough for a villain in *Pirates of the Caribbean*.

Haqqani told me that he had spent most of his life fighting for two goals: to free Afghanistan of foreign intervention, and to implement Sharia law. The first had been achieved. The second had yet to be. "We speak of the Sharia that has been brought to us from God by its messenger," he explained. "That is the Sharia we want."

I told Haqqani that there was confusion about what kind of Sharia the Taliban wished to implement. "There is one Sharia," he replied. "Within Sharia, there is behavior that is neither sinful nor makes one an infidel, and that brings about attitudes of mercy and compassion. We are inching toward that, in order to bring ease to people and yet protect ourselves from infidel behavior."

I asked if the Taliban intended to revive the strict form of Sharia that they had imposed in the nineties. Haqqani told me that, to explain, it would be necessary to counter the negative impressions that had been spread by infidel propaganda. "I will give you one example," he said. "In the past government, did we allow people to take photos? No. But now have we prevented anyone from taking photos? No, we have not. In the previous government, we prevented women from going to the marketplace on their own. What was the reason? The reason was the depravity that existed here, from the Russian era. There was no trust, and we were not confident in the women. That is why we were trying to limit women until we ensured their proper security. Nowadays, though, there are not restrictions on women. They roam freely, they go to work, they are doctors, they are sitting in offices."

Haqqani begged my forgiveness; he had to attend the sunset prayer. While he was out of the room, I thought about the dissonance between the new government's professions of softness and its lingering ferocity. Just weeks earlier, Haqqani's nephew Sirajuddin had held a celebration for the families of suicide bombers. The commander Mokhbit had told me that the men he sent to their deaths were "closer to God than you or I."

After a few minutes, Haqqani returned and continued his thought. "We still have some concerns about the effects of American influence," he said. But, he added, "there is a trust that Afghans will not repeat the actions of the past, and that the actions of the foreigners, and the services that were provided to them, will not be repeated. We try to take a softer approach in all aspects of Sharia, where it does not contradict God's orders." He spoke with the assurance of an all-knowing parent: "Severity is a global principle. Whenever there is chaos in a country, strict measures are put in place, and when things become normal again the strict measures can be relaxed." He went on, "God is patient. If a tribe takes the right path, God will give them ease and comfort, but if the tribe takes the wrong path, denying the Koran and such things, then God gives them severe punishment. This is God's way and the world's way."

ON DECEMBER 3, THE TALIBAN ISSUED A DECREE, IN THE NAME of the supreme leader, which held that women should have some inheritance rights and should not be forced into marriage. But it did not address their rights to work and to pursue secondary education.

The next day, I met with a group of former senior employees of the Ministry of Women's Affairs. They ranged in age from thirty-two to forty-six, and most had been the primary breadwinner in their family. Although female activists in Afghanistan risked violence and censure, all of them were willing to show their face and to use their real name.

Nazifa Azimi, who had been the ministry's IT director, explained that when the Taliban swept into Kabul she and her colleagues went home, unsure what was going to happen. Quickly, though, they decided to stand their ground, and began showing up at the ministry every morning. They found the building cordoned off by guards. "At the beginning, the Taliban guards at the door were polite and would come outside and speak to us," Azimi said. But, after two weeks went by and nothing changed, the women decided to protest.

Shahlla Arifi, who had been in charge of education and culture at the ministry, led the protests. Ever since then, she said, she had been receiving threats, including texts warning her that her husband, a teacher at a school for boys, would be "taken down." Arifi and her husband have five children, between three and fifteen years old. They had considered joining the crowds trying to evacuate from Kabul's airport, but were deterred by the chaos.

Since then, the risks for female protesters have only increased. According to reports, several women in Kabul have vanished after attending anti-Taliban rallies in recent months. All the women I spoke to wanted to leave Afghanistan, convinced that they had no future there. Indeed, virtually every Afghan I met who was not a Talib intended to flee. Many asked for my help. In the end, they believed that what the resurgent Taliban were offering was not a "soft revolution" but, rather, an update of their previous rule. The degree of severity they apply in governing Afghanistan will depend on the circumstances they face. But people who have experienced freedom don't like having it taken away, and many more Afghans will likely seek a way out of the country. Some may fight. The majority, however, especially the poor, will have no choice but to adapt in order to survive.

When I asked Arifi about the supreme leader's decree, she laughed and shook her head. "Their ideology hasn't changed," she said. "There I was in the street, asking for my rights, but they were not ready to give them to me. They pointed a gun at my head, and they shouted obscenities at me. They will do anything to convince the international community to give them financing, but eventually I'll be forced to wear the burkha again. They are just waiting."

Afghan women in burkhas in Kabul, December 2001.

# AFTERWORD

Every country is a never-ending story, and so it is with Afghanistan. Nearly a quarter century after the September 11, 2001, attacks thrust Afghanistan into the global limelight, and held it there intermittently during the two decades of the American military presence, the country has once again subsided from view. Today it exists in a twilight zone, remote-seeming, and, for now, strategically irrelevant. One day, a new reckoning will come to Afghanistan. We cannot yet predict when it will occur or what form it will take. But if past history is anything to go by, it seems inevitable that it will involve war.

Whenever news does come out of Afghanistan, it is almost always because of a terrorist attack—usually carried out by one of the Taliban's extremist offshoots like ISIS-Khorasan—directed against such targets as Hazara Shiite girls' schools. Most other news deals with the repression that has increased steadily since the Taliban takeover. One edict forbade women from speaking outside of their homes, from which they can no longer emerge without burkhas—just as the former women's affairs ministry official Shahlla Arifi predicted to me when we met in Kabul in December 2021. Other decrees had forbidden girls from attending schools and women from working in hospitals or being outside without a male relative as an escort. There is now no place on earth that is more oppressive for women than Afghanistan.

I have written about a good many people in the course of the two decades covered in this book. Many of them are still alive, having survived the violent ructions of Afghanistan's tumult as best they could—but quite a few have also fled into exile. Some have been killed, their deaths chronicled in these pages.

At last word, Mamur Hassan, the warlord of Dasht-i-Qala with whom I stayed in 2001, was still living with his wives and children in his hometown, which is no longer a frontline position in a war zone, just a little trading settlement by a river near the Tajik border. Bashir, the Taliban prisoner who was being kept in a hole by another warlord near Dasht-i-Qala, was reportedly executed in November 2001, shortly after the Taliban defenses in northern Afghanistan crumbled and the Northern Alliance marched on Taloqan.

Over the years, several personal friends and colleagues have paid high prices for being in Afghanistan. João Silva, the photographer, lost both his legs stepping on a land mine not far from where I also spent time in 2010. David Rohde and Sean Langan both spent many months as hostages of the Taliban or their Haqqani allies. The veteran Afghan hand, cameraman Peter Jouvenal, whom I met on my earliest sojourns in Afghanistan in the eighties and saw again on most of my return trips, was arrested by the Taliban a few days after I met him in Kabul in 2021, accused of espionage, and held in prison for six months before being released.

Fridoun, the affable medical student who first guided me around the ruins of Kabul, and also worked with me as a translator, eventually sat for his medical school exams and became a doctor in a hospital in

Herat. Fridoun married and began a family, with his wife giving birth to twin boys. A few years later, seeking a peaceful life, Fridoun emigrated with his family to Sacramento, California. But when the second Taliban takeover came in 2021, Fridoun's twin boys, by then in their first year of college, were on a summer trip to see their grandparents in Kabul. Caught up in the chaos of the American withdrawal, they spent several terrifying days amid the throngs outside Kabul's airport before managing to get on one of the last evacuation flights.

Qais, the young translator who accompanied Thomas Dworzak and me from Kabul to Tora Bora and on to Kandahar—and who also worked with us when we returned to Kabul—went on to become a major Afghan media personality. But he, too, eventually fled, to Canada. In 2021, however, he also had to scramble to secure the evacuation of close relatives who were left vulnerable by the American pullout.

Many other Afghans have been less fortunate, including several I got to know on my last trip, some of whom continue to write me, begging for help to leave their homeland, a place they no longer belong, and which, it seems safe to say, most Americans have already forgotten.

# ACKNOWLEDGMENTS

I owe thanks to a great many people. Thomas Dworzak was my loyal companion during the 2001 war and its aftermath in 2002, and he made our experiences together not only bearable, but quite often an unexpected delight. On later trips, Samantha Appleton, Aaron Huey, João Carvalho Pina, Carlos and Mike Boettcher, and Moises Saman accompanied me as photographers, and proved to be good friends.

Qais, Fridoun, Nabi, Habib, and Lutf were of great help as translators and all-around assistants on my various trips. Peter Jouvenal, Bob Nickelsberg, Heathcliff O'Malley, Julius Strauss, Wendell Steavenson, Andrew Testa, Liz Tynes, Bree Fitzgerald, and Iva Zimova were excellent comrades in the field.

My respective editors Sharon DeLano, Amy Davidson, and Nick Trautwein at *The New Yorker* gave me great backup, as did Dorothy Wickenden and Pamela McCarthy. I'm grateful to David Remnick for letting me return to Afghanistan again and again over the years; to Elizabeth Biondi, Whitney Johnson, Joanna Milter, and their photo departments; to the magazine's amazing team of fact-checkers, including Andy Young and Nandi Rodrigo. Thanks also to Risa Leibowitz, Francine Schore, and Jillian Kosminoff; my agent Sarah Chalfant of the Wylie Agency; Morgan Entrekin, who published the original *Lion's Grave*; and Scott Moyers, who believed in this new book, for which I am very grateful.

To Erica, Bella, Rosie, and Máximo, for understanding why I had to be away from home so much of the time, and for putting up with me when I came back.

# INDEX

*Italicized page numbers indicate material in photographs.*